p/30

CONTENTS

For Dorothy, who has made most of this journey with me.

I wish to thank my colleagues Richard T. Hughes and Ronald C. Highfield, who read and made suggestions on parts of the manuscript. I especially wish to express appreciation to Thom Lemmons, Managing Director of the ACU Press, for his many suggestions and detailed editing. The assistance of all three has made this a better book.

Thomas H. Olbricht
Malibu, California
April, 1996

Introduction: A Point of Departure

In a real sense hermeneutics is the interpreting of God to those who wish to be his. Even God did not propose to do that by a few simple rules. He did not offer rules, but a Son. "No one has ever seen God. It is God the only Son, who is close to the father's heart, who has made him known [*exegeomai*]" (John 1:18). Jesus Christ is therefore the ultimate hermeneutic. If God can best explain himself in person, we can best explain him too in his body, that is, his living church.

As the twentieth century winds down, disputes have arisen among members of the Churches of Christ over hermeneutics—the rules for interpreting Scripture. The charge has been lodged that an age-old consensus is being challenged by malcontents who have proposed a "new" hermeneutic. Through the centuries, those concerned with hermeneutics have had at least two objects in mind: to explain what statements of Scripture meant in the biblical context, and to determine from Scripture what God expected from them and their contemporaries. In Churches of Christ the second intent has predominated. The "new hermeneutic" perceived to be underway in Churches of Christ is alleged to be a recently-devised way of determining from the Bible what God requires.

For several years now students and others have encouraged me to write a book on hermeneutics, but I have resisted on the grounds that what most people are hoping for is a how-to book. I have never felt that books of this sort did justice in providing an appropriate methodology for incorporating the Scripture into the life of the church. It was not clear to me how I might find a channel appropriate for conveying my views. Books on the interpretation of Scripture are legion. Perhaps what is *least* needed is another one. I have published several short pieces on hermeneutics, and several items which serve as *prolegomenas*—introductions—to hermeneutics, especially those on biblical theology.[1] But I have not published a book specifically on hermeneutics. So, why have I decided to publish a book on hermeneutics? I have thought about and spoken on hermeneutics off and on for at least the past fifty years. Over most of these years I have addressed the subject under the title, "How to study the Bible." I have taught such lessons in numerous church classes, sermons, lectureships, workshops, forums and encampments. Only during the past fifteen years, however, has the word, "hermeneutics" surfaced as a familiar term in congregations of the Churches of Christ. I have refrained from using the word in churches since, until recently, few persons knew what hermeneutics were, and most could care less. But now, in the midst of current controversies, the word is in vogue. For the past thirty years I have taught graduate courses in biblical theology, theology, philosophy and early church history at Abilene Christian and Pepperdine Universities, but I have never taught a course on hermeneutics as a separate subject. To be sure, in all these classes I have struggled with and reflected upon the role and interpretation of Scripture in the life of the believer and in the church. Most of my graduate courses have had sections on hermeneutics, and about half of my class on "Restoration Doctrine" was devoted to hermeneutics. I have concluded, after several years of contemplating biblical interpretation, that interpretation must commence with a biblical understanding of God. Since a proper understanding of God is the province of biblical theology, biblical theology and hermeneutics must work hand-in-hand. I have already proposed that one of the aims of hermeneutics is to determine from Scripture what God expects from his people in this time. It soon becomes clear from Scripture that what God expects is, in fact, what he has demonstrated through his own actions. I can quote many Scriptures to this effect, but two will perhaps be sufficient at present. In Leviticus 19:2, God said, "You shall be holy, for I the Lord your God am holy." Jesus, in Matthew 5:48, challenged his auditors, "Be perfect, therefore, as your heavenly Father is perfect." It follows then, that what God expects of his people is what he himself is and does. A hermeneutic which is not sensitive to this central fact seems not altogether biblical. Later on, we will give specific attention to ways in which Paul, for example, determined what God expected. For Paul, God exhibited what he expected in the life and death of his son, and he expects believers to emulate his son. A valid biblical hermeneutic must follow the path Paul has laid out in his writings. The question, then, is this: What are the implications of who God is (as Father, Son, and Spirit) and what he does in regard to his expectations for his people in this time?

For the first half of my teaching career I steered away from frequent use of the word "theology", believing with Barton W. Stone (1772-1844), Alexander Campbell (1788-1866), our other forefathers and some contemporaries, that much damage has been done to Christian reflection through the centuries under the rubric of theology. I still believe that. I believe that Platonic and Philonic influences on Origen (c. 185-254) and Augustine (354-430); Aristotelian influences on Thomas Aquinas (c.1225-1274); Scottish Enlightenment influences on Charles Hodge (1797-1878) and Alexander Campbell; and phenomenological and existential influences on Karl Barth (1886-1968) and Rudolf Bultmann (1884-1976) have skewed the message of the biblical writers when viewed through the lenses of these theologians.

Nevertheless, theology is not, per se, an unwholesome word or concept. It is actually a biblical word in that *theos* (Greek) is translated into English as "God." *Logos* in Greek means a discourse on or a study of a specific topic. Theology, therefore, is a study of God. What can be more biblical than a study of God? That is what the Bible is all about. Studies of God flourish, of course, which draw admittedly on other fountainheads than those in Scripture. For example, the British theologian, John Macquarrie (1919-), who taught at Union Theological Seminary in New York, spoke of six sources for theology: experience, revelation, Scripture, tradition, culture, and reason.[2]

When I say we need an insight into the theological manner in which the biblical writers worked I am speaking about biblical theology. We should not be afraid of biblical theology, since it is not informed by philosophies outside Scripture.

Rather, it focuses upon the manner in which theology proceeds in Scripture. I concluded some years ago that any hermeneutic which ignores how theology and application run hand-in-hand in Scripture will end up as a bare-bone, impoverished, mechanical, how-to-do-it enterprise. If we interpret the Bible properly we do not come face to face with a sure-fire scheme. We come face to face with the living God, through Christ his Son and the Holy Spirit. It is for this reason that I despaired of writing a book on hermeneutics for those with little insight into biblical theology.

In our churches, we still do not have a good mental picture of the manner in which theological reflection in Scripture is based upon the mighty acts of God. It is, however, much better than formerly. I have tried to contribute by publishing *He Loves Forever*, a book on Old Testament theology for use in the churches, as well as in the Living Word Commentary, and in *Restoration Quarterly* articles. I also had hoped to have a similar book on New Testament theology in print by now. I have therefore abstained from prematurely publishing a formulaic hermeneutic, even though some of my students have not been as constrained.[3]

Now, however, because of the dramatic increase of interest in hermeneutics—the result of persons coming to and studying the Scriptures in new ways and for differing reasons—perhaps it is time to break the silence. The question is, what sort of book is to be written? Obviously, it cannot be a how-to book. Likewise, it cannot be a short book, since the effort to see how biblical writers work theologically and then hermeneutically must precede any hermeneutical system.

I have read many books on hermeneutics.

From my perspective some were lifeless, others pedantic, still others misinformed, and miscellaneous additional contributions in these works not particularly helpful for those interested in coming face to face with the living God through Scripture. I have concluded that the last thing we need is another book on hermeneutics which presents a philosophical, cookbook-style program for achieving correct biblical interpretation and application. One may find enough of these in the libraries to satisfy about any theological taste, both literarily and historically.

What may be of help is how to think hermeneutically from a biblical perspective. For some years I have struggled over how this may best be done. I have concluded that in my case it seems best to approach hermeneutics autobiographically. It is true that autobiographical theology is in the air. "Narrativity" is now, in some circles, a buzz word. I have decided on this approach, I think, not so much because narrative is popular, but because in our present discussion of hermeneutics, it may be the only manner by which to raise the pertinent questions for this time in our fellowship. Through autobiography, the emphasis will be more on why I came to certain conclusions, rather than simply setting them forth.

Dangers lurk in an autobiographical approach, and I'm sure I will not be able to avoid all the pitfalls. Autobiography probably cannot avoid being self-serving. It cannot avoid arguing for one's commitments, decisions and actions. I hope in some measure to proceed, not so much, however, toward self-vindication, as to lead the reader out of the various quagmires into which all of us have blundered. I have sometimes taken wrong turns, and even at present struggle with new challenges to consensus interpretations of the past. I hope to present these struggles and reflections in such a manner that the reader can arrive at her own conclusions.

My conclusions about hermeneutics have not come about merely as a class room exercise. They have been hammered out in the crucibles of church involvement across this land and in foreign countries. The reader may at times feel that I have included too many details extraneous to the task at hand. I have done so to make it clear that my perspectives have come about through in-depth involvement with the people of God; in fact, much more often so than in the quiet of a book-lined study. I have spent much more time struggling in the church and in the classroom than in private reflection or engagement with scholars over a theory of hermeneutics.

This book, if I know my own mind and heart, is written so as to provide helpful reflection on how to live under a God whose voice may be heard in his Word. I have little interest in defending any status I may have as a guru or a leader in the "new hermeneutics" movement. I think these assertions are exaggerated so as to secure an *ad hominem* triumph for their authors. I think the controversy over the "new hermeneutics" is basically a shift in the manner in which preachers and people among us perceive the Scriptures. A new set of questions are now being addressed to these ancient documents. Neither am I concerned as to where I may be placed on a theological spectrum, whether middle-of-the-road, left or right. I am much more interested in following the voice of God as it may be heard in Scripture, than in conforming to an appropriate location on a spectrum as constructed by humans.

I have had a role in educating perhaps as many as two thousand preachers over the past forty years and some role in delineating and clarifying changes among our churches. But it would be foolhardy to take credit for the larger cultural and theological winds now blowing. I stated this conviction at some length in a two-part article published in *Image*. In commenting on the changes, I wrote

> First, I contend that the shift is grass roots. In my years of reflecting on reasons for the various developments in Christendom, I have come to believe that the major shifts have always been grass roots. Scholars, for the most part, have identified these shifts, and after the fact, have recommended ways of reformulating theologies and methods. But the impulse for the shifts came not from scholars, *qua* scholars, but from grass roots movements. Some scholars have led grass roots reforms or protests, for example, Martin Luther and Dietrich Bonhoeffer, or pertinent to our own history, Alexander Campbell, through "dirtying their hands" in active front line participation.[4]

In fact, I have expressed my own reservations over certain new directions and views on Scripture and its interpretation as expressed by some, several of whom are former students of mine. Even so, I still cherish them for the hours we spent together, confronted by the Word of the living Lord.

The manner in which I employ the word "hermeneutics" is in some measure undifferentiated.

By the word "hermeneutics" I have in mind the overall enterprise of correctly interpreting the Scriptures. I tend not to make precise distinctions among theology, exegesis, and hermeneutics, even though I believe the centers of each may be delineated. I do so because all three are inextricably interrelated. Despite criticism from some quarters that my treatment of hermeneutics is too broad, I persist. My observation of the alternative approach is that by delineating hermeneutics as an independent discipline, its proponents position it as essentially a technical and methodological discipline and ignore the larger theological matters which are, after all, the central foci of the Scriptures. A hermeneutic which fails to highlight, as central to Scripture, God, Christ and the Holy Spirit, whatever else it may offer, can give no more than superficial discernment of the message of the Scriptures. It is, of course, a hermeneutic, but is it a biblical hermeneutic? That is the ultimate question.

Since I am pursuing a somewhat privatized and undifferentiated perspective on hermeneutics I am obligated to locate my approach in the history of the discipline. The word itself means whatever the person employing it wants it to mean. It is difficult to fault the position of John Locke that words represent an idea in the mind of a speaker.[5] I must, however, point out that regardless of how we conceptualize hermeneutics, the word has a long history which even predates Christianity.[6] The word itself is derived from the name of the Greek god Hermes. Hermes delivered messages for Zeus, the chief god. Paul, for example, was mistaken for Hermes "because he was the chief speaker" (Acts 14:12). Hermeneutics, for the Greeks, had to do with interpreting the will of the gods. By New Testament times the Greek literary critics had developed specific rules for interpreting the poems of Homer and other ancient documents to which they assigned a privileged status.

For several centuries religious scholars have meant by hermeneutics those rules for explaining obscure textual meanings or for setting out the full significance of selected Scriptures. According to Carl R. Holladay in *Harper's Bible Dictionary*, hermeneutics "encompasses both the study of the principles of biblical interpretation and the process through which such interpretation is carried out."[7] Colin Brown, in the glossary of *The New International Dictionary of New Testament Theology*, defines hermeneutics as "The science of the interpretation of written texts in accordance with scientifically formulated rules and principles."[8] I respect these traditional definitions. At the same time, here and elsewhere, I employ a somewhat privatized meaning which is more inclusive in scope. By hermeneutics, I mean the perspectives and commitments from which believers put questions to the Scriptures in order to determine how to hear the voice of the living God and live accordingly.

It is my conviction that one cannot appreciate the hermeneutics of the believers of any era or of a specific subset of believers, without assessing these believers' perception of reality, the role the Scripture plays in it, and the questions they put to Scripture. The sociological and theological background of any confessional group, therefore, weighs heavily upon its hermeneutics. Hermeneutics are shaped by culture and theology, and once formulated, in turn, shape the culture and theology of a specific body of believers.

I have said enough by way of introduction.

The ramifications will emerge as the story unfolds. I am indebted to many persons along the way. The identity of several appear in the narrative, and therefore their names need not be itemized here.

I am convinced that the background from which we come to the Scripture, and the questions we address to it, are determined by our biography. I reject the assertion, however, that since such is the case, that any interpretation is as valid as any other. I agree with Bultmann that no interpretation is without presuppositions.[9] But I reject the implication that we are unable to replace or change our presuppositions for those that come from the Scriptures themselves. In fact, I hope to show in these autobiographical reflections that I have revised my own understanding of Scriptures at certain critical junctures precisely because my presuppositions were not that biblical. While many interpretations may capture a dimension of biblical truth, certain ones, I believe, are truer to the text than others.

As the result of the autobiographical approach employed here, readers are invited to reflect on whether the presuppositions and questions with which they come to the Scriptures are those of their own biography, rather than presuppositions found in the Scriptures themselves. My upbringing has forced me to perceive the Scriptures from a number of different angles. Through the years I have struggled with most of these. The influences upon my visions of reality have suggested different emphases in locating what is of central importance and must be highlighted and applied. These are the larger concerns. It is only after asking what is of first importance from the standpoint of Scripture that we have a way of judging these numerous approaches that surface in our upbringing. Perhaps my background has been yours; then again, perhaps not. Nevertheless, we cannot properly weigh hermeneutical proposals without assessing the particular spectacles through which we have been trained to visualize reality and assess the Scriptures.

---

[1] These items are found in the footnotes and the bibliography.

[2] John Macquarrie, *Principles of Christian Theology* (New York: Charles Scribner's Sons, 1966) 5-17.

[3] For example, Bob Burgess, "New Testament Interpretation: Problem & Probe," *Mission*, Part I, November 1975, Part II, December, 1975, 106-110.

[4] Thomas H. Olbricht, "Hermeneutics: The Beginning Point," *Image* Part I, September 1989, 14, 15, Part II, October 1989, 15-17.

[5] John Locke, *An Essay Concerning Human Understanding*, III, ii, 2.

[6] Gerhard Kittel, *Theological Dictionary of the New Testament*, trans. Geoffrey W. Bromiley, (Grand Rapids: Eerdmans, 1964) II, 661-666.

[7] Carl R. Holladay, "Hermeneutics," *Harper's Bible Dictionary* (San Francisco: Harper & Row, 1985) 384.

[8] *The New International Dictionary of New Testament Theology*, Colin Brown, ed. (Grand Rapids: Zondervan, 1979), Vol. I, 59.

[9] Rudolf Bultmann, *Theology of the New Testament*, trans. Kendrick Grobel (New York: Charles Scribner's Sons, 1955) 237-251.

1

The Scriptures Through the Eyes of Grandparents and Parents

Anyone's interpretation of Scripture obviously is indebted to beginnings—the world into which he is born. We may depart from our beginnings in certain ways through the years, but to a significant extent they remain with us until the end. The late A. D. Nock of Harvard, one of my professors, used to announce with great delight that "we cannot climb out of our own skin."

When I was thirty-five, having completed one undergraduate and three graduate degrees, and having been shaped socially by these educational institutions and the cosmopolitan region of eastern Massachusetts, I thought I was considerably different from my father, son of a German immigrant, who spent his life in isolated regions of western Nebraska and southern Missouri. It was with considerable surprise and no little chagrin that I realized, after spending a week with him, that in most personal manners and ways of thinking I was still very much in his image. It was just that I knew many aspects of Western and even Eastern civilization of which he had only the dimmest notion. It wasn't even so much a matter of admiration or respect. His experiences and insights as a Nebraska homesteader were unique. I thought perhaps I had in some measure outgrown my past, but it was by no means the extent to which I had imagined.

In discussions on hermeneutics in recent years the term employed to describe the background which the reader brings to the text is *preunderstanding*. Duncan S. Ferguson remarked in his book, *Biblical Hermeneutics*, "Indeed it would appear that nearly all perception and subsequent understanding and interpretation of reality proceed in some measure from the preunderstanding of the participant."[1]

My earliest understandings—rather, preunderstandings—of Scripture came from my parents and grandparents, but especially from my mother and her father, and the teachers and preachers in congregations of the Churches of Christ which we attended.

I was born in November 1929 in Thayer, Missouri, to Benjamin J. (1885-1978) and Agnes M. Taylor Olbricht (1898-1978). My father had moved to Thayer from Crawford, Nebraska, when he married my mother in 1927. His parents had moved to Thayer from Crawford in 1910. My grandfather, Henry (Heinrich) Olbricht (1856-1941) was born in Glatz, Germany (now Klodzo, Poland) and was

Roman Catholic. My step-grandmother Bertha Lange Sauser Olbricht (1866-1955) was born in a German-speaking region of Russia, later Poland, and was Lutheran. Although they lived only ten miles away, the roads were unpaved and rocky, so we visited only four or five times a year. They almost never came to see us. I knew practically nothing of their religious beliefs.

T. Shelt Taylor

My religious heritage was that of my mother's father, Thomas Shelton Taylor (1876-1968) born near Couch, Missouri. His father, John Moody Taylor (1829-1909) was born in Bellgreen, Franklin County, Alabama. As a young man, John Moody Taylor, according to my grandfather, heard T. B. Larimore preach. John Taylor left Alabama in 1869 for southern Missouri and northern Arkansas. The Taylors were well-grounded in the heritage of the Restoration Movement. My maternal grandmother, Myrtle Dunsmore Taylor (1879-1969) was born in Iona, Michigan. Her parents were Methodists. She and my grandfather were baptized about the time they were married, in 1896.

My earliest memories are from age four. At that time my grandfather was a leader of the Church of Christ in Centertown, an area of scattered houses about halfway between Thayer, Missouri, and Mammoth Spring, Arkansas. The Centertown church was established during World War I in the house of my grandfather. In 1918 he had built a relatively large stone dwelling. Upon entering the front door one noted, on the left and right, double living rooms. These were specifically designed so as to accommodate the church. In the twenties, a frame church building was constructed on two acres my grandfather contributed, about 300 yards north of his house and across the highway. My parents lived an additional quarter mile north toward Thayer. Many of the members were related to my grandfather.

Some of my earliest memories are of church services at Centertown. We began by singing. We sang out of cheap, paperback books, some of which had torn covers. I always liked the singing.

We had preaching only irregularly. The leading men of the congregation took turns teaching a book from the Bible, almost always from the New Testament, and usually Acts or a shorter Pauline epistle. What I remember were the arguments on topics which pertained not only to the members present, but to the views of people in the various denominations. The exchanges sometimes became heated and even though I didn't always fully understand what they were about, they kept me awake. From these experiences I developed the sense that the Bible was a book to be scrutinized verse by verse, even word by word. The main reason for studying it was to determine who was right and who was wrong.

We sometimes had a visiting preacher, such as Joe Blue from Morriston, Arkansas. These preachers often utilized "chart sermons." This was before the days of photographic projection, or at least before it was affordable to preachers or the churches in our region. The charts were painted on cloth sheets which were attached to the wall behind the pulpit. Other preachers painted their charts on oil cloth, while still others utilized large sheets of paper which they obtained from printers. Some preachers had fifteen or twenty of these charts, all attached to a cross bar which they placed on a stand. In that manner they could flip the charts if they wished to use more than one during the sermon.

The sermons on the charts were mostly in outline form. One of the favorites was a sermon contrasting man's requirements for pleasing God before the death of Christ with those afterward. A large cross was drawn down the middle of the chart. On the left, in outline form, were the commands from the Old Testament and on the right were those from the New Testament. A clear distinction was made between the obligations for believers under the Old Testament as contrasted with the New. These sermons were all topical. They discussed such issues as the authority of the New Testament compared with that of the Old, the establishment of the church, the worship of the church, the history of the church, or the plan of salvation. From these sermons I received the impression that the Scriptures were to be interpreted in light of topics set forth in logical fashion. I also concluded that the chief matters of importance could be summed up in ten or fifteen sermons. Members might argue over specific Scriptures, but when it came down to what really mattered, a few logically arranged topics summed it all up.

Consistency was portrayed as the chief desirable attribute of scriptural interpretation. I was led to believe that except for those of us in the Churches of Christ, most religious persons were woefully inconsistent. I was drilled to argue that if one claims that the Bible is the word of God, then every jot and tittle is the word of God. Likewise, if one holds that commands are to be obeyed, that implies all commands. It is not enough to emphasize repentance and faith in calling sinners to Christ. One must also emphasize confession, and especially baptism.

The sermons were not particularly attractive to a four year old. The delivery was often loud and in a strident, repetitive rhythm. I tended to daydream about digging holes or damming up small streams, my favorite pastimes at that age. The preaching at the two-week meetings held during the summer was much the same—the charts, and the monotonous vocal patterns. I remember going to sleep more than once on the hard wooden benches, since the preaching did not commence until after eight and continued past my bedtime. The benches were made by members and not sophisticated enough to be called pews. We considered "pews" theologically objectionable, if not elitist.

The summer meetings were held in the open. The church building was set back a hundred yards from the highway. Between the highway and the building were several oak trees, some quite large. The benches were carried out of the building and placed under the trees, upon which electric lights were strung. The open space was cooler on a warm southern Missouri night, but there a new problem emerged—flies and mosquitoes. We did not need a brush arbor, which was fabricated by erecting a frame cut from small trees, and then covered with leafed branches, often seen along the roadsides in the summer. We had our own live canopy, and on a clear night, the stars were visible, twinkling through the leaves.

At the end of the sermon we always sang an invitation song, inviting persons for baptism or restoration. At that point I returned either from daydreams or sleep to what was going on in the meeting. On Sunday mornings the invitation was followed by communion. We usually had a few remarks at the Lord's table and occasionally a reading from the Scriptures. The bread and the cup were passed. The contribution, however, proceeded by people walking up in turns and laying the money on the table.

"Why do we do all these things?" I wanted to know. "Because," I was told, "it is like the last supper of Christ with the disciples. And Jesus commanded us to commemorate his supper every Lord's day. We are also commanded to lay by in store on the first day of the week." From these remarks I received early encouragement toward the view that what we practiced came out of Scripture by way of Christ's example or command.

While it was true that the purpose and pattern were drawn from the New Testament, I now realize that specific aspects reflected our British cultural heritage. One hundred-fifty years ago our worship followed Scottish patterns. The singing was often of Psalms put to music, but popular English and American hymns began to invade our services. Many of these songs were generated by groups influenced by the two great spiritual awakenings (1740-1770, 1800-1830) and the heirs of those groups. Some of the songs were African-American spirituals, and a free interchange took place.[2] The words to these hymns were published in books, normally without musical notation, though the names of the tunes were identified. About Alexander Campbell, Forrest McCann wrote, "He objected to the use of musical notes in hymnals, believing that these detracted from the content of the songs. So long as he lived no notes were printed in his own hymnals nor those of the ACMS."[3] Barton Stone and Alexander Campbell both published hymnals, then collaborated with Walter Scott and John T. Johnson.[4] Campbell not only opposed the use of instrumental music, but also the use of hymn books in worship. Books were to be left at home, fostering memorization, he thought. The hymns were "lined out"—a leader read a line, then the congregation sang it.

In these early days of our movement, the services were long, often occupying two hours. The preacher, more often called "elder," was followed by a younger man in training who offered an exhortation and invitation. In most churches the communion was placed on a long table, covered with white linen, which reached across the front of the building. Where practical the congregation literally gathered around the table. The traditional prayer phrase, "As we gather round the table," was not metaphorical. Moses Lard, in his 1863 *Quarterly*, in describing his ideal church, wrote "A table is now prepared extending entirely across the house, and covered with a clean white linen."[5] Laying by in store was also more literal in that each member laid his or her contribution on the table. Lard declared, "The whole congregation simultaneously arose and rushed to the stand in front of the pulpit"[6] to provide funds for a member whose house had burned. When a congregation became so large that it could no longer gather round the table, each person still walked up to the table and placed money on it. In that manner, if one employed discretion, no one knew what he gave, since it was placed behind the communion items. The folding of the table cloth became a ceremony in the hands of some who presided. The linens disappeared when metal and wooden covers graced the communion trays. The linens had a long history in liturgical symbolism, but also a pragmatic mission in obstructing the flies which came through the open windows of the church house in summertime.

My earliest memories of singing in our churches in southern Missouri involved a fluid canon. Our hymnals were almost always paperback and the most frequently employed was that of Will Slater.[7] We used these books frequently—for regular services, summer meetings and special singings. Because of constant use the books did not last longer than two or three years. We were glad to replace them because new songs appeared in later versions. The Stamps-Baxter Music Company regularly published new songs which made their way into our services. We learned these through listening to the Stamps-Baxter quartet on the radio and being present at their personal appearances. Members involved with quartets bought the latest Stamps-Baxter song books. We had Sunday afternoon singings in various churches, as many as two or three a month. We sang congregationally, listened to quartets, male or mixed, or to female trios or quartets. As these songs made their way into the Slater books we usually already knew them. We also learned most of the new songs we did not know. I remember the excitement when we first sang, "If We Never Meet Again this Side of Heaven," and "I Will Meet You in the Morning," both by Albert Brumley, a fellow Missourian from Powell, or Slater's "Walking Alone at Eve."

These early church memories are especially connected with my grandfather. He was often involved in leading public church events. I admired him in many respects, probably above all other persons, and in turn was his favorite. It was either he or my mother who answered any questions I might have. I was always full of questions, in fact so much so that one of my uncles, after a few trips, stopped inviting me to go on with him on gas deliveries—he was a bulk agent for Standard Oil—because I asked too many questions. Though Grandfather Taylor helped mold aspects of my religious attitudes, I regarded certain contributions of my mother more highly.

By the time I knew my grandfather he had operated a gas station and small grocery for some fifteen years. He also sold livestock feed. In addition, he owned four or five tourist cabins situated near the business. His services were analogous to those of a contemporary multipurpose convenience store. The station, as he called it, was on the major highway (U. S. 63), running through central Missouri and southeasterly into Memphis, Tennessee. Many customers were out-of-state travelers, but he also had local clientele. Business tended to be slow at certain times of the day. He always kept a Bible on a long, wide shelf which extended across the expanse behind a display window. In winter he occupied a favorite chair, with his feet extended over the floor grate to the coal furnace. In summer he sat out front, under the overhang. He often read from his Bible.

He was never one to read through the Bible in scheduled fashion, though he probably had done so at one time in his life. He tended to read sections of Scripture which related to topics currently in dispute, thereby hoping to settle them. By time I knew him he had an essentially empty nest, and three unoccupied bedrooms in his home. Since his house was about as modernized as any among the members, and since he loved to discuss the unresolved problems with preachers, he usually kept the summer meeting preachers at his own expense.

In summer, since no one—at least no one in southern Missouri—had air conditioning, he sat in front of the display window, where two or three metal outdoor chairs were placed. I can still see him sitting there, either reading the Bible or napping. He was a light napper, and if a car drove in, he jumped up quickly so that his napping might go undetected. If a visiting preacher was around, he tried to entice him to the station for a discussion. I sat many hours, listening to these discussions.

From age six, I spent much of the summer at my grandparents. From the third through the eighth grade, I was there all year, to help with the station and the forty-acre farm. By the time I was eight I had begun to develop some of my own views on the controversial topics in which my grandfather specialized. But in those days children were to be seen, not heard, so I did not interrupt, at least, while the adults were in discussion.

Grandpa's favorite topic, on which he presumed to have a definitive answer, was how the apostles became members of the church. The problem, noticed by others, was that there is no evidence that the apostles were ever baptized. Lacking such evidence, my grandfather concluded that they weren't baptized. Since we assumed that people had to be baptized to be saved and included by God as members of the church, he was sure that the explanation as to how they came into the church was to be found in I Corinthians 12:28, which, in the KJV, reads, "And God hath set some in the church, first apostles, secondarily prophets, thirdly teachers." The apostles, my Grandfather argued, were set in the church, but everyone else had to be baptized into it. One time I proposed to him that, since John 4:2 says that Jesus' disciples baptized, perhaps they baptized each other. This he doubted, but even if so, in his judgment, the baptism would not qualify, since it occurred before Christ died on the cross. He convinced certain preachers, but others were not so easily persuaded.

It was clear my grandfather had a rule for interpretation, whether stated or not: If a problem arose because of an apparent violation of a presumed biblical imperative, then the appropriate explanation was derived from any statement which seemed to resolve it. The imperative in the above case was that everyone had to be baptized into the church, the favorite prooftext being I Corinthians 12:13. In fact, some persons, arguing against the universal need for baptism, contended that the apostles were not baptized. My grandfather agreed, but held that they were an exception. The rule is an interesting one. It has had a revered career in the Restoration Movement. For example, some of us have believed that it is futile for unbaptized persons to pray, since John 9:31 reads, "God does not listen to sinners," even though the remark was made by Pharisees who opposed Jesus.

My grandfather's study of the Scripture was akin to puzzle solving. The Bible was a handbook of puzzles as well as the means for resolving them.

Agnes M. (Taylor) Olbricht

My mother was twenty-nine and on her way to being an old maid school teacher when she met my father, a forty-one year old Nebraska bachelor who was visiting his parents in southern Missouri. She had attained a college degree in 1924 at Southwest Missouri State Teachers College (now Southwest Missouri State University). She had taught for some years, both before and after obtaining her degree. This pattern was typical for the time. She was a high school teacher in math and the sciences. She spoke occasionally of having had a problem with faith at one stage in her life. She never revealed many specifics, but because of her own struggles, insisted that her children attend a Christian college.

My mother read the Scriptures regularly, mostly to find out how to order her life. She was a voracious reader, much more so than was pleasing to my father. At best, he had attended school for a year and a half. To do even that, he rode a horse about eight miles to a one-room frame building in the open spaces of the western Nebraska prairie. In my earliest memories of him, he occasionally read the weekly *Kansas City Star*, but for news he usually listened to the radio. He was mostly a builder of houses or a painter, but in reality a jack-of-all-trades. At one time he bought and erected windmills. He didn't have much time for reading. His father was a Roman Catholic immigrant, but in Nebraska, Granddad Olbricht lived so far from a church that he attended mass irregularly. The sentiments of my father were the generic Protestantism of the western plains. But he considered himself a Roman Catholic and thought reading the Scripture would damage one's mind. My mother read the Scriptures when he was at work.

Mother was always a storyteller. She loved to tell stories or read to children, later grandchildren. Because she loved not only reading, but disseminating what she read, she entered Harding University and received a master's degree in elementary education at age fifty-nine. She then re-entered the classroom as an elementary teacher.

Some of my earliest memories are of her taking her four children on walks in the fields and woods behind the house. When we grew tired of walking she asked us to sit down, and proceeded to tell a story; either a folk tale, or something from children's literature. Sometimes she might quote a poem. Among her favorite stories were those from the Scriptures—about Samson, David and Goliath, Daniel or Jesus. As we got older she read from Bible story books, especially Hurlbut's. I still remember my reactions. Some of the accounts were interesting and challenging; for example, Daniel, Shadrach, Meshach and Abednego. I marveled at how they succeeded by remaining steadfast to their commitments. I also liked stories about Jesus and his gentleness and concern for children. Some of the accounts, however, were frightening because of punishment by disaster. The pictures added to the alarm—of great disasters such as the Flood, fires from heaven, the earth opening up or the Day of Judgment. These were the sources of childhood nightmares.

My mother so wanted us absorbed in Bible stories that she read them as a bribe, but she had other reasons. Mom was never particularly interested in cooking or house cleaning. My father did a great deal of both. Instead, she loved to read and write. For many years she wrote regularly for *Christian Woman*. My sister Nedra was the oldest. By early elementary years she could read almost anything on her own. Furthermore, she was a tomboy and cared little for house work or dishes. Mother would tell her sons—Glenn, Owen, and me—that if we would wash and dry the dishes she would read Bible stories. My mother set out to motivate us by slipping up on what she thought was our blind side. She considered it good psychology, having studied the subject for pedagogical purposes. We much preferred to dig in the banks of the ditches back in the fields or play ball. But we knew we would have to do dishes anyway and, since we liked Mom—even her "warped," if winsome, ways—we let her read to us while we washed.

The image of the Bible I received from my mother was much different from that of my grandfather, or the focus and approach at church. In neither of the latter cases was the Bible perceived primarily as story. I did not, at the time, see these two contrasting approaches as dissonant, but I tended to favor my mother's somewhat unarticulated agenda that the Bible has more to do with the replication of the lives of those whose stories are told than with argument over words and doctrines. She had little interest in delineating hermeneutical formulas. She was much more into imitating exemplary lives. She emphasized the good qualities, but left no uncertain sound in regard to the evils that befall those who disobey. Mother, however, did believe as strongly as anyone that we in the Churches of Christ were correct on a whole series of matters having to do with baptism, elders and deacons, instrumental music, and weekly communion.

Mother was a great reader and she encouraged all her children to read. Her vision of reality, as well as ours, was influenced by books. Our reading particularly focused on the moral nature of persons, of right and wrong, of guilt, sin, and shame. Success and reward for hard work, goodness, and persistence also could be found, along with love, but the last was mostly of a romantic sort. Focus upon genuine, giving love, reconciliation, and forgiveness was, to some extent, neglected. We walked to the Thayer library once a week to select our books. It was almost a mile each way, and up and down a steep hill. The walk was tiring to short legs. Sometimes, after a spurt of energy, we dawdled behind and complained. Still, we did not wish to miss the adventure into new realities provided by books.

When we were in preschool and early elementary grades, Mother read such works as *Aesop's Fables*, *Arabian Nights*, *Alice's Adventure in Wonderland*, *Robinson Crusoe*, and *Gulliver's Travels*. As we grew older, we read books by Dickens, Alcott, Twain, Stevenson, Cooper, Poe, Eliot, and much poetry, especially that of Henry Wadsworth Longfellow, Carl Sandburg, and James Whitcomb Riley. I read the usual boy's books; *The Rover Boys*, *Mark Tidd*, and even *Rebecca of Sunny Brook Farm*. As I got older I read historical novels: Owen Wister's *The Virginian*, Winston Churchhill's *The Crisis*, John Fox's *The Trail of the Lonesome Pine*, and by high school days, Margaret Mitchell's *Gone with the Wind*.

Mother especially encouraged us to read religious novels. The ones I remember most vividly were Harold Bell Wright's *The Shepherd of the Hills*, Charles Sheldon's *In His Steps*, and several novels of Lloyd C. Douglas: *The Great Fisherman*, *The Robe*, and *Magnificent Obsession*. The two books that at one stage influenced my mother the most were *In His Steps* and *Magnificent Obsession*. They were likewise the books that influenced me, but in reverse order.

It seems almost contradictory now, more than fifty years later, that in the middle thirties my mother was obsessed with *In His Steps*. After all, Charles Sheldon was a part of the social gospel movement which in the 1950s was bitterly rejected by most preachers in the Churches of Christ. As far as I know, Mother was one of the few persons of our acquaintance who read the book and took it seriously. At one stage, she was regarded in our circle as something of a religious fanatic. It was one thing to prove that sectarians are wrong, or to spend long hours on tricky exceptions to biblical rules. It was another, apparently, to take seriously the model of Jesus' concerns for others. In Sheldon's *In His Steps* (first published in 1897) the hero, a minister named Henry Maxwell, challenges his congregation to do nothing without first asking, "What would Jesus do?" and then follow through by acting accordingly.

The thirties were Depression years. My mother was interested in sharing what we had because she believed that was what Jesus would do. We may not have had much, but we had plenty to eat. We lived on a ten-acre farm and grew garden items of all sorts. It seemed that we planted, hoed, weeded, picked, shelled, broke, peeled, and canned all summer long. We had plenty of potatoes, both Irish and sweet. We had apples, pears, grapes, peaches—of which we grew enough to sell—gooseberries, blackberries, raspberries, strawberries, rhubarb, asparagus, and even peanuts. We had a windmill and my father built two large concrete tanks so we could irrigate in dry times, which ordinarily plagued southern Missouri in July and August.

In September, my brothers and I spent long hours picking up walnuts and hickory nuts. Later in the fall and before Christmas, we shelled, cracked and picked out the meats. My mother got the bright idea of giving relatives shelled nuts for Christmas, and they were pleased to receive them. But tediously picking out nut meats became one of the less favorite activities of my siblings and me. We preferred Monopoly, hands-down. Once again, mother sometimes bribed us by reading aloud.

Mother made clothes of all sorts, for both men and women. She wasn't that good at it, but the garments were serviceable. She also made quilts and even bedsheets out of white feed sacks. We shared these, especially with needy people who lived within walking distance of our house. We children went along to carry fruit, or home canned items. In the spring of 1937 there was a major flood on the Mississippi River. Though we lived one hundred-fifty miles away, we were plagued more than usual with migrating bums who constantly stopped and asked for something to eat. They often offered to work, but we soon discovered that they tired easily and exercised little quality control. We tended just to give them food so they would be on their way. Mom always made sandwiches for them out of homemade "graham" bread as she called it. We usually had two acres of wheat which Dad would thrash and grind into whole-wheat flour. Mom filled a brown bag with sandwiches, fruit, or whatever we had available. More than once, a recipient would tell her she gave them too much—that she should offer less so as to have plenty for the hoboes who came along later.

At this stage mother was especially interested in Scripture's call to help the needy. She was clear about why she was doing it: because that was what Jesus would do. Most of the people we knew were not kind toward the bums. They might occasionally give them food, but drifters were generally said to be lazy. If they really wanted to provide for themselves they could, it was thought.

At seven, I didn't have much religious motivation for helping vagrants. We children tended to be afraid of them and were encouraged in that direction by our parents. Once in a while, Mother had us hand them a bag of food, but warned us not to get far from the house. Some of them were talkative, but most seemed to be loners and were glad to move on and eat. I thought Mom was doing right, but overdoing it, as my dad agreed. I didn't mind for others to help people, but I saved most of the money I earned or was given. All of us had a savings account at the bank, and we had read in the children's success stories how people had grown rich from saving pennies. I dreamed of doing that. Along with everyone else during WWII, I bought savings bonds as I could, always in the lowest denomination. A twenty-five dollar bond could be purchased for $17.50. I would have preferred not giving much at church, but mother encouraged us and then watched or called for an accounting. By time I was in the seventh or eighth grade I had developed my own commitment to benevolence, mostly by putting money in the collection plate at church.

I don't remember when I first read Lloyd C. Douglas's *Magnificent Obsession*, but it left an indelible impression. The novel is about a doctor who ascertained that Jesus charged those he helped not to reveal his help. Instead, he told them to keep quiet and not tell anyone. The doctor decided that the secret to God-given success in life was to help people without their knowledge. This was his magnificent obsession. He took extreme measures to conceal his gifts and ways of helping people. I concluded that the obsession was commendable, but I didn't know how to implement it except by occasionally doing extra chores, such as emptying waste paper baskets, cleaning the basement, and mowing or hoeing. But that didn't really qualify, since my parents or grandparents noticed and concluded I had done it. I could do extra work, but it always tended to get credited. By the *Obsession* yardstick, known efforts did not qualify.

Magnificent Obsession left me mystified, intrigued—and confused. What happens to a boy who, on the one hand, dotes upon wonder, fantasy, story, and fiction, but on the other, lives in the real world of men and adores a father and a grandfather who disdained gullibility and make-believe and much preferred facts and reason? I have already introduced this dichotomy in my upbringing. In order to develop this struggle in more detail, I must introduce my dad.

Benjamin J. Olbricht

We never referred to him as "Father," since every good student of Scripture knew that no one on earth may be called "Father"—this title was reserved for the Father in heaven (Matthew 23:9). My dad's mother died before he was four. He lived a few years with a maternal aunt and her family in New Jersey. Henry Olbricht, his father, migrated to Nebraska to homestead in 1892. A year later, all the children except the youngest followed, accompanied by the family of my dad's fraternal uncle. He never knew the care of a real mother and his relationship with his German-born father was detached and non-emotive. In his opinion, his father was mostly interested in the work he got out of him. Dad remained at home, unmarried. In 1910, when Dad was twenty-five, my grandfather tired of Nebraska blizzards and bought a farm in southern Missouri.

My father, who, in 1906, was homesteading an adjacent section, bought my grandfather's farm.

In Germany, my grandfather apprenticed as a tanner. Upon migrating to New York in 1878, he worked in tanneries. When he moved to Nebraska, he built a tannery on his ranch. According to my dad, Grandpa tanned while making his son do the demanding ranch work of planting wheat and potatoes and cutting hay. At first, my grandfather tanned local hides: deer, bear, wolf, coyote, cow, horse, and sheep. Later, he placed ads in national magazines, and once received a shipment of alligator hides from Florida.

My earliest memories of my father were of his bedroom. My mother and father were married in 1927. Six years later, in 1933, there were four children. Some of the children slept in Mother's bedroom; by 1933, Dad slept in his own room. His floor and walls were covered with hides my grandfather had tanned. He had a bearskin and wolfskin rug and other hides on the walls. There was no heat in my father's bedroom: he liked it that way. We were not permitted to play there for fear we would damage the animal skins. A few years later the room was badly contaminated with moths, so my mother made him destroy his cherished furs.

I do not know the extent of the influence of my grandfather on my father because I never really knew my German grandfather. He was seventy-three when I was born. He said very little to kids. I remember once accidentally coming upon him in the barnyard when I was about eight. He never said a word, and I was not about to venture anything, since I normally only saw him at the house with my parents present. It may well have been the absence of any real relationship with my grandfather which influenced my father the most.

My father was strictly business when I was young—he didn't talk very much. He was the very opposite of "touchy-feely." I spent my early years with him, so I was too young to recognize anything unusual in this, or to do anything about it if I had. My son Joel, when he was three or four, sometimes snuggled up to him, but my father pushed him away. He was very uncomfortable with any sort of physical contact. I am sure that represented and resulted from his relationship with his own father.

Grandpa Taylor—Mother's father—liked my dad because he was a "worker"—and that he was. He kept busy from sunrise to sunset. There was the cow to milk, eggs to gather, and the garden to tend. At one time my father raised broiler chickens, sometimes as many as a thousand. We kids did not care for the feeding and cleaning chores, but we loved the baby chicks when they arrived from the hatchery—so soft and furry. But he also worked away from our small farm, usually building houses and barns with my mother's cousin, Rob Hicks. They constructed houses for two of my mother's brothers. My father also constructed houses, which he then rented. These he built himself with some help from his young sons. He also painted houses and commercial buildings for others.

My father did little reading, and he did not believe in stories. He interpreted the world according to the current realities, according to facts and reason. He was a hard-working pragmatist. My mother's brothers, who had gone to college, could usually explain why things worked. But my father, who could fix almost anything, did not worry so much about why they worked, but how they worked. He fixed things that stymied my uncles. He had certain designations for story-tellers: they were "wind bags", "windjammers," and their achievements were "all in their heads." Whenever we helped him, his constant admonition was, "Shut up and work!" He also was quick to say, "Don't brag about it—do it!"

Some of my earliest memories of my father are of his disinterest in religion. He did, however, go to church. Religion seemed like so much talk to him, reflecting on matters which were mostly speculation. While he considered himself sort of a Catholic, he did not admire that church. He believed the church was too interested in dictating to the American government and to individual people. He saw it as too engrossed in mystery and superstition, and as excessively wealthy and greedy.

I remember when my father was baptized. I was eight. Mother had been hoping, but not pressuring. It was during a summer gospel meeting. I remember going home for him to get a change of clothes, then driving to the mouth of Warm Fork Creek, where it emptied into the stream which flowed out of Mammoth Spring. The atmosphere seemed numinous—out the ordinary. I had been to several baptisms, but this was my own father. For some reason, his baptism seemed to distance us even more. But I also remember how he changed. Before, he had always been gruff and impatient. Now he seemed mellowed; more helpful. While he was never outgoing, from that point on he took on certain responsibilities which he perceived as characteristic of Christians. As summer meetings approached, he invited people to attend, even those who I think he realized were highly unlikely to come. In summers, after all the chores were done, he sat out in a swing attached to a box elder tree. We knew most of the people who walked by on the highway. He would greet them from the distance of his swing, and invite them to attend the meeting. He also invited the people whose houses he painted.

When my father became a Christian he took up reading the Scriptures. I'm not altogether sure what he was looking for, although I'm certain he did not see the Bible as story. He was so impatient with controversy that he surely didn't read it to solve the puzzles, as my grandfather did. He thought people in church spent too much time arguing the same old things, which, in his opinion, could not be resolved. He was against "speculation," as he called it—matters which may have been related to the facts, but far enough removed so as to be mostly personal opinion. He was never much interested in people's personal opinions, considering them simply that. I think he mostly read Scripture to fix it in his mind, since he liked to be knowledgeable. He was a good listener in classes and during sermons. He said very little. He wanted to know the Scriptures so he could judge himself whether the preacher or teacher stuck to the facts. He was little concerned, however, to discuss his conclusions with others, though he and my mom occasionally talked over certain points, mostly in the middle of the night. My father usually went to bed by nine or nine-thirty, but my mother didn't sleep much: her first priority was reading. It was not unusual for me to wake up at 3:00 A.M. and hear them talking in bed. After conversing for thirty minutes or so, they usually went back to sleep.

Dad had his criteria for a good preacher. A good preacher mostly preached the Scripture. He was a person with a positive outlook. My father did not like a "sore head" who always ran down other religions, but he didn't mind clear exposition which showed specific religious views to be wrong. He tolerated passion or emotion in a sermon, but he did not like stories extraneous to the Scriptures, especially stories which stirred up excessive emotion, such as deathbed stories. For him the Scriptures were chiefly a composite of right facts and conclusions and were to be interpreted by staying as close as possible to those facts. He had little interest in distinguishing between different sorts of facts—command and example, for instance.

Clearly, my father retained a healthy skepticism of any point of view which strayed from the data of his experience or from an authoritative source, such as the Scriptures. I loved the stories of my mother. I loved novels, especially historical novels. My father, however, cared for none of these. I admired my father, and in some way I imitated his healthy skepticism of all fictions and "stories." But unlike him, I still relished the stories. I was the child of both my father and mother: like her, I enjoyed the stories; because of his influence, I always worried about which events actually happened, and which did not. When someone told a story, I always listened with great interest, but my father usually got up and left when the talespinners commenced. He had work to do—I stuck around. I loved a good story, but given the chance I would ask, "Is that really true?" I constantly sought to hone my skills at getting at the truth which my father required in the stories which my mother loved.

I think more than anyone I knew of my age, I was determined to delineate the true from the false in stories. Adults sometimes smiled at my reaction to a long-winded tale. A penurious neighbor often came to my grandfather's station on long winter nights, spinning drawn-out stories about the business deals in which he had been involved and at which he had made several hundreds of dollars. My father called him a windbag. After one long session when the storyteller had departed, I said to my grandfather and an uncle (my dad was not present), "Well, Ed certainly made a lot of money tonight," thereby indicating that I did not believe a word of it, even though I took it all in. They laughed, as if to say, "No one is going to put anything over on this kid!"

I was greatly influenced by my father to develop critical acumen. Since I read much more than he, I possessed a much larger body of data on which to exercise my skills. I struggled with the separation of facts and fiction in a variety of materials he would never have touched. Stories people told about their religious experiences, especially if they were extraordinary, were always weighed carefully. Neither my father nor I were impressed with stories of people, such as James A. Harding (after whom Harding University was named), who had to get somewhere, had no money, prayed, and saw someone walk up and put money into their hands. That never happened to us and we doubted that it happened to others. We also had little patience with faith-healers or people who reported miraculous cures after fervent prayers, either privately or in prayer meetings. My mother also doubted many aspects of these reports, but she believed somehow that God, in his providence, rewarded humble, hidden service.

Scripture, however, was something different. It was inspired of God and not to be doubted, even when reporting eerie events and unusual miracles. But the age of miracles was past, since we accepted the idea that miracles ceased when the Scriptures were completed, quoting I Corinthians 13:10. And, when it came to interpreting Scripture, the usual cautious, healthy skepticism had to be maintained. What anyone said in regard to a Scripture's meaning was to be perceived as personal opinion until it passed the test of critical examination.

Even though I was my father's and my grandfather's child in regard to keeping as close to the facts as possible, I sometimes wished the world of stories, romances, and mystery were the real world. I wanted to believe in the magnificent obsession, but since, at that stage in life, I did not have an adequate means of putting the obsession to the test, I pushed it to the back burner and stuck to the business of saving as much money as possible for a wealthy future. I especially disliked spending my own money on clothes and school supplies. My parents should do that, I thought. I sometimes had to battle with my father over this, especially after the third grade, when I lived with Grandpa Taylor, and when I went to high school while living with my mother's brother, Cleo Taylor.

As I grew older I continued to read novels. I checked them out at school and public libraries. I was an inveterate reader. My father, aunts and uncles and others suggested I get out of the house and play. I preferred to read, but felt somewhat shamed by their constant exhortations, so I would put down my book and wander outside. My mother, according to my father's judgment, ruined me for life by instilling in me her fixation on books and reading.

I was aware of certain dissonances in my vision of reality, but I did not find these troublesome. I hoped that life could be both factual and romantic, but admittedly, experienced mostly the factual, emotionless side. I knew I was liked, especially by my mother and her father, and by aunts and uncles. But we were not affectionate or physically demonstrative in our relationships. Perhaps the reason I relished the romance in novels so much was that they provided a future prospect which was lacking in my present.

The implications of all this for hermeneutics are perhaps obvious. I came to the Scripture, as we all do, with a preunderstanding of reality. This, in turn, deeply influenced the manner in which I perceived Scripture. For my mother, the Scriptures consisted first of stories, but mostly stories pertinent to an earlier age when miracles occurred. Consideration had to be given to outcomes of obeying God now, as compared with former times. The stories from Scripture provided models. The heroes were to be emulated. My mother's favorite Longfellow poem, "Psalm of Life," contained this line, "Lives of great men all remind us/ we can make our lives sublime/ and departing leave behind us/ footprints on the sands of time." Noah, David, Daniel, and Jesus were to be followed as examples of being about the Father's business. Story interpretation was, therefore, very important. The chief end of interpreting stories was to ascertain how the life of the model was to be imitated. The emphasis was more on action than understanding. We did, however, presume that right understanding preceded right action.

My grandfather did not overtly reject this aspect of Scripture, but he had little interest in it. He was more concerned with the Scripture as a guide book for church disputation and practice. He viewed it as the one authoritative source for conduct of all church matters. He did not emphasize its "constitutional" similarity, though he would not have rejected this analogy. Neither did he conceive it as primarily a handbook of rules. He was mostly interested in Scripture for the manner in which it provided resolution of enigmas. He was not interested in the esoteric and cryptic materials of the Bible. He did not seek to unravel John's Revelation, for example. He considered that beyond his capabilities, and not of immediate practical application. He limited his struggle to matters that interested preachers and Bible teachers. These mostly had to do with wrong interpretations of religious neighbors and eccentric church members. The payoff was practical and immediate, and the insights were be shared in conversations and in classes at church.

My father's legacy was a determination to stick to the facts. One should never be misled by opinions. Scripture contained much useful information and insight. These were to be found, however, more in explicit statements, rather than in analogies or stories. I accepted his premises, but went further than he in exploring stories for factual content. Because of a love for science and other influences, I drifted from the stories of my mother as I moved into my teenage years. I began approaching Scripture mostly as a book providing factual answers for correct thought and action.

---

[1] Duncan S. Ferguson, *Biblical Hermeneutics: An Introduction* (Atlanta: John Knox Press, 1986) 7.

[2] Nathan O. Hatch, *The Democratization of American Christianity* (New Haven: Yale University Press, 1989) 146-161.

[3] Forrest W. McCann, "The Hymnals of the Restoration Movement," *Restoration Quarterly*, 19 (1976) 31.

---

[4] McCann, "The Hymnals of the Restoration Movement," 23-38. The 1864 edition consisted of 511 pages, titled *Christian Hymn Book,* and the title page read, "Psalms, Hymns, and Spiritual Songs, Original and Selected. Compiled by A. Campbell, W. Scott, B. W. Stone, and J. T. Johnson, Elders of the Christian Church; with Numerous and Various Additions and Emendations Adapted to Personal, Family, and Church Worship by Alexander Campbell."

[5] Moses E. Lard, "My Church," *Lard's Quarterly* 1 (1863) 150.

[6] Lard, "My Church," 147.

[7] Will W. Slater, Editor-in-Chief, *The Church Hymnal* (Fort Smith: Will W. Slater, Publisher, 1938). There are about 250 hymns. It contains several Stamps-Baxter songs—songs written by J. R. Baxter, Jr. and Virgil O. Stamps—such as, "Let Me Live Close to Thee," 1927. It cost $28 per hundred. Other persons listed on the title page are Flavil Hall and Johnnie Payne.

2

Interpretation in the Churches: 1938-1947

In the final years of the Depression before World War II, a mighty harvest of new members entered Churches of Christ, especially in small towns and rural regions. In these years evangelists journeyed from town to town, holding summer meetings, which almost always extended through three Sundays, usually reporting ten to a hundred baptisms per meeting.

Economic and technological factors of the thirties permitted a less demanding life. In August, farm operations slowed because of the heat and dryness. Television was still in the future. Movie houses abounded, but many religious persons resisted attending them, and money was not available for frequent patronage in any case. A gospel meeting was, therefore, an event; one of the diversions of the summer. The singing began at 8:00 P.M., at dusk when the air cooled, and work ceased for everyone except the switchboard operators. Our meetings were held outside in a large tent, seating three hundred or so persons on benches or folding chairs. A public address system, with speakers pointing toward the streets, enabled an unlimited audience. At Mammoth Spring in 1937, for example, the congregation numbered about one hundred-ten persons. By the final night of the meeting, five hundred or more occupied the tent, stood outside, or sat in cars. The town itself had only eight hundred people, but visitors came from Thayer, as well as from outlying areas. In summer meetings of 1937, 1938 and 1939 in Mammoth Spring, G. K. Wallace reported a total of one hundred five baptisms, which equaled the membership in 1937.

Our Revivalist Roots

While precedents for outdoor preaching may be found in the New Testament—in the "Sermon on the Mount" and "Sermon on the Plain," for example— the mystique of our gospel meetings was more indebted to the great camp meetings of the second American Awakening than to the Scripture. Barton W. Stone, of Restorationist fame, was a leader in the greatest of these—the Cane Ridge camp meeting, gathered near Lexington, Kentucky, in 1801. In prior years, evangelistic efforts extended two or, at most, three days. In the camp meetings, the sessions sometimes lasted up to a month. As these evangelistic methods were adopted by congregations, or in the towns, they were designated "protracted meetings" and popularized by Charles Grandison Finney and Dwight W. Moody.[1] It was not until after the Civil War that protracted meetings became standard among our churches.

Central to and climaxing the preaching in the meeting was the invitation to come forward, which in our case, meant presenting oneself either for baptism or restoration. The invitation, likewise, was a new measure launched in the camp meetings. The earlier American custom was for individuals struggling over their conversion to repair to the woods in order seek God's mercy and obtain his outpouring of love. Barton W. Stone, Elias Smith and Abner Jones all depicted a sylvan setting for their conversion experiences. With so many persons wandering in the woods at the camp meetings, however, relations other than religious sometimes ensued. So, the preachers made a "pen" from poles, and invited individuals to enter the enclosure to culminate their struggles. When this new measure was carried into the churches, a bench was set aside and identified as the "anxious," or "mourner's" bench, or sometimes "the mercy seat."[2]

Barton W. Stone reported that he asked people to come forward to present themselves for immersion as early as 1815, but did not continue to do so because no one responded.[3] It was Walter Scott on the Western Reserve in 1827, designated that year as Association evangelist for the Mahoning Baptist Association, who claimed to have launched the practice of extending the invitation for persons to come forward to be baptized. The Mahoning Association soon abandoned the Baptists, as did Alexander Campbell, Scott, and others, to undertake the restoration of the ancient order. From that time until now, extending the invitation has been a revered restorationist practice.

Gospel Meetings in Southern Missouri

The Depression impeded the movement of persons to the cities, since little work was available there. In fact, population increased in southern Missouri and northern Arkansas because a family could at least survive by tending gardens and orchards, and by heating with wood, which was plentiful throughout the region. Jobs were available in the rural areas through the programs of the New Deal—the WPA, PWA, and CCC. These government agencies built court houses, town halls, sidewalks, curbs, county roads, state highways, and dirt roads in rural areas and national forests. The dust bowl of the early thirties resulted in some migration from our region to California, but the percentage was not as great as from Oklahoma, Texas, and parts of Arkansas.

Various factors contributed to the harvest of newcomers. Our evangelists were aggressive, experienced, and possessed a degree of charisma. We sought out the best available, which meant men imported from distant parts of Arkansas and especially from Texas. They attracted the crowds.

Our vision of reality corresponded well with that of many in our era and region. The twenties had been a time in which progressives flurried at the cultural leading edge, urging expansiveness, experimentation, and liberated emotionalism. We resisted these new developments, for the most part. Our fellowship expanded rapidly in the twenties, mostly among the middle class in the small towns and in the countryside. The converts were persons who reacted negatively to avant-garde aspects of the Roaring Twenties. Our preachers criticized the rich, the powerful, the indigent—especially those who participated in the government programs—the flamboyant, the artistic, the propagators of evolution, innovations, and higher criticism of the Bible. With the onslaught of the Great Depression, the twenties' cutting edge in the metropolitan centers was largely blunted.[4]

In the thirties, many people spent their time in the struggle for basic goods. The resulting mood reclaimed the American propensity for close scrutiny of empirical facts. Emotionalism and ecstatic expressions of religious fervor became suspect in many quarters. The Pentecostals and "holy rollers" grew, but only on the fringes of society. Our movement, in part as the result of its historical epistemology, thrived. We perceived reality through the spectacles of John Locke, as mediated through the Scottish Enlightenment. All the early leaders of our movement emphasized facts and reasonableness, and negated "enthusiasm"—especially Alexander Campbell, Walter Scott, Raccoon John Smith, and to a lesser extent, Barton W. Stone. British empiricism widely influenced most Americans in the 1800s, especially in the frontier regions of Kentucky, Ohio, and Tennessee. Not only was Locke widely read, but Baconianism became a catch word for this new wave of empiricism. The first college in our movement was, in fact, named Bacon College, founded at Georgetown in central Kentucky in 1836, with Walter Scott as president. The emphasis on science, beginning in the latter part of the nineteenth century, escalated the importance of the factual, empirical data of the Enlightenment.

Many of the persons who migrated to our area came from Kentucky and Tennessee. It is known, for example, that fifty miles east of us, around Pocahontas, Arkansas, immigrants arrived as early as 1806 who had embraced the views of Barton W. Stone and, later, of John Mulkey. Among the early settlers were the ancestors of Reuel Lemmons.[5] Many of the preachers who came to Thayer and Mammoth Spring were descendents of these early settlers. My great-grandfather, John Moody Taylor, came to our region in 1869 from Alabama. In the late 1840s two sisters of his wife, Amy Waite Taylor, had moved to an area northeast of Thayer near Couch, Missouri. One was married to Colonel Norman, an important early settler. From people who inhabited this region came several preacher-teachers, some of whom are my distant relatives, including the late Ray F. Chester and James Thompson. James can trace his great-great grandfather to the Mulkey region in Tennessee, and to those early restorationists who attached themselves to the Stone movement.

In the late thirties, we emphasized the inspiration and authority of the Scriptures, the literal and factual interpretation of it, the need for the church to have the same characteristics as those of the New Testament church, and salvation by faith through baptism. We were against innovations of all sorts, as well as evolution, higher criticism, premillennialism and sometimes, communism. We were opposed to large churches, expensive buildings, located or high-salaried preachers, divorce, dancing, drinking, smoking, card-playing, and, sometimes, movies. Our preunderstanding was a vizualization of the Scriptures as a fact book, a book of rules, or a constitution for the church and everyday morality. This was our beginning point for interpreting the Bible—in other words, our hermeneutic. We grew by leaps and bounds in the late thirties because this philosophy was congenial to many people in our region, especially so among the hard-working, aggressive, middle class persons aspiring to education and upper mobility. We were in the country or on the other side of the tracks, but we believed we were not destined to stay there, and we didn't! Furthermore, when we moved to the other side of the tracks, we took large numbers of our friends, relatives and neighbors along.[6]

The Churches in Mammoth Spring and Thayer

By 1938 there was no longer a church meeting in Centertown. I don't know all the reasons. It may have been that frictions within the church contributed. In the early thirties a church was meeting in Thayer in the town hall library, but by 1938 it had constructed a native sandstone building which seated one hundred-fifty and had a full basement, where the children's classrooms were located. The church in Mammoth Spring had met for a number of years in a frame building. It was an older, larger, and more stable congregation. In the thirties it constructed a sandstone building which seated two hundred but had no basement. Both congregations grew rapidly from that point, despite internal problems.

For some reason—perhaps because of the church leadership—most of my relatives who had been members at Centertown, transferred to the church at Mammoth Spring. The congregation was closer to my grandfather's house than the one in Thayer. Sometime in the late thirties or early forties my parents began attending at Thayer because of the Bible classes for children and the building's proximity to our house. But the rest of my relatives continued to go to church in Mammoth Spring, including my Uncle Cleo who lived in Alton, Missouri, and our cousin, Bynum Dunsmore. Both of them drove past the building in Thayer to get to Mammoth Spring for church services. They were deeply involved in the warp and weave of the congregation. In fact, Bynum later became an elder and Cleo a deacon. My grandfather was respected by the older members. The father-in-law of Bynum and Cleo (they married sisters) was president of the Mammoth Spring bank, and the heaviest contributor to the church.

The congregation in Mammoth Spring was typical for our region. The church was without a preacher until 1942, when Leroy Miller moved there from Kentucky at the invitation of the elders. There were no Bible classes for children, since certain key leaders argued that the early church had only one assembly. To have more than one class at the same time divided the assembly, they held. The matter of classes was discussed only occasionally, since most of the country congregations met in one-room buildings and didn't envision the need for Bible classes. It was more a matter of tradition than of theology, except for a few leading persons in the Mammoth Spring congregation.

The congregation assembled on Sunday morning at ten o'clock. The men took turns teaching. They normally pushed their favorite doctrines until the congregation became exasperated and requested a change of teachers. I remember listening in on long conversations of my mother and her sisters in regard to the teachers. They also discussed these matters with other women and influenced the outcome through their brother and cousin. One teacher with a bit of flair, when permitted to teach, always pushed his view of the second coming and the thousand-year reign of Christ. Members soon tired and demanded a change. His usual response at that point was to temporarily transfer to another congregation.

A topic discussed in the region at length in those years was the situation of the deceased between death and the judgment. The standard conviction was that at death everyone entered Hades. Those who had obeyed God entered into the paradise region of Hades, while those who denied him, entered Gehenna. Long discussions ensued over whether those so consigned were conscious. A literal predilection for interpretation was obvious. Most people held that the parable of the rich man and Lazarus was the key for understanding the afterlife. Persons awaiting the final judgment were indeed conscious since the rich man was shown as being aware of his plight. He was also aware that Lazarus was in paradise, that is, the bosom of Abraham. A few argued that at death the soul sleeps, as in earthly sleep, in a semi-conscious state, awaiting the great judgment. They argued that there would be no purpose for the final judgment if one were already judged as soon as he dies. The parable of the rich man and Lazarus was therefore not to be taken literally, they thought, but rather as an allegory which teaches a point about deciding for God in this life. The story was no true basis for assuming the existence of consciousness after death, they believed. I listened in on these discussions with great interest because this was the topic in which I specialized—the distinguishing of fact from fiction. I tended to place parables in the category of fiction and believed with several that the separation of the good and the evil only occurred at the final judgment.

Another topic which engrossed most members was whether believers would know each other in heaven. The consensus held that they would not, but someone could always be found who affirmed that they would. The argument against knowing each other in heaven was that if we knew each other we would soon discover who was there and who failed to make it. If, example, our mother was not there, we would be so distraught that heaven would be a place of torment rather than rejoicing. For heaven to be a place of comfort and joy it is necessary that we not recognize our friends and acquaintances. The parable of the rich man and Lazarus was again brought to bear, since the rich man recognized Lazarus in Abraham's bosom.

From these remarks it is clear that decisions on matters of life and death drew upon scriptural information, but were weighed, sifted and decided, more likely than not, according to cunning extra-scriptural arguments. Our theological conclusions were more than the simple facts of the Scriptures. They rested in sophisticated inferences drawn from matters of experience—for example, our sentimental attachment to our parents. At that time I was not troubled by the incongruity of arguing for the Bible alone as the sole authority in religion while basing its proper interpretation on the force of pragmatic and shrewd arguments. That crisis was to come later.

The preoccupation of the church members with problems of death and afterlife, though certain to draw discussion, was disturbing to some, including my mother. She was of the view that, while these topics should not be dismissed, they could not be conclusively resolved because of the absence of clear-cut biblical data. It was best, therefore, to push such matters to the periphery and focus on the church, obedience to God, and the moral life. Among our various teachers it was difficult to find someone who would simply take up a book of the Bible and explain its teachings without mostly pouncing on statements relating to the teacher's pet interests. Such a man was finally found in Lem Lewis, a former high school teacher then working as a bank cashier. He was a good speaker, had an educated manner, and tried to teach and explain whatever was in the text. He was also a man of commitment and prayer. The Bible was more to him than a book for resolving puzzles and conflicts. It was a book which called women and men to an understanding of God and a dedicated spiritual life.

In these years we considered ourselves a minority. We did not dwell on the inadequacies of the sectarians who surrounded us. We believed they were wrong, but still felt their error had to be proved by the Scriptures. We did not try to push people into the corner with the fact that we were the true church. We assumed that as a minority we had to pay proper respect to the majority. It was the meeting preachers who sometimes launched a sharp attack on the Methodists, Baptists, and Pentecostals, calling them by name and excoriating their abominable doctrines. My mother and her sisters had long discussions on these combative approaches. They did not object to teaching the truth on these matters. They did, however, feel that explicitly naming the different denominations and singling them out for ridicule caused more alienation and ill will than conversions. They encouraged making arrangements with those meeting preachers who preached the truth from Scripture without scalding the sectarians by name.

They did this both on the grounds of Christian charity and the need to avoid unnecessary persecution as the result of our minority position.

I enjoyed the esoteric topics, but I, too, was troubled by whether they emphasized the important aspects of the Scriptures. The Scriptures seemed to me to be more about strengthening the church, helping people, and living a proper moral life in action and speech. Very clearly, as indicated by the hot topics in our churches, interpretation of the Scriptures depends on our interests and our judgment as to what is of consequence in the Bible. Since we thought that the important topics had to do with death and judgment, then we always interpreted the Scriptures from that perspective. We were not just teaching the Scripture and the Scripture alone, we were also teaching a theological perspective on Scripture by deciding in advance what was important and proceeding to interpret Scripture accordingly. Our preunderstanding led us to emphasize certain topics in Scripture far more than others. We often professed to teach the whole oracles of God (I Peter 4:11), but we ourselves very much determined which topics to highlight to the neglect of other, more important matters. We therefore had a theological commitment or agenda which was prior to the Scripture itself. These matters worried me, but not enough so as to cause me to form a better theological beginning point. All I knew—and in this I agreed with my mother—was that these matters, though of great concern to us, occasioned little attention in Scripture.

The focus of the messages in the summer meetings was different. Our "hot topics" about the specifics of life beyond the grave were not discussed at all. But then, we didn't expect it. The meetings were designed for unbelievers—those who had not been baptized. The meeting preachers of these years followed a conventional unfolding of topics. The meeting opened on Sunday, and the sermons that day were designed for the members, to reconfirm them in the glories of the church, and to incite them to invite their relatives, friends and neighbors. Ephesians usually played a key role in the Sunday morning and night sermons. Christ's church was portrayed as sublime because "God placed all things under his feet and appointed him to be head over everything for the church which is his body, the fullness of him who fills everything in every way" (1:22, 23). In the evening the focus was on the characteristics of the church Christ established: its name, its organization, its doctrine, and its music. These topics might also be individual sermons of the next few days.[7]

Defining the Church: Historical Roots

Such a focus on the church has a long and honorable history in reformation and restoration traditions. The young Alexander Campbell, in the *Christian Baptist*, launched in 1823, focused upon the ancient order in the early issues. We can ascertain more precisely what he meant by the "ancient order" since under this title he published a series of thirty articles, discussing the Lord's supper, fellowship (contribution), bishops, love feasts, purity of speech, deacons, hymns, church discipline, names, and titles. All of these involved activities and actions within the church.

The presuppositions underlying restoration theology and hermeneutics can best be understood against the backdrop of the Swiss and English reformations and their interest in the centrality of the church, and from the Anglo-Scottish enlightenment's vision of reality and texts. In order to understand the hermeneutics of the Churches of Christ it is important to perceive that the primary questions put to the Scripture concerned the church's overt characteristics.

Restorationist theology owes more to the reformed theology of Calvin and Zwingli than to that of Luther because it is Scripture- and church-centered. Luther argued for a Christocentric interpretation. Calvin rejected the Christocentric, arguing that "...Scripture itself is the authority for Christian belief rather than any Christocentric interpretation of Scripture."[8] More specifically, however, theology in the Churches of Christ resounds with echoes of Zwingli (1484-1531) who

> ...had the same basic aim as Luther, but highlighted the purification of the Church by the proclamation of the Word of God which involved necessarily not merely the revivification of its faith and reconstruction of its doctrine, but the overhauling of every department of ecclesiastical life and practice.[9]

Our connection with the Swiss reformers, though not direct, is not accidental. One can mention first the influence of Zwingli on John Knox and Scottish Presbyterianism, and thereby on the Campbells, who came from Scottish Presbyterian backgrounds. But there is also the connection with English Puritanism and their effect on the British independents of various stripes. While these disparate groups may not have been genetically connected in every case, yet they were from the same milieu and believed that what Christianity needed most of all in order to return to the ancient paths was the purifying of the church.

The connection between the Zwinglian reform and the British scene may be specifically documented. Various English exiles in the time of Mary Tudor (queen, 1553-1558) made their way to Zurich. Already some influence from the Swiss reformation had occurred through the correspondence of English church leaders with Johann Heinrich Bullinger (1504-1575) who succeeded Zwingli as chief pastor of Zurich. Somewhat later because of opposition, Martin Bucer (1491-1551), the successor to Zwingli as leader of the Swiss reform, made his way to Cambridge (1549) where he was appointed Regius professor of divinity.[10]

From the time of Henry VIII (1491-1547), the focus of English Christianity had been on the church. The battles of Henry and his successors were the struggles of royalty and the ruling classes to define the contours of a specifically English Church over against a Christianity politically directed from Rome. Henry broke ties with Rome and became prince and defender of the church. He confiscated the church's lands, closed the monasteries, and declared the right of the English government to try church functionaries. For a growing group of church leaders—later designated Puritans—most of what Henry accomplished was simply a tinkering with the politics of the church. Under the influence of the Swiss reform they wanted to go much farther and purify the liturgy and life of the church. Ahlstrom says of the Puritans that

> From the outset these reformers were determined to achieve a three-fold program for purifying the visible church: through a purging of popish remnants and the establishment of "apostolic" principles of worship and church order, through the implantation and teaching of Reformed doctrine, and through a revival of discipline and evangelical piety in clergy and laity alike.[11]

More specifically, the Puritans launched a major attack upon the Church of England, especially in regard to the details of worship such as vestments, ornaments, surplices, the sign of the cross, organs, rochets, and ecclesiastical courts. They demanded explicit scriptural warrant for all such matters, regarding whatever was without such as idolatrous, popish and superstitious. The Puritans championed plain preaching and heralded simplicity of proclamation and life. In terms of polity they were Presbyterian or congregational, but in America the congregational aspect won out. They brought to Christianity the rhetoric of a pure church over against the state church.

While the Campbells and other early restoration leaders had no direct ties to Puritanism, they were heirs of many of its principles.[12] The Campbell movement grew rapidly in a country founded on Puritan principles. But in America there was a difference. In America, by Campbell's time, only the vestiges of a state church existed to rally against. However, multiple churches were visible on the scene. The Campbells championed the ideal of one unified church over against multiple churches. The question therefore was to define the parameters of this one church. The solution was to reject all creeds and rebuild the Church of Jesus Christ, plank by plank, from the oracles of God—the Scriptures, and especially the New Testament. In the minds of certain right-wingers from the beginning of the movement, the manner of proceeding was to compare church with church and declare the restorationist church the obvious winner, based on clear mandates from the Scriptures.[13] The America of the Campbells was specifically one in which the denominations were organizing and testing their wings, as Jon Butler has argued in a recent book.[14] As the growing churches competed for the minds and hearts of Americans, certain restorationist leaders, to gain a competitive edge, specialized on scriptural warrants for a church which avoided denominationalism.

Dispensational Hermeneutics: The Scripture that Really Counts

Since our beginnings as a movement were so rooted in establishing the differences between ourselves and the denominational world, it may come as no surprise that a frequent topic for the summer meetings during my boyhood was the authority of Christ in the church. The distinctive features of the church were not to be determined by man made creeds, it was alleged, but by the words of Christ—the New Testament. Our preachers taught that not all the Bible was authoritative for the church. Instead, the New Testament—especially Acts through Revelation—was to be the standard for determining proper practice. Such delineation of parts of the Bible as authoritative for the church was set forth in a sermon typically titled something like, "Rightly Dividing the Word of Truth." The text was usually II Timothy 2:15 in the King James Version. "Study to show thyself approved of God, a workman that needeth not to be ashamed, rightly dividing the word of truth." In this sermon the three dispensations were set forth: the patriarchal, the Mosaic and the Christian. Each of these dispensations had its law. The law for Israel, that is, the Jews, was the Mosaic law. But when Christ died on the cross he removed the Mosaic law and replaced it with the Christian law. A consensus agreement was that since the Gospels preceded the cross, they belonged to the previous dispensation, not the Christian. Therefore, the characteristics of the church must be determined by Acts and the epistles. This obviously was a hermeneutically-driven decision. The authoritative aspects of the Scriptures for the church are narrowed down to what scholars designate as a canon within a canon—in our case, Acts through Revelation. Despite the contemporary focus on command, example, and necessary inference in the current discussion of hermeneutics, the hermeneutical rule of the three dispensations has probably been more pervasive in shaping our interpretation of Scripture.

It is interesting that Campbell's 1835 "Principles of Interpretation" were not carefully coordinated with dispensationalism, nor with the command-example-necessary inference formula. The latter is not even mentioned in the "Principles of Interpretation" nor in the seven general rules at the end, though the dispensational principle receives passing mention.[15] The same holds true in later books on hermeneutics in our movement, notably those of Lamar, Dungan, and Thomas.[16] A student at Freed-Hardeman University raised a perceptive question when he asked me what the "new hermeneutic" furor over command, examples, and necessary inferences was all about, since none of the classic books on hermeneutics in our movement discuss this tripartite formula.

As the meetings entered the second week, the evangelist turned more attention to the unimmersed. The gospel plan of salvation was now set forth and some preachers took a night for each of the five steps in the plan of salvation: hearing, believing, repenting, confessing, and being baptized. These sermons were resplendent with appropriate Scriptures. The preachers who impressed us the most were the ones who quoted from memory. We followed along in the text or from our own memory to determine if the preacher left out a word or substituted phrases. The meeting preachers had preached these sermons many times, so actually the whole sermon was essentially memorized through repetitive delivery. The sermons on the final Sunday concentrated on heaven and hell. The preacher tried to make them, respectively, as attractive and unattractive as possible. These were the motivating sermons in case anyone seriously considering baptism had delayed until this point. The last night was typically the most productive in terms of respondents. The song "Oh Why Not Tonight" was often reserved for this grand finale. We repeated the song as long as people kept streaming forward, interlaced with a few additional exhortations by the preacher. I can still hear the point of the sermon repeated in the words of the song, "Tomorrow's sun may never rise…" This was scary to an impressionable but reticent ten-year-old.

Certain evangelists held early morning services on weekdays. The time was 7:00 to 8:00 A.M. so that people could get to their jobs in the stores. My mother was dedicated to attending these, as well as those at night. Since my dad often went to work before seven, we walked. It was about a mile-and-a-half. Occasionally, someone on the way to the meeting saw us along the highway and gave us a ride. Those attending were the dedicated—the majority of whom were women—and a sprinkling of farmers, ninety percent of the audience consisting of church members. The attendees numbered about a hundred, and since it was fairly cool that early in the morning, the services were held inside. The evangelist I best remember for the morning sermons was Reuel Lemmons, later famous as longtime editor of the *Firm Foundation*, who was the Mammoth Spring gospel meeting preacher in the early 1940s. Reuel preached on subjects I had never heard before: the need for a deep spiritual life and family devotions, prayer, and the necessity of Bible study and regular church attendance. He stressed evangelism and parables of the kingdom's growth. He called for an abandonment of worldly pursuits. He encouraged care for the needy and the support of orphanages. At that time he preached in Tipton, Oklahoma, and had connections with Tipton Orphan's Home.

Reuel's preaching resulted in something of a spiritual renewal in the Mammoth Spring church, which accelerated as the result of World War II, with its catastrophic deaths and uncertainties. In addition, Lemmons encouraged the church to a new vision of organization and growth. He pointed out that the persons baptized at a gospel meeting often backslid, only to request restoration at the next year's meeting.

Even though the congregation should have had above two hundred present after the one hundred five baptisms in 1937-1939, two months later the attendance settled back to about one hundred-fifty. Reuel attributed it to the lack of good preaching. He encouraged the employment of a full time minister and sacrificial giving by the congregation to support him. Soon afterward the congregation decided that this was a move in the right direction. Reuel also encouraged the church to start a mid-week service.

Our preachers made little effort to defend the weekly flow of our services by the Scripture except for the meeting upon the first day of the week. The favorite prooftext was I Corinthians 16:2 which speaks of the early Christians meeting "On the first day of every week." Early in our movement, churches which had available buildings often met on Sunday morning, in the afternoon, then again at "candle time"—when it grew dark enough to need artificial light. This was especially the case if visiting preachers showed up. But the indispensable time was on Sunday morning. In small communities in which public buildings were shared with other groups, one service per week was the norm. The mid-week service is not mentioned in Scripture, nor does it have a long genealogy in church history. It is basically an American phenomenon. Of course, on special church calendar occasions, such as Lent, churches met during the week, starting as early as the third century A. D., but not throughout the year. The regular mid-week service became the norm when popularized by Charles Grandison Finney and Dwight L. Moody, and especially after the Prayer Meeting Revival of 1857-1859.[17] Not many of the churches in our region had regular mid-week services until sometime during World War II. When

Leroy Miller came to Mammoth Spring, he instituted "mid-week" services, but they fell on Saturday night, because the farmers came to town on Saturday. As time wore on and these practices became ingrained, some believed them to be "biblical"—but on the basis of inferences rather than commands or examples.

The task of the early forties in our churches was to solidify and capitalize upon the growth of the thirties. We were challenged with a new vision of a church on the march, founded upon sound doctrine. The activities and developments at the congregation in Thayer were much like those in Mammoth Spring—typified by the gospel meetings and the baptisms. The responses in Thayer were somewhat fewer in number, but still significant. The congregation in Thayer was a bit slower to employ a preacher. The excitement of growth pushed the teachers away from the older controverted topics of death, judgment and the second coming. Discussions now centered on the work of the church, the growth of the kingdom, and ways of encouraging new believers.

The church at Thayer at the beginning was much like the surrounding small country churches. One cup was employed for the "fruit of the vine", and there were no Bible classes. Neither issue was as much a matter of theology as of tradition. I remember the problem which pushed the congregation toward multiple cups: the specter of polio, which traversed the land in the mid-1930s, perhaps with greater trauma than the AIDS epidemic, since everyone was known to be susceptible, especially the children. Several cases arose in our area. Since polio targeted children, we were scared out of our wits. I remember Mother insisting that we walk a longer route to school to avoid a house where one of our fellow students was quarantined with polio. My mother and her sisters were college graduates and knew how diseases spread. They insisted that the congregation obtain multiple communion cups. The leaders of the congregation were not quickly moved. They argued that since it was the Lord's supper, God would protect the participants. But as more and more children came down with polio, members became concerned. The elders, however, didn't think we had the money to send away for communion trays. Some of the women of the church decided to acquire multiple cups by utilizing small glasses in which tuna was sold. The women in the congregation agreed among themselves to purchase as many of the small containers as they could. Mother bought several. We had not eaten much tuna up to that point, and I relished the fallout from the purchases, since I had acquired a taste for tuna. We did not have refrigeration, so we had to eat it as soon as we opened a glass. Thanks to the willing efforts of myself and others, in a few weeks enough containers were available so as to provide one for each person who partook of the fruit of the vine.

The congregation at Thayer was one of the first in the region to have Bible classes for children. That was the reason my mother determined to go there with her four children, ranging from age four to nine, despite the fact that all of her relatives attended at Mammoth Spring. At first there were only two or three classes, so the children in each comprised a considerable age span. We had a few women elementary teachers in the congregation and they were prevailed upon to do the teaching. The developments at Mammoth Spring were different.

Certain influential men in the congregation opposed the introduction of classes. One of these was the banker father-in-law of my cousin—an elder—and Uncle Cleo. Opposition continued even through the war years. After the war, the soldiers returned, married and settled into the community. The economy boomed. Several children were born. Certain parents in the congregation started agitating for classes. Finally, since the elders took no action, a group of the younger families broke off to meet on their own. They comprised about a fourth of the congregation. My relatives were divided on the matter, and the division was viewed as a scandal.

After a few months, the former preacher, Leroy Miller, was invited to return and see if a reconciliation could be effected. He preached on love and the need to work out differences. Finally, an accord was achieved. Classes were not to be held in the church building, but in an old structure across the street. The teachers were to be males only. One of the first was Lem Lewis, who had been a success as an adult teacher. At first there were only two classes. In a few years and after a death or two, the congregation added an educational wing to the church building and females taught eager young hearts.

The employment of full time preachers expanded considerably the amount of Scripture covered by the church. The church at Mammoth Spring employed its first located preacher during the war years. The church at Thayer waited until the late forties or early fifties. Much of the preaching was topical, and mostly duplicated the subject matter of the meeting sermons, such as the proper name, organization, and worship of the church. With year-round preaching, new issues came to the fore. What made the deepest impression on me was preaching on the parables of Jesus. This was a return to the story attributes of Scripture which I had relished as a youth. I remember hearing for the first time complete sermons on the Prodigal Son, and an especially memorable sermon by Boyd Morgan at Thayer on the Good Samaritan. There were also sermons on the sower, the mustard seed, the hidden treasure, the lost sheep, the tenants, the great banquet, the talents, the ten virgins, and the sheep and goats in the final judgment. It was different to hear sermons that were narrative rather than step-by-step logical progressions.

The arrival of the full time preachers also meant that now we had both a Sunday morning class and a preaching service. The preacher sometimes taught the class, but not always. More and more, books of the New Testament were discussed in the classes verse by verse, in an effort to look at the whole document, rather than centering in on "hobby" items. The latter wasn't altogether avoided, however, because we knew little about some of the details in the text. We did not, for example, study Romans, since we found it too difficult both in language and concept. I recall discussions about whether to study Romans and hearing the arguments for studying I and II Timothy instead. The book of Acts remained the favorite study because, as we thought, it focused on conversions. Acts was also important because it focused upon the church and how to enter it, that is, upon the New Testament church and the gospel plan of salvation. We were inclined to interpret the whole of the Scripture in the light of our two central interests: ecclesiology (defining the church) and soteriology (matters essential to salvation). We were recipients of a tradition which involved a hermeneutical emphasis, but we did not often bother ourselves with the question as to whether that emphasis itself was scriptural. With the preachers present, we were now bold enough to tackle the Gospels and the narratives of the Old Testament.

The churches introduced mid-week services by the middle forties. We did not have "prayer meetings," since those were denominational. We called Bible things by Bible names. For some reason, Wednesday nights were at first avoided, perhaps because that was the night of the denominational prayer meetings. The church at Thayer met for a time on Thursday night, while at Mammoth Spring, Friday or Saturday was perceived to be the best choice. It wasn't too long, however, until school conflicts, especially with basketball games, thrust the mid-week meetings to Wednesday. The schools did not schedule activities on Wednesday night in deference to the churches. It is amazing how long-ingrained traditions may change quickly when the interests of church members take new directions. Before the Church of Christ became the only act in Mammoth Spring, not many basketball players were members. But after World War II the scenario changed. High school basketball skyrocketed in importance and the sons and daughters of many members of the church were involved. It was not long before members saw their way clear to meet on Wednesday night so as to avoid a conflict between church and basketball. The elders were not oblivious to which would win out should the conflict persist. Even so, the consciences of many were troubled by this surrender to the "world."

The focus in the mid-week service was some book of the Bible. We studied the Old Testament very little prior to the arrival of the preachers, since the

Old Testament was for the Jews and had little to do with Christian salvation. Furthermore, it was sometimes difficult to understand, especially when reading the prophets. I remember the murmurs which surged in the congregation when Leroy Miller proposed, a few months after commencing the Friday/Saturday night "mid-week" service, to study the book of Genesis. He was persuasive, however, so we launched into the book. It was different since it was in narrative form. In the discussion, several unanswerable questions arose—where Cain found a wife, for example. But, for the most part, a new excitement emanated from the study. We were treading on new turf: the focus now was upon God, and not so much on the church.

Over the course of a decade a considerable shift occurred in the teaching fare of the churches. In turn, the questions addressed to the text were new and different. A new hermeneutical focus arose. In the past, the main concerns had related to judgment, death and the second coming. The Bible was the source book with the answers. The gospel meetings offered up a different set of topics: the authority of the Scriptures, the church, and the proper steps to salvation. Along with these considerations were the historic emphases on the abandonment of creeds, the unity of believers, anti-sectarianism, and the restoration of the New Testament church. Perhaps my memory is faulty, but though I remember hearing the latter topics, they did not seem to be at the forefront in our churches. The stress was rather on the truth found in Scripture on miscellaneous topics, and the effort to pattern the church on the blueprint found in the New Testament. With the numerical and spiritual growth of the churches, we began to look at Scriptures on topics we had not previously scrutinized: the kingdom parables, prayer, dedication, and sacrificial giving. We plunged into whole new sections of Scripture previously unexamined: Genesis and even the Psalms, for example. A whole new range of subjects lifted the horizons of our vision. A new agenda was set for the theology of the church. Naturally, these changes did not occur without charges from some quarters that we were abandoning the old paths.

Christ now entered the picture anew. He was the head of the church and the authority for its regulations. His blood shed upon the cross provided the ground of salvation. The preaching moved quickly from the foundational beginnings, however, to ramifications in the life of the church. The details still consisted of the name, the organization, and the worship of the church. Little attention was paid to the manner in which a loving and forgiving God informed the organization and worship of the church. The emphasis was more on the rules as rules—on commands and examples. We seldom heard messages on the cross as the radiating point from which a Christian launched a life of sharing with other believers and serving the church and the world.[18] The cross was a key item in salvation because it was where Christ's body was broken and his blood shed. But the cross was not shown as the ground for defining the life style of the believer. I seldom heard such Scriptures as "I have been crucified with Christ and I no longer live, but Christ lives in me" (Galatians 2:20). Or, "If your brother is distressed because of what you eat, you are no longer acting in love. Do not by your eating destroy your brother for whom Christ died" (Romans 14:15).

We now had new interests which set the agenda for the teaching in the churches; for determining what we found in Scripture and why. This in turn demanded a "new" hermeneutic. Remember that hermeneutics has to do with the topics or matters which are addressed to the Scriptures. I have spent some time setting forth the historical backgrounds of some aspects of our church life—the invitation and meetings on Sunday and Wednesday nights, for example. This history lesson may seem far afield from the matter of biblical interpretation, but the point is that while we have often assumed that the details of church life have been spelled out in Scripture, various aspects have actually arisen because of history and culture—in this case, American history and culture.

My Decision

While I, too, was absorbed in the new directions in the churches, I had my own personal spiritual struggles and decisions to make. Church activities and discussions of grandparents, aunts, uncles and cousins regarding them took up much of our time in the late forties. For our churches it was an era of genuine spiritual renewal and growth.

The matter of responding to the invitation started to trouble me as early as age nine. That year my sister Nedra was baptized. She was essentially a loner at church: there were no girls her age with which to associate. But she was serious, and read the Bible a lot. It seemed natural for her, though perceived as being somewhat young at age eleven, to request baptism. I, too, was alone, having no boys my exact age at Mammoth Spring, where I usually attended with my grandparents and, later, my uncle. We had no youth groups or teen Bible classes. I was generally reluctant to discuss my own personal feelings and beliefs, even with my mother, though she encouraged me to do so.

Matters came to something of a head in the summer of 1940 when I was ten. Reuel Lemmons stayed with my grandfather during the meeting that summer, as did I. Reuel was on the outlook for people to baptize and he considered me a prime prospect. He told me in the presence of my grandfather that I should consider becoming a Christian. I was not quick to respond. I lowered my head: the proposal was an embarrassment. My grandfather then spoke up. "Oh, he's only ten. He's big for his age." Reuel responded that he thought I was older, and I was off the hook. It was not that I rejected the idea of becoming a Christian: I thought about it much of the time, especially during the meetings. But I was a very private person. I preferred reading books to talking with people, though I didn't mind being underfoot to listen in as others conversed. I rarely volunteered for any role in school which required talking in front of people, such as in plays. If I were pushed into parts, they were always secondary and required little speaking. At that age I could not fathom the time when I might muster enough courage to walk down the aisle during the singing of the invitation hymn. That, in my view, and in the view of most people in our churches, was the only way to become a Christian: one had to make a public confession. I was troubled by my reticence and I knew at some time in the future I would take the step, but I was so anxious over the whole matter that I could not envision when.

As I passed twelve and thirteen the reticence was intensified through reading the Lloyd C. Douglas books. His views of Christian commitment seemed to place discipleship beyond my grasp. I thought he was right: Christianity was demanding. One did not take the decision to become a Christian lightly. If one put one's hand to the plow, one had to be fully committed to not turning back. In the preaching, I didn't hear much about the help of God. The view prevailed that I had to walk the new road of discipleship alone and through sheer determination. It seemed, too, that I had to walk it by myself, since none of the few boys I knew at church were committed to living like Christians. If I took this step, I would be alone among my peers. The demands were high, and the encouragement of companions was absent.

The decision became an albatross around my neck, especially during the summer meetings when the pressure was on. I wanted badly to step out, but I just couldn't bring myself to it. I reproached myself constantly for cowardice, but to no avail. I was filled with fear and trepidation when I envisioned pushing people aside so I could step out into the aisle. I intentionally sat in the middle of the long seats so I could justify inaction on the grounds that it was not easy to get out.

I considered myself basically a good person, not so much because of any great willingness to befriend and help others, though I had some inkling of this challenge through reading *In His Steps* and *Magnificent Obsession*. However, on the basis of the moral life—the major emphasis of the meeting preachers—I thought I shaped up well. I did not play marbles for "keeps." I studiously avoided telling lies (though on occasion I might not speak up for the truth and may have told a few "white" lies, but I prided myself in these being very few). I did not play cards, knew nothing about dancing, and was never around alcohol so as to be tempted. I did not smoke, even though I could have taken cigarettes from my grandfather's store without him knowing it. My brothers and I, on a few occasions, did resort to smoking dry grape vines while hiding in the woods where our parents couldn't see us. My friends were basically of the same disposition. I was a good student and a keeper of the rules. I had to watch my "P's" and "Q's," since one my of my aunts, Alice Taylor, taught home economics in the school system at Thayer while I went from first through eighth grade. Then, when I attended high school at Alton and stayed with Uncle Cleo, he was the vocational agriculture teacher, so I knew I could not do anything at school without my aunt and uncle hearing about it. As a result, I was generally rule-abiding and moral, by any measure I could determine.

I did, however, believe that if I became a Christian, I had some changes to make. The conviction about these grew as I passed fourteen, fifteen, and sixteen. First, I needed to give more when the collection was passed: I was something of a miser and dreaded parting with my money. My grandfather paid me periodically, often with a silver dollar. In summers, my uncle paid the magnificent sum of a dollar a day for working from sunup to sundown on his farms. He also provided room and meals. He paid the same to a full time adult farm worker and furnished a house. Even so, I viewed my money as hard-earned, and being a cheerful giver, as commanded by Scripture, was difficult for me. I also knew I had to increase my reading of the Scriptures. I read them from time to time, but not with a great deal of enthusiasm. Novels and movies seemed much more exciting.

But there were two other problems which I knew too had to be addressed. The first was off-color jokes. I heard such jokes from traveling salesmen in my grandfather's store, from men who worked on my uncle's farms at harvest times, and from some of my schoolmates. Around adults I mostly listened, wide-eared. Around my male schoolmates in private I repeated several of the jokes, as they shared ones they had heard. On trips to high school basketball games, some of my friends and I sat in the back of the bus, away from the girls, and exchanged dirty jokes. Though I had an eye for the girls I was too timid to muster up the courage to sit by one or suggest a date. By joining the boys of like disposition and cracking jokes, I was let off the hook. But I knew if I became a Christian I would have to clean up my act. I did not swear or use foul language: one can maneuver through even sexually-related jokes and avoid most of the bad language.

The other matter had to do with sex itself. Sex was a mystery which was discussed occasionally, often by way of jokes. My friends, for the most part, were intrigued—but only as theorists, not as activists. These days were prior to the sexual revolution, and most teens of my generation were fearful of indulgence on the grounds of pregnancy, disease, and disdain afterward by the companion. My interest in sex was perhaps accelerated by my mother, who intended the opposite. For example she was always concerned when we went swimming in the creek if there were girls anywhere near. At her insistence, we swam in long pants, rather than in swimming trunks . She grilled us if we had been out of her sight for a time. Her perceived nervousness made us wonder what it was all about. As I moved toward the teens the impulses were there. It was clear to me that they had to be repressed—certainly not acted upon.

As I passed through the teenage years, then, I knew that if I became a Christian it would be a major decision. I wanted to be a person who was helpful. I wanted to be a faithful reader of the Scriptures, to study for deeper spiritual insight. I felt that even with the changes in our churches, there was still too much focus on what was wrong with people in the sects, too much argument over inconsequential matters, too much preference for disputations instead of Christian action, and too much hypocrisy. A Christian needed to be a person of prayer, kindness, biblical knowledge, and total commitment. He had to avoid the temptations into which I had, to some degree, plunged.

In the summer of 1946 my two brothers, Glenn and Owen, a friend named Paul DuBois, and I discussed being baptized at the gospel meeting in Thayer. We made up our minds as to what night it would be. And, slowly but surely, the fateful moment approached. I was ready, but I feared the public display. The invitation song commenced: "Are you washed in the blood of the lamb?" My heart raced, my breath grew short and my hands perspired as they had many times in the past when I contemplated walking up the aisle. But this time I had committed myself not only to the Lord, but to my companions. We cleared the long seat and made our way to the front. When the song ceased, we stood one by one before the congregation and confessed that Jesus is the Christ, the son of the living God. People seemed pleased but there was little public display: that was our way. A person or two dropped by and said, "Thomas, we are pleased that you have taken this step." We drove home from the church building to pick up a change of clothing, then headed toward the deep pool in Warm Fork Creek, which was also our swimming hole. Cars drove to the bank, and the headlights were directed downward. The beams crossed the stream and provided adequate illumination as the preacher plunged us beneath the waters in the name of the Father, the Son, and the Holy Spirit. It was a new day. I had now taken the step I had longed to take for at least four years.

My baptism occurred shortly before the commencement of my senior year in high school. I would have been fearful had I thought my school companions would learn of my decision, but I went to high school at Alton seventeen miles away, and my brothers and Paul DuBois went to school in Thayer. There was not a Church of Christ in Alton, though there was one in the country about four miles out—Hickory Grove. I did not have to worry; my secret was safe. I could work out the details of my new life without fearing taunts from friends.

I became a person of regular prayer. I resolved to read through the Bible, starting in Genesis. It went fine, since it was narrative. The same was true of Exodus, but I got tangled up in the legal jargon of Leviticus and limped along for awhile. Finally, I stopped completely. After six months of bad conscience I decided to take up my reading anew. I was sure, however, that I would fail if I started where I left off, in Leviticus. So I commenced again in Genesis. It went well. Exodus was better. But once again, I got bogged down in Leviticus. I was several chapters along, but I just couldn't go on. Soon the resolve passed to read through the Bible from cover to cover, never to be made again. I continued with the same companions, but I avoided telling dirty jokes. I don't know what they thought. We never discussed it.

The decision to become a Christian was, at the same time, a hermeneutically-driven decision. It was a decision about the matters most important for the Christian life. It was a decision about what the church should discuss. It was a decision about what parts of the Scripture were to be read and how they were to be interpreted. I appreciated the teaching of grandparents, parents and members of the church. Their role had been inestimable. But I had read the Scripture, heard the sermons, and read the novels. I had developed my own ideas as to how the Bible was to be envisioned and what it meant to be a Christian. I hoped that my vision was a better one, informed by taking seriously more of the Bible. I especially believed that interpretation—hermeneutics—was more than an exercise of practical reason and logic designed to gain an advantage over friends, relatives and neighbors. I believed that the Scripture had to be translated into life, however inadequately I understood the far-reaching ramifications of this decision at that stage. I did not construe, however, my decision so much as taking up a new relationship with the living God, His Son and Spirit. It was, rather, the embracing of a new set of rules from the book which God inspired.

From these observations I conclude that for each of us, the interpretation of the Scripture depends upon those interests which absorb our attention. When we take up the Scriptures, it matters whether we conceive them as revealing the parameters of life beyond the grave, the answers to church puzzles, the features of a perfectly patterned church, the dynamics of a growing, powerful church, or the contours of a spiritual and moral life. Not only do we, from some *a priori* agenda, determine which Scriptures need highlighting and interpreting, but these decisions also effect our hermeneutic method. In the case of defining the perfect pattern for the church, the hermeneutic may well feature commands and examples, as well as inferences. The establishment of a spiritual and moral life, may, in addition, depend upon searching the narratives in both the Old and New Testaments so as to discover traits of life exhibited by revered men and women.

---

[1] W. G. Travis, "Protestant Revivalism," *Dictionary of Christianity in America,* Daniel G. Reid, ed. (Downers Grove: InterVarsity Press, 1990) 1012-1015.

[2] M. G. Bell, "Altar Call" (*DCA*) 39.

[3] Thomas H. Olbricht, "The Invitation: An Historical Survey" *Restoration Quarterly*, 5:1 (1961) 6-16.

[4] For the history of our churches in this period see: Earl West, *Search for the Ancient Order* (Vol. I, Nashville: The Gospel Advocate Co., 1949, Vol. II, Indianapolis: Religious Book Service, 1950, and Vol. III, Indianapolis: Religious Book Service, 1979, Vol. IV, 1988), Robert Hooper, *A Distinctive People: The Churches of Christ in the Twentieth Century* (Nashville: The Gospel Advocate Company, 1993) and Richard Hughes, *Reviving the Ancient Faith: The Story of Churches of Christ in America* (Grand Rapids: Eerdmans Publishing Company, 1996).

[5] Boyd E. Morgan, *Arkansas Angels* (Paragould: College Bookstore and Press, 1967).

[6] For general religious background to this period see Martin E. Marty, *Modern American Religion*; Volume I *The Irony of It All, 1893-1919*; Volume II *The Noise of Conflict 1919-1941* (Chicago: The University of Chicago Press, 1989, 1991).

[7] The content of these sermons may be gleaned by reading Leroy Brownlow's *Why I am a Member of the Church of Christ* (Fort Worth, Leroy Brownlow, 1945).

[8] Robert M. Grant and David Tracey, *A Short History of the Interpretation of the Bible,* 2nd edition (Philadelphia: Fortress Press, 1894) 96.

---

[9] *Zwingli and Bullinger,* ed. G. W. Bromiley (Philadelphia: Westminster, 1963) 29.

[10] C. Hopf, *Martin Bucer and the English Reformation* (Oxford: Oxford University Press, 1946).

[11] Sydney E. Ahlstrom, *A Religious History of the American People,* (New Haven: Yale University Press, 1972) 125.

[12] For an insightful comparison of the thought of the two, see Dwight Bozeman, "Alexander Campbell, Child of the Puritans?", in *Lectures in Honor of the Alexander Campbell Bicentennial, 1788-1988,* (Nashville: The Disciples of Christ Historical Society, 1988) 3-18.

[13] See Richard T. Hughes, *Reviving the Ancient Faith,* in which Hughes traces this frame of mind in the movement from the early nineteenth century to the present.

[14] Jon Butler, *Awash in a Sea of Faith: Christianizing the American People* (Cambridge: Harvard University Press, 1992) 257, 258.

[15] Alexander Campbell, "Principles of Interpretation," *Christianity Restored* (Rosemead: Old Paths Book Club, 1959, Reprint) 96-98.

[16] J. S. Lamar, *The Organon of Scripture* (Philadelphia: J. B. Lippincott & Co., 1960) Reprint, D. R. Dungan, *Hermeneutics* (Cincinnati: The Standard Publishing Company, n. d.), J. D. Thomas, *We Be Brethren* (Abilene: Biblical Research Press, 1958); *Heaven's Window* (Abilene: Biblical Research Press, 1974).

[17] N. A. Magnuson, "Prayer Meeting Revival (1857-1859)"; T. H. Olbricht, "Prayer Meeting" *Dictionary of Christianity in America,* editor, Daniel G. Reid (Downers Grove: InterVarsity Press, 1990) 922.

[18] See the book by Bill Love, *The Core Gospel: on Restoring the Crux of the Matter* (Abilene: ACU Press, 1992).

3

Expanding the Base of Scriptures to be Interpreted: 1947-1949

In September 1947 my grandfather took me, a suitcase of clothes, and some cookies Mother had baked to Harding College (now University) in Searcy, Arkansas. I wasn't too excited about going to Harding because I wanted to major in agriculture, then take over my father's Nebraska ranch. Furthermore, most of my relatives and teachers thought I was making a mistake because they said my records and intelligence scores were such that I would do well in a much better college or university. I wasn't too bothered by the latter, however. From earliest memory, I wanted to farm in Nebraska. I had never seen the farm, but it sounded glamorous in the occasional stories my father told. To prepare myself for farming I stayed with my mother's brother, Cleo Taylor, in Alton, Missouri. The high school in Thayer at that time did not offer agriculture. Uncle Cleo was the vocational agriculture teacher at Alton, and had several farming operations going. By staying with him I not only could study agriculture, but obtain much practical experience.

The application to Harding was at my mother's insistence. I objected little, however, because Nedra, my sister, preceded me there by a year and liked it very much. I, too, with my mother, thought that taking Bible courses was appropriate, since there was not a Church of Christ anywhere near the Nebraska farm and I would have to start one. My parents further assured me that I could transfer to the University of Missouri and obtain my degree in agriculture after two years at Harding. Mother also threatened that my dad would help financially only if I went to Harding. That was not as powerful a motivation as she thought, for by the time I was ready to go to college I had saved $2,000 from work, and from cattle and hog enterprises. In 1947, that was enough money for two years of college. I planned to work during the school year and summers, so I knew I could make it on my own. Uncle Cleo had even been able to bank money while attending Southwest Missouri at Springfield in the early 1930s. But, then again, I was more than willing to let my father pay for whatever he wished. If they thought I was going to Harding because he was paying, that was fine with me.

Harding College in Searcy, Arkansas was, in 1947, one of six mostly struggling colleges operated by members of the Churches of Christ. It was founded in 1924 in Morrilton, Arkansas, then moved to Searcy. The other five were David Lipscomb

College (1891), Nashville, Tennessee—at that time a two-year school—Abilene Christian College (1906), Abilene, Texas; Freed-Hardeman College (1908), Henderson, Tennessee—also two-year—Pepperdine College (1937), Los Angeles, California, and Alabama Christian College (1942, later Faulkner University)—a two-year school—in Montgomery, Alabama. All these schools since have replaced "College" with "University." At the time, Pepperdine was the only one of the six accredited by a regional accrediting association, and with viable financial resources supplied by its launching angel, George Pepperdine, founder of Western Auto Stores. All these colleges were entrepreneurial. Since Churches of Christ are fiercely congregational with no ecclesiastical structure larger than the local church, colleges are founded by individual members for their own reasons, and usually receive no funds from churches. The schools are financed by tuition and monies solicited from foundations and wealthy individuals, many of whom are not members of the Churches of Christ.

Even though these colleges have no hierarchical supervision from the churches and minimal capital funding through resources of the Churches of Christ, they have still rigorously reflected the outlook and theology of the Churches of Christ. The reasons are that the administration and faculty have been drawn overwhelmingly from the Churches of Christ, and perhaps more importantly, above ninety percent of the students come from Churches of Christ. Pepperdine has been the exception in this regard, in its almost sixty years of existence, seldom having had more than twenty percent of its students from Churches of Christ.

I arrived at Harding during the throes of post-World War II overcrowding. During the war, Harding had less than 300 students. By 1947, with the arrival of war veterans, the number had swollen above 800. Housing for men was all temporary, having been moved in from army bases. Veterans had first choice on the better housing, and the rest had to settle into 15-by-15 foot hutments. Four persons were assigned to each hutment, which was constructed with an exposed internal frame—no inside walls—and covered with a composition material through which one could easily throw a baseball. In fact, a baseball-sized hole or two were visible in the hutment where I lived. The furniture consisted of two sets of bunk beds, four small tables with chairs, and pegs and lines for hanging clothes.

Upon arrival, my grandfather and I talked with William Font Mattox, Dean of Students, later founding president of Lubbock Christian College (now a university). He had an apartment in the east end of Godden Hall. He handed me a hutment housing assignment, showed us where they were located, and we found my hut. My grandfather looked it over and was very upset. The hutments were crude, somewhat unkempt, and with the latrine two hundred feet away—inconvenient. My grandfather declared that he would not raise chickens in a building like that. He ordered me to leave my suitcase in the pickup and said I should go back to Thayer and make arrangements to go to the University of Missouri. Like myself, he was not overly sold on Harding, even before he saw it, and especially not after. But I was never a person to look back, once a commitment was made. After I assured him I didn't mind that much, we went to talk with Dr. Maddox who said that perhaps later, after a few students dropped out, I could live in one of the dormitories. My grandfather finally acquiesced even though he thought I was making a big mistake.

My strategy was to take as much science and Bible as possible. Bible was required each semester. I also took English composition, American history, German and economics. In two years I took enough biology and chemistry to obtain a minor in each. My life seemed to waste away in science laboratories, since most afternoons required four to five hours of lab. I struggled, especially with English composition. Still, my mother's inculcation of a love for poetry persisted, and I joined the poetry club and published several poems in the literary magazine. Some of my peers viewed my interest in poetry as incongruous. A pre-agriculture major writing poetry? To further the anomaly, I was thought of as a muscular he-man. I never bothered to extol or exhibit my physique, but a fellow student, Bobby Mock, who was interested in weight lifting, always complimented me and kept telling me I should take up weight lifting.

Despite my difficulties with some of the academics, I endured, perhaps especially because of the mentoring of Dr. Kern Sears, my chemistry professor, who was, significantly, a sponsor of the poetry club and a practicing poet. I had difficulty with organic chemistry and quantitative analysis, the first because it was mostly memory with no applications, and the latter because it required a level of math which I had not attained. But Dr. Sears was a great encouragement.

On the other hand, I flourished in Bible, history, biology, biochemistry, entomology, and especially genetics. In fact, Dr. Jack Wood Sears, who took his doctorate in genetics from the University of

Texas, asked me to take over his classes when he was out of town. On more than one occasion, I bailed him out when he got confused in working through genetic formulations. I loved science, especially when it revealed secrets about the physical universe and immediate applications with which I could amaze my peers. I always enjoyed being identified as a science whiz, even if it entailed being something of a nerd.

New Preunderstandings: Andy T. Ritchie, Jr.

My first course in Scripture was under Andy T. Ritchie, Jr. at the recommendation of my sister. Not only had she taken Bible from him, she had spent several weeks in the summer of 1947 with a group of Harding students on campaigns which he directed in New York and Massachusetts. She was impressed with his deep spirituality and commitment to evangelism. Perhaps we had read about these qualities in the books our mother stumbled upon in the library, but they were not modeled by anyone in our home churches. Brother Ritchie was as committed as anyone to our fellowship's perspectives on salvation, worship, and church organization, but especially in respect to morality. He was far more demanding on moral matters than anyone we had known. He situated morality in the context of spirituality. He was not opposed to laying down the law, but he rarely set out a series of "don'ts" which would result in eternal damnation. Rather, he reflected on the sources of morality and why certain actions were improper from a Christian perspective.

My advisor was not going to let me take Brother Ritchie, since his classes were full. Andy was in great demand, indicating the influence he wielded over the students. Again, consistent with my demeanor when something really mattered, I held out with bulldog determination, and they finally let me enroll. The influence of Andy Ritchie was felt not only through his classes, but through his once-a-month preaching, his song leading, his devotions, and his Tuesday night personal evangelism meetings. After about a month I was hooked on whatever Andy did. Wherever Andy spoke, I was present. I also wanted to take voice lessons from him, but that one I couldn't swing—he himself declared that he couldn't accomodate another student.

Andy Ritchie attended David Lipscomb College his first two years. He finished his B.A. at the University of Louisville. He also attended Louisville Presbyterian Seminary, but didn't take a degree. That he didn't hold a graduate degree was something of an embarrassment to the administration since they were trying to move rapidly toward accreditation by the North Central Association. He trained in voice, both in school and privately. He had sung in numerous concerts and for a time performed regularly on a radio program. He had a powerful, rich baritone/bass voice. I spent two years in his choruses: first, the men's glee club, then the main chorus. Sometimes, when, in his opinion, we were not putting out, he chided, "I can overpower the whole chorus," and proceeded to do it. All this is pertinent because not only did Ritchie have new content in his sermons, his vocal approach was considerably different. His voice was resonant, varied and without repetitive "preacher" patterns. His delivery was fairly slow, as he waited for the points to sink in. For me and most of my peers it was a new style, a paradigm change in preaching. Ritchie was respected, but not a noted meeting preacher, since he did not fit the mold.

Ritchie's Bible course was on the Gospels. From church life I experienced a smattering of the Gospels, especially the condemnations (as in Matthew 23) and, later, the parables. But we never systematically studied the Gospels. In fact, the argument, going back to Alexander Campbell—though his version was a bit different—was that the instructions in the Gospels preceded the cross. It was supposed that Christians were to live only by the biblical books written after Jesus died on the cross, since that was when God "nailed to the cross the handwriting of ordinances which are against us" (Colossians 2:14). Some conceded that the Gospels contained valuable teachings, but they argued that whatever is required is repeated in Acts or the epistles, written after Jesus' death. The Sermon on the Mount was worthy of study, but its demands were perceived as too idealistic for contemporary Christians. None of us could live up to its requirements, and in fact, we didn't have to, since they were not for us. They were, rather, for the persons who lived during the time of Christ's ministry. They were designated by scholars as "interim ethics," a designation popularized by Albert Schweitzer. The Sermon on the Mount anticipated the opposition and persecution leading to Christ's death, and those perilous days required a special set of rules, it was thought. But after they were past, the rules, with their extraordinary demands, were no longer in force.

Ritchie bought none of this, though, as I remember, he argued little against the standard views of our churches. He simply plunged into the Gospels as if these utterances applied to us. What struck me about the Gospels and the emphasis of Ritchie was a shift from the focus in our churches. In the churches of my region, we were mostly concerned with whether we had replicated the blueprint of the New Testament church. It was important to go to church and to be moral, but no real demands were made on one's individual time or money. Ritchie, in contrast, emphasized the inner life of the believer. The focus was not on the structures of worship, organization, or mechanical obedience, but on the love of God in the human heart. He was interested in the commitment behind the skeletal superstructure.

We had to keep a notebook to outline the Gospels and their implications and applications. We also had to memorize several key passages to be repeated on exams. Several sayings of Jesus made a deep impression, but two stood out because they demanded a change of direction.

When statements in Scripture cause life to take a drastic turn, an interpretation is obviously involved—a hermeneutic. The question is, what sort of hermeneutic? Perhaps we may speak of internalized or existential hermeneutics. Was Ritchie something of an existentialist before anyone among us knew what it was, or how appalling as a philosophy? Perhaps! Certain existentialists claimed they were indebted for their ideas to Jeremiah, Jesus, Paul and Augustine, and Ritchie was indebted to at least the first three.

The two disconcerting statements of Jesus with which I felt the need to wrestle were: "No one can serve two masters. . . You cannot serve God and wealth" (Matthew 6:24), and "Seek first the kingdom of God and its righteousness and the rest of these things shall be yours as well" (Matthew 6). To this point, my life, in part, had centered on saving money. I can't say I was avaricious—I had no special plans to be unusually wealthy. But I did think that money was to be saved, not spent. I picked this up from my father, whose major strategy for money management was to avoid spending it. Money itself may not have been my master, but certainly the retaining of it was.

Before coming face to face with Jesus in these statements, I had never questioned the propriety of my rationale for saving money: to possess it, to be able to draw upon it in a time of dire need. But, if Jesus was to be master, something had to give. With this new focus on Jesus, it became clear to me that I was trying to serve two masters, that I was living like a circus rider with a foot on each of two horses. The second Scripture, "Seek first the kingdom of God", emphasized that trust is not in possessions, but in God. If one trusts God, he assumes God will provide in the day of tragedy. The one who trusts God places his primary energy into the work of the kingdom.

I faced a decision. I had no intention of spending money promiscuously, but somehow I had to overcome the inclination to keep it in the bank, even when the causes for saving it were good—buying clothes, for example. I somehow had to sidestep the pursuit of banking money as if this were the whole purpose of life. The aim of life was now to follow Christ, wherever he led. He was to be *the* master.

I knew it was not going to be easy: I knew I needed God's help. But I determined from that point on to serve only one master to the best of my ability: Jesus Christ, the son of the living God. This was a major shift in the manner in which I interpreted Scripture. Was it a paradigm shift? Was this shifting of my preunderstanding—the matters which guided my interpretation of Scripture—for good or ill? In my judgment, from the perspective of Scripture itself, it was for the good.

Andy Ritchie not only emphasized these Scriptures, he placarded them with his own life. He had four children; two boys and two girls. He lived in a plain, frame, one-story house in a relatively poor neighborhood. He always wore black suits and white shirts. His wife did not cut her hair, but wore it in a bun, and she dressed plainly. The children were neat and clean, but not stylish. The only luxury Andy allowed himself was ownership of a large Buick with Dynaflow—the Buick version of the automatic shift. He was quite apologetic about driving what many considered a luxury car. His rationale was that, as a diabetic, he was beginning to lose his sight, and his wife Kathryn now had to drive. Since she had difficulty mastering the art of clutch shifting, he felt that owning a vehicle with an automatic transmission was justified.

Andy was perceived as a deeply spiritual man, and he encouraged others to mature in spirituality. I still remember a sermon which vividly demonstrated what he perceived as the fountainhead of spirituality. It was based on the story of the woman with a hemorrhage of blood, from Mark 5:24-34. This woman, in order to obtain the blessing of Jesus, pushed through the crowd. The person who truly desires to be spiritual must exhaust every avenue to be close to and emulate Jesus, Ritchie preached. She must turn her back on a run-of-the-mill existence. She must push through in order to be in the inner circle.

For Andy, spirituality was especially characterized by its positive attributes. It had to do with prayer, the reading of the Scriptures, and the feeling of the love of God through meditation and music. This was before the fad of "quiet time" arose; Ritchie simply believed that one had to spend time alone with Jesus, just as Jesus did with God. He believed that hymns needed words with genuine spiritual depth, not mere sentimentality. The tune, in turn, needed to lift persons into the presence of God, not simply provide a rhythm attractive to the senses. In a life filled with these Christlike attributes, no leisure was available for the inroads of sin, he felt. Ritchie emphasized the saying of Jesus in which a demon, though cast out, returned with six other demons to fill the vacuum, since nothing positive had assumed the space (Matthew 12:45). Ritchie made the point over and over that a spiritual offense is the best defense against sin. A catalog of items to be avoided so as to keep the rules tended to be self defeating, he thought. The one who seeks first to be God's person does not have time for dancing or card-playing.

Brother Ritchie had a code of proper action which he thought should characterize Christians. They shunned physical contact with dates, dressed modestly and simply, and wore little or no cosmetics. They devoted their leisure time to study, prayer, meditation, and sharing the Gospel. They did not have time for movies, and they avoided the devastating effects of alcohol and tobacco, since the body is the temple of the Holy Spirit. They revered God's name and avoided vulgar, immoral language. Ritchie did not hesitate to lay down the law in these matters, but he was no legalist, if that means one who emphasizes mere rule-keeping, with no mention of motivations or reasons premised upon the nature of God and his Son.

Andy also stressed the need to share the Gospel with others. He wasn't too impressed with the effectiveness of the standard Gospel meeting. He certainly believed in preaching evangelistic sermons to those who had not accepted the Gospel, but he believed the best results accrued when persons went about the neighborhood sharing the teachings of Christ, one-on-one. He emphasized personal evangelism, preaching on such texts as "Go home and tell," and discussing the manner in which Jesus told of the love of God wherever he went. He, along with Otis Gatewood, was one of the first evangelists in the Churches of Christ to take groups—with Andy, it was mostly Harding students—to small churches in mission regions of the United States. He usually went on summer campaigns to the northeast.[1]

The focus of the Tuesday night meetings was trusting in God for one's life. The one who trusts shares the love of God with others, he taught. She makes summer commitments to campaigns and long-range commitments to mission areas. Andy's activities did not appeal to everyone, especially those who aspired to be big meeting preachers or debaters. But those interested in personal evangelism and foreign and domestic missions studiously attended the Tuesday night meetings. The encouragement and inspiration which Ritchie had to offer went far afield from Searcy in the late 1940s and early 1950s.

My perception, in 1947, was that Ritchie was unique and therefore uncharacteristic of the Restoration Movement. He represented a distinctive, if not altogether new, paradigm. Those of us influenced by his life and views believed that we were ushering in a new day in the Churches of

Christ. I wasn't aware at the time that strands of Ritchie's outlooks had resided in the Restoration Movement from the beginning. These were strands more in tune with the awakening perspectives of such revered leaders as Barton W. Stone, as contrasted with Alexander Campbell, who was more influenced by the Scottish Enlightenment in its various forms. These Stone evangelicals presumed a strong role for emotion in conversion, and in preaching and motivation for the Christian life. Later in his life, after merging with the Campbell wing, Stone remarked, "We have done away with the mourner's bench, but I fear also with the mourners." Stone's people were pessimistic about the prospects for human progress. They conceived humans as basically sinful and that human governments of necessity shared in this sin. They were convinced that a major change in human life could only come about as the result of God breaking in upon the human world. It is only the kingdom of God which can negate the pernicious pervasiveness of sin, they held. The Christian should therefore commit his time and resources to the kingdom of God—to the church for which Christ died.

The heirs of Stone stressed a warm personal piety, an interest in spiritual worship, an indwelling of the Holy Spirit, and a rigorous evangelistic and moral life. At the same time, they negated political involvement and trust in material accumulation. Many of these attributes impressed such persons as David Lipscomb and James A. Harding, who founded the Nashville Bible School, now David Lipscomb University. Ritchie attended David Lipscomb as a young man, and came to hold many similar views. These outlooks contrasted with those of the young Alexander Campbell and such persons as William Winans and Jacob Crifield, all of whom were deeply influenced by the empirical, rationalistic presuppositions of the Scottish Enlightenment.

Richard Hughes has patiently tracked this strand of the restoration in his book on the Churches of Christ.[2] While these strands are not always as easy to delineate as may be desired, and do, in fact, take different forms and consist of different combinations, nevertheless we have a more profound perspective on our own history when we come to grips with these differing modes and methods. The churches in my region were mostly influenced by a right-wing, rigid version of the Campbellian restoration. It was no wonder, then, that I perceived in Andy T. Ritchie, Jr. a breath of fresh air which I did not identify with our movement.

Preaching: The Emotive Side

By October of my freshman year I had volunteered to give a talk or two in the devotions we held in the hutments. My long-standing reserve before a group caused anxiety and loss of sleep as the time approached. But at least I was among friends. I was especially encouraged by Rodney Wald, a roommate, and George Pledger, who lived in a neighboring hut. Once we got to know each other, George and I popped corn, in the evenings at about 9:00 P.M., with great regularity. I was also comforted to some extent by the conviction that speaking out for Christ might indeed involve agony. I doubt now, however, that the stress of overcoming reticence is the suffering Jesus had in mind as the result of confessing him before men.

While my speaking skills did not particularly excite anyone, I was commended for the ideas and sincerity. Toward the end of the semester I mustered the courage to speak in Monday Night Meeting. At each meeting, several aspiring preachers spoke for about five minutes. Certain persons were invited to speak by prearrangement, but the majority decided to do so on the spur of the moment. For those of us without experience, considerable prior preparation went into an "impromptu" talk. I kept wanting to get up and speak, but it was at least a month before I mustered the courage. When I finally arose, I have no recollection at all of what I said. I remember, rather, the rapidly increasing heartbeat, the shortness of breath, and the eerie strangeness of observing myself so distraught that I was alienated from both ideas and audience. As time went on, I volunteered again, but never in the two Harding years was I so free from anxiety as to achieve true *rapprochement* with the audience.

By Christmas time I began to give thought to preaching. I did not have in mind a career; in fact, few of my peers did. They had wanted to teach or engage in some other occupation to make their livings, and preach as an avocation. Indeed, at Harding in 1947, no one was permitted to major in Bible alone. They had to double-major so that if they did indeed preach, they had another occupation by which to support themselves. Few preachers survived by preaching alone during the Depression and war years. The numbers of full time preachers were just now beginning to accelerate. If I planned to take over the Nebraska ranch I would have to start a congregation and probably do the preaching. Any experience I could gain beforehand would come in handy.

The standard way to get launched was to go on Sunday with an upperclassman who owned a car and who had established a preaching route. There were probably ten or twelve men who did this, along with a few faculty. Classes at Harding were held Tuesday through Saturday, precisely so that persons who preached a hundred or more miles out did not have to be in class on Monday morning after having arrived home after midnight. Burl Curtis, an upperclassman I knew, preached every Sunday in the vicinity of Harrison, Arkansas. His home was nearby in Lead Hill. Someone had arranged two preaching places just east of Conway, Arkansas, fifty miles from Searcy. One of these was in Vilonia and the other at a small Baptist church along the highway in the countryside nearby. I was told that I could preach at the Baptist church if I wished. I was told that another Harding student had preached there a few times. I thought it over a day or two. I believed I could justify preaching in a Baptist church if I preached the whole council of God. I was not sure what my mother and grandfather would think, but I need not tell them. I worried just a little about my future reputation. Dare I ever let it be known that I preached my first sermon in a Baptist church? On the other hand—if my first sermon bombed, perhaps it was best that it occur in a Baptist church.

Over a two or three day period in the middle of January 1948, I prepared a sermon. I don't exactly remember the topic, but I counseled with friends as to what I should say. It was to be something with which the Baptists could agree, but we decided I must interject some item on which we thought the Baptists could stand a bit of enlightenment. I think I started speaking on the inspiration of the Scripture and may have ended with why salvation is not by faith alone, but includes baptism for the remission of sins. I worried about being able to preach thirty or forty minutes. By no means did I have a gift of gab: as indicated earlier, my father immediately nipped in the bud any tendency toward loquaciousness. In the 1990s a fifteen-minute preacher might prove a sensation. But in pre-television days in Arkansas, a fifteen-minute preacher was a wimp: a real preacher could hold forth for at least an hour.

I woke up that Sunday morning with a great deal of trepidation, but I had committed myself and wasn't going to back down. At least, I thought, if I got egg all over my face, it would not get back to campus. As we rode south, then west, we talked about our preaching assignments and sang a few church songs. The encouragement of the brothers was helpful. I was let out at my assignment almost two hours before services started. I went over my sermon several times. Finally, people arrived—about forty or so. I felt fairly comfortable when I got up to preach. I got off to a good start, but bogged down in the middle. I managed to end, however, with some flourish. I had utilized about eighteen minutes, and I was somewhat relieved that I had spoken that long. But I knew it was not enough to qualify as a bonafide sermon. A person or two made a kind remark. I don't remember whether they invited me back, but that was not necessary if I wanted to return. As I recall, they paid me five dollars, two dollars of which went to Burl Curtis for the ride. No one invited me to dinner, so I waited at a cafe for the arrival of the person preaching in Vilonia. He and I planned to hitchhike back to Harding. Neither place we preached had night services, but those going north did. We had a terrible time obtaining a ride. About the time we were ready to give up, after walking about three hours, a man picked us up who was going all the way to Searcy. I certainly saw the day as an adventure in faith. I had stuck out my neck for God and I needed him in the worst way. I thought he had not let me down, but, on the other hand, nothing happened which elicited glowing praise. I had recently learned the song "Under his wing I am safely abiding/ though the night deepen and tempests are wild/ still I can trust him I know he will keep me. He has redeemed me and I am his child." I sang it several times: it meant much to me. I learned in these hours to address new topics to the Scriptures. I searched in memory and in Scripture for any statement relating to the assistance of God when involved in his work. I had not been particularly interested in those passages before.

The Encouragement of Rodney Wald

The person who acted as a mentor and encourager more than any other was my roommate, Rodney Wald. We had two other roommates who were from Florida, not much interested in religion, and didn't stay around the hut. One of them moved out before the semester ended. Rodney was from Nelson, Wisconsin. He was six or seven years older than the rest of us and was something of a loner, so we didn't ordinarily attend campus activities together. We had regular talks in the hut, however. He was baptized at a Church of Christ in Madison, Wisconsin, in the midst of World War II. He decided he wanted to preach, but elected to attend undenominational Bible colleges in Los Angeles and Philadelphia. At that time these were unaccredited and only taught courses in the Bible. After two years he decided he wasn't getting what he needed. He berated himself as having been too stubborn to go to a college like Harding, but he had repented and now he was there.

Rodney felt that at his age he had to make up for lost time. He therefore dedicated himself completely to his studies, to religious activities, to church, and personal meditation. He never wasted any time. He went to bed about 10:30 and was up at five every morning, spending the first hour mostly in prayer but also reading the Scriptures. He was the most disciplined person I had ever met. Before an exam he would sleep only two or three hours. He had very good grades, but that was not important to him. What was important was that he employ his time wisely, as a servant of God. He was a great encourager. As I stated earlier, he encouraged me in my efforts to speak and went over my talks with me ahead of time. He also inspired me to take up personal devotions. On occasion he chided my lack of discipline, but in such a manner that I did not take offense. He spoke at some of the campus sessions, but did not aspire to preach out of town. He thought he should dedicate himself to his studies.

Rodney opened up new worlds for me. He was from the north, with different habits, mannerisms and outlooks. He was dedicated to our fellowship's basic views on baptism and instrumental music, but not altogether so in regard to amillennialism. But neither did he identify with the premillennialists on campus, of whom there were above forty. He was not wed to many of our practices or traditions, although he was also not critical. He was very kind and considerate. He continually reflected on practices in the light of the Scripture in a way that was new to me. Rather than seeking proof texts for current practices, he carefully weighed the biblical evidence. He could do this better than I since his experiences were so much wider. Though he thought members of the Churches of Christ were right on a number of points, he identified various weaknesses. He felt that many members lacked a seriousness of purpose and spiritual depth. He did not see them as persons of prayer and meditation as were his peers and professors at the Bible colleges. Still, he was patient and non-judgmental. He prayed constantly for members of our churches, soliciting for them a newfound spirituality and dedication.

Rodney modeled for me an evangelical piety and inspiration of which I was only dimly aware, except perhaps through the novels of Lloyd C. Douglas. He introduced me to the sermons of Dwight W. Moody and Charles W. Spurgeon, which could be purchased in cheap paperback editions at the Harding bookstore. He, along with Andy Ritchie, encouraged me to acquire a love for the Psalms. It was also through him that I took up reading the Gospel of John, a favorite with evangelicals. In our circle, John was perceived as a bit too elevated and full of hidden meanings. Perhaps this new interest which Rodney quickened in me was not a change in hermeneutics, but it certainly involved putting new questions to the Scriptures—questions about inspiration and devotion; matters which were of little concern in my home region. Even my mother hadn't developed much taste for the Psalms as far as I know, though she had us memorize the twenty-third.

Rodney also introduced me to an aspect of our movement of which I was little aware. He was particularly tuned to the concept of nondenominationalism. He was aware that the fathers of our movement were non-credal and attacked sectarianism. He knew that we still did this. But it was his view that we ourselves were sometimes unknowingly sectarian. We needed to develop a greater passion for undenominationalism. To do so, he believed, was to follow the Bible wherever it led, regardless of whether the directions were counter to our prevailing views and practices. He also thought we were sectarian in the resources and models we were willing to utilize. In his view, to be non-sectarian meant to welcome whatever resources were available from all quarters. The only question to be raised was how they stood up in the light of the Scriptures.

The Churches of Christ in Wisconsin where Rodney Wald was converted had particularly stressed non-denominationalism as a ground for getting a foot in the door. At that time there were only about seven or eight Churches of Christ in Wisconsin. Our traditional views did not have the ready appeal in this land of Lutherans and Roman Catholics that they had in southern Missouri and northern Arkansas. In Wisconsin, the forward-looking preachers highlighted the importance of difference on biblical and undenominational grounds. Rodney's views and actions in this regard prepared me for future tasks and added a new dimension to my biblical interpretation. Rodney's perspective helped me lay aside the blinders that may have been superimposed by upbringing, and elicited a fresh reading of Scripture. I began to understand that we could only be truly undenominational if we pushed aside views and emphases which were more traditional than biblical. A sermon by Dean L. C. Sears also made a lasting impression. The sermon was on the search for truth wherever it led, and Sears argued that we in the

Churches of Christ should never claim to have discovered all the truth in Scripture, although we should certainly stand on whatever truth we had discovered. But, he preached, we should always talk to others with an attitude of openness to whatever truth they can show us and, in turn, hope they will consider the truth we present. It is only in this way, he argued, that we can be undenominational.

I was being encouraged along new paths in my journey of faith and Scripture. It was a time of exciting discovery, reflection, and growth. The influence of Andy T. Ritchie, Jr. and Rodney Wald nurtured seeds already planted by my mother and the books she encouraged me to read. On the other hand, different forces in the Harding experience and in my preaching fostered the retention and maturing of the empirical and factual emphases of my grandfather and father.

Preaching: The Empirical Side

I didn't go back to the Baptist church. Not that it was such a bad experience: what discouraged me more than anything was the hitchhiking. Because of my temperamental reticence I did not enjoy hitchhiking and I was not good at it. My classmate from Thayer, Paul Dubois, who also attended Harding, loved to hitchhike. He went everywhere and seldom had long waits for rides. But I was not Paul. I soon arranged to go to appointments where I was assured of a ride both ways. A student named Johnny Clark from Del Rio, Texas, took budding preachers to a group of churches northeast of Batesville, Arkansas, and I was invited along to preach at a country congregation at a place called Antioch; a church of about a hundred people. Again,

I was worried about how long I could preach, though I had prepared a new sermon. A few minutes into the sermon I blanked out. It seemed like an eternity before I came up with something to say, and the shock of the pause was devastating to me. I was afraid it would happen again, and because of the anxiety I again only managed about fifteen minutes. When the service was over, the person counting the contribution told me to hold out my hands. As I wondered why, he poured all the money into my hands—it was all change. Upon later counting, it totaled the magnificent sum of $3.23. That was from a hundred people, many of whom drove the new Fords and Chevrolets which were just becoming available after the war. Again, two dollars was to go to Johnny for transportation. I never went back to Antioch, either because they didn't want me or because I was too embarrassed.

Instead, I started going to my home region. I felt more comfortable there, though I avoided preaching where too many knew me. A disabled veteran named Ike Hall drove regularly to his home in West Plains, Missouri. I began preaching at a church in a small town called Brandsville, and also at a country cross roads named Lanton. I also preached at Jeff, a hamlet east of Thayer: my step-uncle, Ernest Sauser, was an elder there. The first Sunday I was there he said he wanted to speak with me after the service. Since he was a man of few words I was a bit surprised, but I stayed around. He told me that they had decided to appoint two new elders and wanted me to install them that night. I had borrowed my grandfather's pickup for the drive out to Jeff and my grandfather had gone along with me. We talked on the way back to his house—about ten miles away—about how to proceed with ordaining the elders. That night I returned with great confidence, having now developed a sermon or two on which I could elaborate for twenty-five to thirty minutes. I was also bouyed by the weighty task of installing elders. After I preached, I announced the installation according to the instructions of my uncle. I asked the two candidates to come forward. Nothing happened. Finally, one of the two said, somewhat hesitantly, "Whose idea is this?" I had assumed all along that it was the will of the congregation and those to be appointed. Somewhat deflated but still confident, I named my uncle. There was again a pause. My uncle didn't say anything. The man who spoke up said, "I think we'd better discuss this matter in another meeting, and postpone the installing until later." I was greatly embarrassed, and my exaltation ended in chagrin. I never returned to preach at Jeff. I was not too upset at my uncle, since I was sure his intentions were good. But I thought it might embarrass him if I returned. One of these men, as I recall, was installed as an elder a few months later.

In those days, the sermons I preached were essentially like those I had heard while growing up, and the reason I did so was because of my intimate knowledge of what our people expected in a sermon. I had heard sermons discussed, mostly by relatives, from earliest memory. The variety of what one may learn from a homogenous population—such as relatives—can be limited, but there were plenty of them, and they differed, sometimes violently, among themselves. I knew our people preferred factual, well-organized sermons, with the accurate quoting of numerous biblical texts. The believers preferred sermons which spent more time challenging the views of others than raising questions about their own. They didn't mind being exhorted about sin, but the designation of church members as worldly or greedy was to be avoided. They were bothered by talk of deep spirituality, which seemed too emotional and, therefore, denominational.

I'm not sure why I was committed to the view that the audience was the most important component in communication. I suspect, however, it came from the example of my grandfather and mother. Grandfather probably never actually heard the phrase that the customer is always right, but his forte in business was going out of his way to please the customer: he was the consummate salesman. He had little "brass," but a very winning manner, and my mother had copied these skills from him. If company came, it meant that she dropped everything and set out to make the company comfortable and to provide something to drink and eat. I don't remember ever seeing her exhibit a negative attitude toward a visitor. I assumed almost instinctively, then, that if I was to make it as a preacher, I had to please those who heard me. I intended to change certain emphases, but I did not presume to do it overnight, or bring it about through unsettling people. I memorized Scripture, used the standard kinds of outlines, but incorporated new insights from my teaching, reading and reflection. At certain points I probably leaned over backwards to sound traditional.

In the spring of 1948 I was in a car load of student preachers headed northeast of Searcy for churches around Hickory Ridge, Arkansas. That morning I was let out at a little country church, and as starting time drew near, there were still only fifteen or so women present. One informed me that I would probably be the only man, so I would have to do everything. In Churches of Christ, of course, preachers normally confine themselves to preaching, and male members of the congregation lead the singing, the prayers, wait on the Lord's table, and take up the contribution. But that morning, in addition to anxiety over the sermon, I had to worry about correctly carrying out the other functions. I probably had been involved in all these duties, but not regularly. I remember it all going fairly well, but the sermon suffered a bit because I could not give it undivided attention. That night Howard See, an older Harding student who preached regularly at Hickory Ridge, decided that three of us less seasoned fellows should do the preaching. I was elected to end with an exhortation and the offering of the invitation. If there was anything at which I thought I might excel it was offering the standard invitation. I mentioned the five steps of salvation: hearing, believing, repenting, confessing, and being baptized. I emphasized the importance of each step, arguing that none could be left out, and ended by saying that the last—baptism—was the most important. I don't know that I ever actually ever heard a preacher say as much, but I would now argue that such was certainly the implication of many a meeting sermon. On the way home a student I had grown to respect, Bob Roe from Newcomerstown, Ohio, asked if I really thought my statement about baptism being the most important could be supported from Scripture. I was somewhat taken aback, and set out an argument which was somewhat lacking in conviction. By the time we had reached Searcy he had convinced me that, according to Scripture, faith was the most important, though none of the others could be bypassed.

My near-total involvement in scientific education further influenced my predilection for the factual. Information about scientific breakthroughs in the war, such as radar, atomic energy, and the laser, were just beginning to be disseminated in detail in the academic community. It was an exciting time. Various synthetic chemical products, such as margarine, were hitting the market in a big way. My work in chemistry and biology enabled me to understand such phenomena as fission and fusion. All of these breakthroughs employed theoretical physics, but the applications were achieved through careful, painstaking, empirical experimentation. Following the war, as Thorton Wilder declared in "The Skin of Our Teeth", calm reason was the ideal. Any emphasis on emotion was perceived as a return to the superstitious and primitive.

My preaching, therefore, involved an analytical approach, moving from one point to another in logical progression. An example was a sermon, the outline originally provided by an older student named Guy Sims, based on John 6:66-71, containing the account of many disciples abandoning Jesus. First, I noted the reasons they abandoned Jesus: because his teachings were too outlandish and demanding—such as his comments on eating his flesh and drinking his blood. I then identified sayings which were a stumbling block to people today—the need to be baptized, for example. I then showed that Jesus turned to the twelve and asked them if they also would leave, and talked a bit about why the disciples might leave: they might prefer to return to fishing, which paid well and was secure. I made current application by telling of the northern Arkansas preacher I heard of who went to Oklahoma in the oil boom of the 1920s, got wealthy from oil, and quit preaching. The final point was the major one, expanding on Peter's question, "Lord, to whom shall we go?" The disciples might return to their old Jewish ways, I said, but that was not an option, since life was found in Jesus, not the law. They might return to their former occupations, but that, too, was insufficient. To follow Jesus was the only option if one hoped for eternal life, I preached. Though I spoke briefly of the reasons given in John's text, I spent most of the time on current applications.

I also developed sermons by trying to exhaust and categorize biblical data through the use of a concordance. My scientific training convinced me of the value of rigorous examination of discrete data. One of my favorite studies was an examination of all the conversion accounts in Acts. From this study I found that not all the steps of salvation were reported in each case, but if one examined all the cases, one discovered that converts heard the proclamation of the gospel, they believed that Jesus was the Christ, the son of God, they repented of their sins, they confessed with their mouths that Jesus was the Christ, and they were buried in baptism. I was not bothered that some items were missing in some cases, or that sometimes the data did not exactly fit my categories. The manner in which salvation comes about in Acts makes it clear that God is involved in specific ways, and the plan of salvation is not limited to the "five acts," as often preached in Churches of Christ. In some cases, as with the conversion of Lydia (Acts 16:14), God worked by opening Lydia's heart to the word preached. In other cases it is clear that salvation includes the gift of the Holy Spirit (Act 2: 38, 19:6). Still, it did not occur to me that I was fitting the data into a predetermined classification, rather than developing classifications from all the data at hand. My study seemed to me to be very scientific. The data was, after all, scrutinized and classified.

Regardless of my immersion in science, under the tutelage of teachers such as Kern and Jack Wood Sears and J. D. Bales, I began to see science in a new way. Before arriving at Harding, science was sacrosanct: it provided concrete, definitive answers which were beyond dispute. Science was the wave of the future, the hope of humankind. But these men encouraged me, rather, to highlight its limitations. Day in and day out, they made it obvious that there were many questions which scientists could not answer and probably never would. There was much in the physical universe a scientist would never see—an electron, for example. Furthermore, science had no clues as to the major questions: where did we come from, what is human life all about, and what is our destiny? Finally, it was slowly dawning on me that science, rather than being the hope of the future, might well be the doom of the future. It was only two years after atomic bombs had fallen on Japan, and there was already a big scare about next step up—the hydrogen bomb. Perhaps science would bring an end to civilization, rather than being its salvation. Partly for these reasons, I began assigning a higher and higher priority to my preaching.

In the spring of 1948, Don Horn, from Black Rock, Arkansas, persuaded me to go with him to DeKalb, Illinois, to start a congregation there. It was a time of church planting throughout the world: in suburbs, in cities, in regions of the United States where Churches of Christ were unknown, and in many foreign countries. I was only eighteen and Don was somewhat younger, but we had few doubts that we could get the job done. The only commission we had or needed was that of the Lord Jesus Christ himself: "Go into all the world and make disciples of all nations" (Matthew 20:19). Don knew a number of people in DeKalb and the surrounding area who had grown up in Black Rock and the Church of Christ. Most importantly, however, his brother lived there, and he hoped to reclaim him for Christ. The details of the DeKalb years will appear in the next chapter, but the reason for bringing it in at this point is that in the spring of 1949, I faced the decision of whether to transfer to the University of Missouri and pursue an agricultural degree or go to DeKalb in order to preach and attend what was then Northern Illinois State Teachers College. I had already applied and been admitted to Missouri.

The decision was not easy. Northern Illinois, like Harding, did not have a major in agriculture. If I went to DeKalb I would probably be putting aside my childhood dream of farming in Nebraska. Still, I decided to preach in DeKalb. I would attend Northern and major in speech, which I thought would be very helpful for my preaching career.

I was very sensitive about my communication skills, and considered them inadequate. The way I talked was often the cause of comment and sometimes even ridicule. It was more idiosyncratic than regional: I talked much like my father, who also defied regional categorization. He replicated elements of his German immigrant father's idiom, which was an amalgam of his native tongue, speech patterns from New Jersey, and the Nebraska frontier. My father did not talk like a native southern Missourian and neither did I. In addition to sounding like my father, I spoke in something of a rhythmic pattern, because when I was three, my mother thought I was going to be a stutterer. Her remedies grew out of her reading. She read somewhere that the proper therapy for stuttering was the recitation of poetry with emphasis on the rhythm, since that helped overcome the erratic stuttering patterns. It worked—or at least something did—but that is a long story. The outcome was that my peers thought I talked strangely—I was a man without a verbal homeland.

My plans were to help the church in DeKalb, improve my speaking skills, receive a bachelor's degree in speech, then take up the study of agriculture at the University of Missouri. In retrospect, I think this strategy was more to delay for myself and my father the need to face the fact that I was giving up a dream of ten or twelve years' standing. I was never one to renege easily upon a commitment. I think by this time, I had decided that the fundamental reality which really mattered was God and his love for the world as revealed through Jesus Christ. I could not permit myself to spend my time in chemical laboratories, or in chasing butterflies and classifying them, or even in planting and harvesting wheat, when that which was most needed was to proclaim that Jesus alone has the words of eternal life.

The traditional aspects of my approach to interpreting the Scriptures were nurtured by two persons: Guthrie Dean, a fellow student, and J. D. Bales, professor of Bible. I gravitated toward them after I started preaching because they both preached regularly and seemed more in tune with the mindset of most Arkansans. I fell in with both of them upon returning to Harding for my second year, after a summer in DeKalb. Guthrie lived in a hutment north of mine. J. D. Bales, through my arrangements, started preaching at Mammoth Spring during a time when the congregation was without a preacher. I rode with him on several occasions so as to preach at one of the previously mentioned nearby congregations. My conversations with him were chiefly during the long rides from Searcy to Mammoth Spring and back, since I did not take a class from him. I also heard him in debates with a Mormon in Hardy, Arkansas, and with an atheist named Teller on the Harding campus.

Despite my father's displeasure with polemic, I was often captivated by it. I loved the excitement of an argument. It was argument, after all, which kept me awake in church at age four. I was still, and probably always will be in some measure, an heir of my grandfather: I might run scared of someone who could physically beat me, but I discovered early on that there were not many who could best me in argument. I had a talent for locating the crucial issues and I read widely, so that I frequently had facts unknown to others. I exulted in the facility of advancing these facts one after another so as to create an irrefutable case. I may have questioned the contribution of public religious debates, but I was exhilarated by arguments as long as they didn't become the tail wagging the dog.

I remember two arguments I carried on with Guthrie Dean. Guthrie was from Shreveport, Louisiana, and was a Bible and speech major. A fluent and cogent speaker, he was on the college debate team and did very well. He loved an argument even more than I. In fact, I think his Christianity chiefly revolved about argument over the correct point of view. He seemed uncritical of the positions taken at Harding, but shortly after he graduated he gravitated toward those who later opposed the Herald of Truth arrangement, whereby funds were sent from congregational treasuries to the Fifth and Highland church in Abilene, Texas, which supervised the program. The Herald of Truth was the first radio program from our churches to be broadcast over one of the national networks. For the critics, this arrangement represented a departure from the congregational independence displayed in the New Testament.

One of the matters which concerned Guthrie was whether children's homes should be administered by a single congregation or whether they could be responsible to a board of trustees made up of men from various congregations. He held that they could be either, but that if they were under a board and not a single congregation, then other churches could not directly contribute funds to them. A few board-directed homes existed, but they gladly accepted funds from any and all congregations who would send them. In the minds of some, the practice was identical with a Christian college accepting contributions from the treasury of a church. The majority view held that churches could not contribute to Christian colleges, since they were an institution larger than a local congregation.

The threads of this argument run back to the nineteenth century controversy over mission societies. David Lipscomb and others who were very influential in formulating our fellowship's thinking had opposed mission societies or boards on the ground that they took over the work of independent congregations and therefore violated their independence. These men persuaded churches not to send money to the mission boards. If churches wished to do mission work they should undertake it themselves, it was thought. If they wished to help a missionary they should send the funds directly to him.

As I remember, it was in my discussions with Guthrie that I first explored the ramifications of commands, examples, and necessary inferences. I had, no doubt, heard the formula before, but it had not been indelibly impressed upon my mind. As I recall, I may have agreed with Guthrie that a church should not send money to a children's home which was under a board of trustees, but I didn't feel as strongly about it as he did. We agreed that Christ commanded a concern for children (Matthew 19:13, 14), as did James, and that this applies specifically to orphans, since James states that pure religion consists of caring for "orphans and widows in their distress" (James 1:27). There are no explicit examples of persons caring for orphans in Scripture in either the Old or New Testaments. Since there is a command to care for them, the question is—how? One might suppose that the best way would be to take them into one's home. As far as we knew, there were no orphanages in Palestine during the time of Christ. But what if a church should decide to spend money for child care? From our reasoning, since there was a command, the church had a duty to do so. The question of method, therefore, seems to involve necessary inference. If child care by the church is to be undertaken so that its congregational independence is not violated—-so that someone from another church or churches is not making the decisions—then the individual church must run its own orphanage, and must not contribute funds for child care to other congregations.

It is interesting that we have so often regarded the command-example-necessary inference triad as the universal formula for interpreting the Scripture, since there are several topics to which we have not applied it. The only matters settled by this hermeneutic rule were those having to do with concrete action about the worship of the church or the use of the money in its treasury. Matters having do with understanding the nature of God or how to grow spiritually perhaps could be addressed from the command-example-inference basis, but ordinarily are not. When we discussed whether the Holy Spirit dwells in the Christian we did not bring to bear commands, examples, or necessary inferences. No one even thought to bring up this hermeneutic when the Holy Spirit was discussed.

As with other methods and modalities, we did not always subject our presupposition of the necessity of applying commands, examples, and necessary inferences to the scrutiny of the Scripture itself. Since this hermeneutic has been in our blood for a long time, we tended to accept it without question. But where did it really come from? It may surprise some that this formula has a prior life in the church reformers.

Command/Example/Inference: Origins

In determining what specific matters were to be adapted, Zwingli spoke of both the commands of Christ and biblical examples.[3] I have not found, however, a statement in which Zwingli brought the two together as a clear hermeneutic principle. An English contemporary of Bullinger named Edward Dering (1540-1576), a Puritan, offered what may be one of the earliest statements on commands, examples, and inferences, in his argument for the theological importance of inferences. He insisted that a conclusion based on Scripture and drawn from "proportion, or deduction, by consequence, ...is as well the Word of God, as that which is an express commandment or example."[4] This formula became popular in those churches interested in patterns of polity: the Zwinglian reform, the Scottish Presbyterians, the English Puritans, and the various British independents. I am not aware that this formula preceded the sixteenth century, though it would be well to examine earlier reform movements, such as those of Wyclif and Hus. The writings or perspectives of various Anabaptist, Socinian, and Unitarian groups should also be examined.

The formula appears to be already widely accepted in the earliest printed document of the Campbell movement, the "Declaration and Address" of 1809. "Express terms and approved precedents" were granted without question, but inferences were suspect. Thomas Campbell conceded that inferences may be useful, but rejected their ecclesiastical role on the ground that they divide believers.

> Therefore, no such deductions can be made terms of communion, but do properly belong to the after and progressive edification of the Church. Hence, it is evident that no such deductions or inferential truths ought to have any place in the Church's confession.[5]

Unfortunately, this formula has not had the sort of influence in the life of local congregations of Churches of Christ envisioned by its early proponents. Instead, its chief employment has been in religious debates and in polemical writings in the journals. In regard to church rule, the formula has been applied as in the following example.

The officers of the church authorized by the New Testament are elders and deacons. A command to appoint elders may be found in Paul's instruction to Titus, ". . .appoint elders in every town, as I directed you" (Titus 1:5). Several examples exist of elders in the New Testament, such as Acts 11:30, and 14:23. Sometimes, however, a cognate term is employed—bishop. According to the argument, we do not know explicitly from the New Testament that these terms designate the same office. We know this, however, from inference. In his letter to the church at Philippians, Paul addressed the "bishops and deacons" (Philippians 1:1). In Acts 14:23, the officers appointed in each church were "elders". Therefore, we conclude that "bishop' and "elder" must be the same office. One puzzle is that in Titus 1:5, the command is to appoint elders in every town. The question arises as to what happens if more than one congregation exists in a town. By inference, the argument goes, we know that each church in a town is to have elders because of the Acts example of Paul appointing elders in every church. But another puzzle is that in some of Paul's letters he does not address these important leaders—in Romans, Galatians and I Corinthians, for example. According to some scholars, these churches did not have elders. But by inference, so our polemicists have argued, these churches had elders, since Paul appointed elders "in every church" (Acts 14:23).

The tripartite formula has had a checkered career in its five-hundred-year history. It has largely been employed by churches intent on restoring overt ecclesiological patterns, but less so by those interested in restoring a more pious life style—such as the Anabaptists and the Amish—or those focusing on the charismatic gifts, such as Pentecostals. In churches where the formula once was important, such as the Congregationalists (originally Puritans) and the Presbyterians, churchmen have lost even a memory of it. But, then, they are no longer committed to restoring the ordinances of the primitive church.

Our tripartite dispensationalism has likewise played a decisive role in the manner in which we have interpreted the Scriptures. This formula was first explicit in our literature in Alexander Campbell's famous 1816 "Sermon on the Law," as presented to the Redstone Baptist Association. Even before that, however, the authority of the New Testament over against the Old for re-establishing the primitive church was implicit. In the "Declaration and Address," Thomas Campbell wrote

> The New Testament is as perfect a constitution for the worship, discipline, and government of the New Testament Church, and as perfect a rule for the particular duties of its members, as the Old Testament was for the worship, discipline, and government of the Old Testament Church, and the particular duties of its members.[6]

Since that time in our movement, we have been adamant against employing the Old Testament to support any Christian practice. The address as presented to the Redstone Baptist Association was denounced by leaders who realized, if somewhat later, its ramifications and departures from the typical Baptist attitude toward the Old Testament. In fact, this relegation of the Old Testament to a non-authoritative status ran counter to the reformed positions of Calvin, Zwingli, Knox, and the Puritans. Luther, in contrast, found employment for the Old Testament, but only as a counterpoint to the Gospel. Alexander Campbell rejected even Luther's proposal, commenting pointedly, "There is no necessity for preaching the law in order to prepare men for receiving the gospel."[7]

Campbell's perspective on the three dispensations was indebted to the federal or covenantal theology of the Dutch scholars, especially Grotius (1583-1645) and Cocceius (1603-1669).[8] Cocceius held that with the failure of the covenant of works with Adam, God instituted the covenant of grace in three dispensations: the patriarchal, the Mosaic, and the Christian.[9] This dispensationalism not only established a groundwork for what is authoritative in each dispensation, it also provided a means of relating the dispensations. In effect, it became a biblical theology, featuring promise and fulfillment. An example of a biblical theology so organized in the restoration movement was Robert Milligan's often reprinted work, *An Exposition and Defence of the Scheme of Redemption.*[10]

American dispensational counterparts may be located in various other quarters: for example, in the lectures on Jewish history of David Tappan (1752-1803), a moderate Calvinist and Hollis Professor at Harvard.[11] More than a century before, Grotius had emphasized the need to understand the Old Testament in its own right, rather than simply for whatever light it might shed on Christology. As David Steinmetz noted, this relegation of the Old Testament to its own segregated context delimits its use by Christians.[12] The Campbells were also probably influenced by Locke and his heirs, who chiefly sought to root Christianity in the Gospels and—secondarily—in the letters of Paul. The Campbells, in contrast, focused upon Acts and the epistles, rather than the Gospels.[13] It is interesting that in the nineteenth century in works explicitly on hermeneutics, the tripartite dispensational formula is always present, but it has dropped out in the twentieth century when hermeneutics are discussed.[14]

J. D. Bales

J. D. Bales impressed me as a skilled polemicist. I knew he read much and kept files on all sorts of subjects. He seemed to be a person of spirituality, but he was given to argument. He lived in near-poverty because he put all of his resources into buying books, papers and journals, and in publishing his own books. Bales was born and orphaned in Georgia, coming to Harding from an orphanage in Valdosta. As a student, he was a debater of some note. He married a Canadian and studied for a time at the University of Toronto, where he also preached. He later obtained a Ph.D. in education from the University of California in Berkeley. Bales reflected, in some ways as much as anyone, the empirical rationalism of the Scottish enlightenment. But he wasn't bound by mere fact and logic. On some matters,—worship and family life, for example—he recognized the power of inspiration and love. He did not shun examples having to do with people and their problems. Still, I came to discern that he did not carefully weigh his evidence—he aimed to overwhelm his opponents with sheer volume. I, too, was a connoisseur of evidence, but believed, because of the Spartan training of my father, that you went with the best, not the most.

What impressed me most about Bales was that he had definite reasons for everything he did. He drove a new large Buick. He had a large family, but the reason he drove a Buick was because he was always in a hurry either to read or write something. He drove as fast as he thought safe, so he needed a new, heavy car. When I started riding with him for preaching assignments to Mammoth Spring, he had begun to get interested in communism. During World War II he was a pacifist, but when the war was over, consonant with Dr. Benson's focus on Americanism, Bales became intrigued by the danger of communism. It was the great scourge because it was atheistic. Since this seemed to justify Christians going to war, Bales rejected his former pacifism. It was about this time that the famous radio show of Herbert Philbrick, "I Led Three Lives for the FBI" went on the air. One station we could receive enroute broadcast it on Sunday night, so the climax of the night's return to Searcy involved listening to that program. The roads from Mammoth Spring to Cave City, Arkansas were about sixty miles of unpaved gravel. Furthermore, it was an open range area, so it was legal for cattle to graze along the highways. Where possible, Bales would floorboard the Buick and we would roll along at about seventy-five miles an hour. This was somewhat infrequent since there were so many curves in the road. He decided, because of the gravel and the cows, that it was dangerous to go that fast without better illumination, so he had a spotlight installed on his car. He drove with one hand directing the spotlight far down the center of the road and around the curves.

The last Bible course I took at Harding was under S. A. Bell, whose better-known brother, R. C. Bell, was a Bible professor at Abilene Christian. It was a course on the prophets of the Old Testament. Brother Bell was elderly and not the most exciting teacher available: he tended to drone on and on. I had a very difficult time with the course even though I was interested in the subject matter. His approach to the prophets focused almost totally on his effort to interpret their writings in the light of Messianic prophecy and its fulfillment in Jesus and the New Testament. He presented the views of various authorities, all of whom seemed to limit their interests to such fulfillment, then presented his own. I had the feeling that something was wrong, though I didn't know exactly what. But I had the impression that there must be some manner of studying the prophets which wasn't so deadly dull and which really had a message for Christians. That, however, had to wait a few years for a different teacher. Since hermeneutics deal with the questions addressed to the text, I infer that Bell's hermeneutic centered on which prophecies were fulfilled, and why. Because these were his only questions, that is all we obtained from the text. It was clear that for Brother Bell, that was the sum total of the prophets' meaning. But a different reading with different emphases reveals that the prophets were much more interested in addressing the religious commitments and outlooks of their contemporaries.

The Harding years were good ones, and there is much more to relate than space permits. I think most of all I was influenced there by the models of spirituality, dedication, and sophistication of my teachers and visiting preachers. At home I had been exposed to preachers of some education, but, excluding the Scriptures and church papers, I had probably read more books, novels, and poetry than they. Their style tended to be rural and either didactic, accusatory, or exhortational. At Harding, the style was different; it was a new paradigm for preaching. It tended to focus more on inspiration and dedication. The style, particularly that of persons like Dean L. C. Sears and his son Kern, was more sophisticated. The speakers drew on a larger range of reading and experience, sometimes quoting from the classic canons of literature, such as Shakespeare. I was impressed by F. W. Mattox because of his historical insights. I didn't know how good a historian he was but I was impressed, because I had not been exposed to church history before. I was also impressed because he argued that we could fellowship a person who disagreed with us on some matter, even one like premillennialism. He spoke of his father, a premillennialist. Mattox said that on some points he disagreed with his father, but he was still a brother in Christ. That was not the manner in which Leroy Miller treated premillennialists. He believed they should be disfellowshiped. I had not had a conversation with a genuine premillennialist in the Churches of Christ, as far as I know, prior to attending Harding. At Harding I became friends with a few, and Mattox's position was helpful. I came to think he was right.

In the Harding lectureships, which occurred at Thanksgiving in those days, I relished and was astounded by the preaching of some of the brotherhood greats. I especially remember Alonzo Welch for his literary style and cogent outlines. He had training in both literature and law. I was also impressed by his interest in orphaned children. G. C. Brewer was impressive as a speaker. When he was at his best he could speak for an hour or more and it seemed like only twenty minutes. He was impressive when he talked about grace and legalism: I had not heard much about grace in my upbringing. A. R. Holton seemed like a gentle, yet firm and dedicated man. Burton Coffman, who caught my attention because of his powerful and resonant voice, once presented a lecture on God which greatly influenced me for a number of years, since it was the first I had heard on the subject. Frank Pack was a young but impressive speaker who introduced me to the church as presented in the New Testament. I didn't know that much about early church history, but from our preachers I had concluded that it was mostly irrelevant. Frank did not shun to mention the problems in the early church, but he also provided information on the positive developments and achievements and suggested that we could profit from reading about these early Christians. I was impressed with the demeanor of E. W. McMillan, who was stately, yet inspiring. J. P. Sanders was a fairly young man, but he was one of the most fluent speakers I had heard. He had a way of bringing in profound insights and details while at the same time keeping the uneducated listener interested. I did not know until later that his training was in philosophy. That might have bothered me at that stage because I thought, as did many of my professors and peers, that philosophy should be avoided because of its secular and atheistic tendencies.

My years at Harding were full of joys, challenges, and opportunities for growth. They were an indispensable preparation for what was to follow.

---

[1] Thomas H. Olbricht, "Featuring Andy T. Ritchie, Jr.: Campaigning and Counseling," *North Atlantic Christian* (October 1962) 24-26.

[2] Richard T. Hughes, *Reviving the Ancient Faith: the Story of the Churches of Christ in America* (Grand Rapids: Eerdmans, 1996).

[3] *Zwingli and Bullinger*, trans. G. W. Bromiley (Philadelphia: The Westminster Press, 1963) 25.

[4] Edward Dering, *The Praelections. . .upon. . .Hebrews* in Dering, *Workes*, 447-448. Quoted by: Theodore Dwight Bozeman, *To Live Ancient Lives* (Chapel Hill: University of North Carolina Press, 1988) 70. This document was probably published in 1572.

[5] "Declaration and Address," in: Charles A. Young, *Historical Documents Advocating Christian Union* (Chicago: The Christian Century Company, 1904) 110.

[6] Young, 109.

[7] Alexander Campbell, "Sermon on the Law", Young, 263.

[8] See especially Robert Frederick West, *Alexander Campbell and Natural Religion*(New Haven: Yale University Press, 1948). Also for the role of these scholars in biblical criticism, Simon J. De Vries, *Bible and Theology in the Netherlands* (New York: Peter Lang, 1989) 5ff.

[9] "Johannes Cocceius," John McClintock and James Strong, *Cyclopaedia of Biblical, Theological, and Ecclesiastical Literature* (New York: Harper and Brothers, 1895).

[10] Robert Milligan, *An Exposition and Defence of the Scheme of Redemption* (Cincinnati: Carroll Publishing, 1868).

[11] David Tappan, *Lectures on Jewish Antiquities; Delivered at Harvard University in Cambridge, A.D. 1802 & 1803* (Cambridge: W. Hilliard and E. Lincoln, 1807).

[12] David Steinmetz, "The Superiority of Precritical Exegesis," *Theology Today* 37 (1980).

---

[13] See the insightful article on the centers of Alexander Campbell's biblical studies, hence his theology, by M. Eugene Boring, "The Formation of a Tradition: Alexander Campbell and the New Testament," *The Disciples Theological Digest* 2 (1987) 5-54. Also Thomas H. Olbricht, "Alexander Campbell as a Theologian", *Impact* 21 (1988), 22-37.

[14] In the intramural battles of the 1950s this formulation dropped out of our explicit hermeneutic since it was assumed by all controversialists. J. D. Thomas did not mention it in *We Be Brethren* (Abilene: Biblical Research Press, 1958), though in *Heaven's Window*, an effort at total hermeneutics, Thomas mentioned it, mostly in passing.

4

A Constant Interpreter in a Growing Church: 1949-1951

Several factors eased the decision to help start the church in DeKalb, Illinois. First, there was the encouragement of Andy Ritchie and my peers to be involved in evangelism, and I was eager to test my wings. The preferred way to go was to spend the summer with Andy in a campaign. I could have done this, but in order to do so I would have needed to ask churches and relatives for funds. This would also have made it difficult to add much to the next year's college expense fund. While I believed that money was to be spent in order to do good, I resisted expecting others to foot the bill. I needed to make it on my own. Don Horn and I—although mostly Don—had talked with Andy about starting the congregation in DeKalb. Andy was excited about the prospect and was very encouraging. Don assured me that I would have no trouble finding employment. He had worked during the summers in DeKalb while he was still in high school. He assured me I could work for California Packing Company, which canned peas and corn, or the DeKalb Agricultural Association, a hybrid seed corn company. California Packing, under the Del Monte label, harvested peas in June and corn in August and September. DeKalb Ag employed several high school students in July to detassel corn. The outcome was that I could make good money and at the same time do evangelism. As it turned out I saved over five hundred dollars that summer, which went a long way toward paying for my second year at Harding. My uncle had hoped I would return to Alton and work for him but had I done so, I would probably have saved less than two hundred dollars.

The experiences in northern Illinois were crucial in laying foundations for the future. I had to move quickly from being a connoisseur of biblical interpretation to actually interpreting Scripture for application to real life. I could no longer play games, as with Guthrie Dean, and relish being a sharp-witted devil's advocate. I sensed that I had to be a sincere interpreter of the Word if I were to gain respect. I knew it would not be easy and that I was inadequately prepared, but I was confident that I knew, as well as any my age, our central commitments—the topics our people relished hearing—our approaches to interpretation, and the appropriate homiletical methods. I now shudder to realize that my confidence resided more in knowing what my auditors expected than in knowing the Scriptures. I still believe, however, that good preaching must interpret Scripture for a specific audience, and therefore I cannot say I was completely unprepared for the task which lay ahead of me during those summers. I learned rapidly. I grew in communication skills, through work in speech and experience in debate. I became more confident of my interpersonal skills and more outgoing, and as a result, less reticent and private. I learned to explore parts of the Bible I had not examined before, and some of the helpful tools for such exploration. Before long I became acquainted with new varieties of preaching, interpreting, and conceptualizing the message of the Bible. I made a few major decisions, including pursuit of a relationship which ended in marriage. I also found myself in the midst of controversy—its flames fanned by those immersed in theological education—over new directions in the church. These struggles were the early harbingers of more serious strains and stresses which shook our movement in the late 1960s and early 1970s.

The First Summer in Madison, Wisconsin and DeKalb, Illinois: 1948

The first week of June 1948, I returned home from Searcy for a short visit, then boarded a bus for Madison, Wisconsin. That was the first time I had been more than five hundred miles from home and it was indeed an adventure, encompassing both eager anticipation and anxiety. I thought we would never get in or out of Chicago: I could not imagine a city that large. The reason for the Madison side trip en route to DeKalb was that James D. Willeford, one of the co-founders of the Herald of Truth, had written Andy, requesting that he hold a campaign in

Madison. Andy decided he could not schedule the campaign, but mentioned in personal evangelism sessions that Willeford had pleaded for campaign workers.

I wrote Willeford and he encouraged me to come. He informed me that I would stay with him for a few days, at first. I called him at home when I arrived on Capitol Square in Madison. He gave me directions for taking a bus to his house on the east side. I was apprehensive about making it there on my own since I had only been on city buses in Kansas City. The tune, "Under His Wings" passed again through my mind. Despite my misgivings, I arrived safely at the Willeford home. They were very hospitable, encouraging me and kidding nicely about my being a Missourian and a Harding student. On Monday I started going down streets, knocking on doors, inviting people to the nightly meetings. Since I was the forerunner of workers to come, I walked the streets by myself. The church had printed 20,000 brochures for distribution, so it was anticipated that we would knock on 20,000 doors. Madison had about 40,000 dwellings at that time. My old nemesis, fear of talking with unfamiliar people, caused me anxiety and made time seem to crawl, generally resulting in a great deal of misery. I could make it for a time if I found someone that was receptive. These were, unfortunately, very few. Most said they were Catholic, Lutheran or some other sort of Protestant, and that they were not interested. A few slammed the door in my face. Others ordered me off their premises. Some refused to meet me at the door, then yelled at me in the street for leaving the brochure on the doorstep. Some less unfriendly types promised to attend, but, as far as I knew, only one or two did.

On Wednesday, two Freed-Hardeman students, Weldon Wells and Neil Lightfoot, arrived. I later became a colleague of Neil's at Abilene Christian. They were both from Waco, Texas, and connected with the Columbus Avenue congregation where Willeford had preached, and which now provided part of his salary. Trine Starnes, who was a later campaign evangelist, preached for Columbus Avenue. Weldon and Neil worked together and I continued by myself. A member of the congregation was supposed to help, but he never showed. Finally, toward the weekend, a high school junior from Blanchardville, Wisconsin, whose family attended the Madison church, showed up. She was assigned to work with me. I was hesitant at first. If she proved more reticent than I, we were in big trouble, I thought. Fortunately, it turned out that she had a great deal of self-confidence, much more than I. We talked together as we walked the street, took breaks, and ate our lunches. I soon learned that she was dedicated and hoped to grow in spiritual insight and commitment. She had volunteered for the campaign, hoping that the activities and the meetings would contribute to that growth. I was impressed by her confidence, her spiritual longings, and her communication skills.

During the preaching services, I sat with her most of the time. When I left to work in DeKalb we wrote letters. But, I learned, her father was disturbed. I had two strikes against me: first, I was a preacher. Though a church member, he wasn't particularly dedicated, and thought preachers were lazy and didn't really earn what they were paid. Second, he didn't like Southerners. Actually, I was a bonafide Yankee, having been born a mile north of the Mason-Dixon line. But the way I spoke—very slowly and countrified, in his opinion—clearly identified me as a Southerner. Furthermore, he already had a husband picked out for his daughter, a Wisconsin lad who would soon be given a dairy farm by his parents.

Despite her father's objections, we corresponded occasionally when I returned to Harding. After Christmas I received a dear Tom letter, saying I should not write anymore. When I returned to Madison the next summer, however, she had graduated and had moved there, having been employed by the Oscar Meyer company. She quite willingly sat by me at church, and nothing seemed to indicate that this was the same girl who had written the goodbye letter. I later found out that the letter was written because of pressure from her father. That high school junior whom I met during my first Madison campaign tour was Dorothy Kiel. Two years later, on June 8, 1951, we were married at the church building in Madison, with James D. Willeford performing the ceremony.

I now turn from these pleasant memories to comment on the strategic approach of the campaign. The brochure we distributed focused on the undenominational posture of the Churches of Christ. Our identity, we insisted, was not that of "just another church." We were not an ecclesiastical body, we had not been sent by any earthly board or authority, and we had no geographically-identifiable headquarters. We were neither Catholic, Protestant nor Jew. We were simply New Testament Christians living according to the dictates of the New Testament. We invited people to attend the meetings with Bibles in hand so they could determine whether, according to Scripture, what we preached was true. We welcomed discussion and assured our prospective hearers that we would make any change in faith or practice that could be documented in Scripture. We were also interested in the unity of the church, but not of just any kind. It had to be based on explicit instructions from the Scriptures.

This approach appealed to a few. Five or six were baptized—not anything like the numbers in other regions of the country. Still, we were pleased. Several contacts had been made which might lead to future baptisms. This was an interesting shift in the role of Scripture from the meeting sermons of my youth. There, the Scriptures were seen as the sum and substance of all religious truth. From them one could establish the error of denominational ways. Now, the Scriptures were a work to be examined. Its truth cut every direction—possibly even against us. We advocated rooting out all sectarianism, even that of which we ourselves might be guilty. We were not interested in what the Churches of Christ taught. We focused upon what the Bible taught. Our hermeneutic did not consist of prooftexting to prove what we already practiced. Rather, it was heuristic—designed to help us determine what God required, without prior reference to the practices of any religious group, ourselves included.

The evangelist for the campaign was Raymond Kelcy, who preached for the Trail Lake congregation in Fort Worth, Texas. Raymond also was working on a Th.D. at Southwestern Theological Seminary. He later spent his life as a Bible teacher and departmental chair at Oklahoma Christian in Oklahoma City. I found Raymond Kelcy's sermons well-structured and interesting. He had a modified version of the older meeting formula, discussing such topics as proofs for the inspiration of the Scriptures, the challenges of science and evolution, how we know that the Bible is from God, and great slogans of the Restoration Movement. He also spoke on the identity and undenominational nature of the church, the plan of salvation, and true Christian unity. Raymond was well-educated, compared with many of our preachers. He portrayed the best qualities of the older generation of preachers, but was moving toward a new style of preaching. He addressed a new set of questions to the Scriptures, based on the perceived attitudes of people in Wisconsin. His sermons made a good logical flow from one subtopic to another. He had excellent support for his subpoints, his evidence coming from the Scriptures and his own experience. When he was at his best, he preached with a degree of passion, though he tended to be more rational than emotional. He spoke effectively, but with a southwestern, nasal quality. He was the best all-around preacher I had heard, up to that point. I can't say that the sermon on great slogans of the Restoration was the one that impressed me the most, but it was the first time I had heard it. The slogans were: "We speak where the Bible speaks and are silent where the Bible is silent"; "No creed but Christ, no book but the Bible, no name but the divine name"; and "In faith, unity—in opinion, liberty—and in all things, charity." I think that Raymond, more than any other preacher I had heard to date, preached in a manner which incorporated the basic thrusts of movement from its beginning. His manner of interpreting Scripture, therefore, was attuned to a longer range of brotherhood experience. Most of the other preachers I had heard were not so aware of the brotherhood's past.

That first year, I left Madison with some reluctance. I had been warmly received by the

Christians there and I knew it would be different in DeKalb. Then too, there was this girl I had met. . . I stayed in Madison a week longer than anticipated. When I arrived in DeKalb, I went right to work for California Packing Company. I told them I wanted to be located in the canning factory because that would make it possible for me to attend church and take my turn at preaching. For the first two days I was sent out to a farm where we labored all night loading cut pea vines on wagons. Soon, however, I was in the cannery, working on the machine that put caps on the metal cans.

Don had been in DeKalb about three weeks. He and some of the members arranged for a meeting place in a room of the Masonic temple. The group had already met twice when I arrived. The room was available on Sunday afternoons only. That was a good arrangement, since it gave people from the neighboring congregations (the closest being more than forty miles away) a chance to attend and lend encouragement. The majority of these visitors were from the West Jefferson Street church in Rockford, but a few came from congregations in the western Chicago suburbs. The ties with the church in Rockford were important since they assured future assistance. Don and I did most of the preaching, but R. E. Van Tassel, minister of the West Jefferson congregation, preached a time or two. We thought he would appeal more to some of the older members.

There were about twenty locals who attended the afternoon services. Most of these were people from Black Rock who knew Don. Don's brother came a few times, mostly when Don preached. He was a disappointment to Don, who had hoped that he would be challenged by the beginning of the church and agree to serve as one of the leaders. As the result of an advertisement in the DeKalb daily paper which announced our services, a few other members surfaced. Several had lived around DeKalb for years but none among them had attempted to start a church. Most of these, other than the Black Rock constituency, were from the areas of Danville, Kentucky or Greenville, Tennessee. They had come north to work on the farms and in the factories. R. E. Van Tassel was especially good at locating members who had moved to northern Illinois. He visited in their homes, chatted with them at length, and asked about relatives or others they knew from their home regions who had ties with Churches of Christ. When I returned to DeKalb in the summer of 1949 to work for the DeKalb Ag construction crew and preach for the church, there were forty or forty-five persons meeting. The doubling occurred entirely from former members Van Tassel had located.

My preaching that first summer was a good experience. It was the first time I had preached several different sermons to the same set of people. The circumstances were difficult, however, and I did not feel confident about most of my presentations. Several times I had gone without sleep before getting up to preach. I worked an average of fifteen hours a day for Cal Pac on a swing shift. One day I was even paid for twenty-two hours, though my boss told me to take a nap in the wee hours of the morning. Since I was interested in saving money for school, I did not complain. We were paid ninety cents an hour, and time-and-a-half after ten hours. I had some trouble with my boss, who was a hard-working, dour, fiftyish German. He was not about to let me off on Sunday afternoon, but I insisted. I told him I would have to quit if I couldn't take off. I think he respected me for my loyalty and skills. I was one of the few persons in our crew who could transfer cans from the capper, which had an eight-place vacuum lift, at the rate of three hundred cans per minute. They had to slow down the machine for most of the others. So, he let me off, but I think he never really believed that I was going to church. I thought much about how, under these new circumstances, it was not easy to keep one's Christian commitments without persistence and having to endure disdain—even a certain amount of criticism. I believed I was experiencing what it meant to suffer as a Christian (I Peter 4:12-16).

I had kept good notes of Raymond Kelcy's sermons and borrowed strongly from them. As a result, I preached somewhat more traditional sermons than Don, who followed more in the mold of Andy T. Ritchie. Since these small-town, border state people were more accustomed to hearing the type of sermons I preached, I was perceived by many as the better preacher, but not because of my communication skills. Don was much better in that regard. Probably one of the reasons I stuck to more traditional sermons was that I knew people were hindered by my slowness of speech, and sing song rhythm. I tried to overcome these as much as possible, but they were always evident, so I compensated by preaching in the style I thought the members liked to hear. I had always liked illustrations in sermons so I also captured interest through examples from my own experience, other brotherhood preachers, and the sermons of Moody and Spurgeon—especially from Moody, who utilized a number of colorful and excellent illustrations.

The Return to DeKalb as Minister: 1949

As the fall drew near, both Don and I headed back to Harding. The next summer Don decided not to return, since his brother had moved. I, however, opted to return to DeKalb. I liked the pay, compared with what I could make in southern Missouri. Don and his brother had worked for the DeKalb Ag construction crew the summer before. The hours were regular—nine hours a day and five on Saturday, for a total of fifty hours per week. The pay was about a dollar an hour. While I could make more working for California Packing, I would be in better shape to preach working the DeKalb Ag schedule. From Harding, I wrote letters to Van Tassel at Rockford. The Rockford church would be pleased for me to return to DeKalb to preach for the summer, he said. They furthermore proposed that I go to school at Northern Illinois and take over the work full-time. They said they would help support me. Don suggested I write the crew boss for DeKalb Ag, a man named Fred Kulow. I had met him the summer before, and Don thought he would be amenable to giving me the spot Don was vacating. As I hoped, Fred said if I showed up he would employ me.

My brothers, who were still in high school, were recruited to go with me to work for California Pack and detassel corn as I had done the year before. We took off from Thayer early in June, in a 1930 Dodge which Don and I had bought in DeKalb the summer before. I had been in touch with James Willeford. They were doing another campaign and Raymond Kelcy was again scheduled to preach.

Willeford invited my brothers and me to come and help distribute brochures. We decided we could spend a week at it. I suppose the anticipated presence of Dorothy Kiel had some part in the decision. It went better that summer, since I had the help and support of my brothers. Sometimes the three of us worked together. At the proper time we left Madison and arrived at DeKalb, where I went to work for the construction crew and my brothers began canning peas for Cal Pack. My brothers returned to DeKalb the following several summers. They also brought several other Harding students with them. After a few years, California Packing Company even recruited on the Harding campus, initiating a long tradition which continues to this day.

I don't remember much about the content of my preaching that summer. What I do remember is that by now I had a portable typewriter. I decided I needed a system for preparing and saving sermons. I had one speech course at Harding, but it was very broad and focused little on preaching. The teacher was more interested in oral interpretation and drama than public speaking. True to my mother's example, I decided I could improve myself by reading on the subject of preaching. I bought the book used at Harding as a text, John A. Broadus's *On the Preparation and Delivery of Sermons*. Broadus discussed four different sermons types: topical, expository, exegetical, and logical. Of these I had preached mostly in the topical mode, since most of the sermons I had heard in the Churches of Christ were of that type. I also had heard several expository sermons—presentations that developed the meaning and application of a text, such as a parable. But I had yet to hear a preacher do exegetical sermons—

go entirely through a book in the Scripture and take up the material as he came to it. But now I had lots of sermons to prepare and preach.

Broadus convinced me of the need for a system, the need to start with a biblical text, and the value of expository sermons, in which the text itself determined the subtopics. As a system, I decided to start typing all my sermon outlines so I could save them. I bought a loose-leaf notebook, about eight inches by five inches in size, with a leather, zippered cover. I normally got one sermon on a sheet by using both the front and back. The reason for this system was that the paper could be taken out of the notebook and put in a Bible without overlap. In this manner I could save my sermons. In some cases I might preach them again at a different congregation, but I decided early that I would seldom preach the same sermon twice. At that stage I discovered that the excitement of preaching something new normally resulted in a better sermon. That seemed not to be the case with most of my peers—they seemed to get better results from polishing a sermon with repeated presentations. I discovered, in contrast, that I tended to lose interest and do poorly.

There were other reasons for keeping sermons, however. First, this made it easier to recount what topics I had covered over a period of time and determine if the congregation was receiving a balanced diet—the "whole council of God." Another reason was that, having always had a historical perspective, I thought the sermons should be saved for someone in the future who might wish to do a study of them—a bit egotistical in my case, since I did not anticipate that I would become a noted preacher. In fact, when I left Pennsylvania some years later, I left behind my collection of sermons. I left them in the attic of the house which we sold to a colleague, intending to retrieve them, but never doing so.

The preachers I heard from youth normally did not start with a text. Rather, they started with a topic—the organization of the church, for example. The use of a text seemed denominational to them, somehow. They did not employ one text, but many. The more Bible verses a preacher quoted, the better he was thought to be. To employ one text, therefore, exposed too little Bible in the sermon. In fact, we heard of preachers who put together sermons which were little more than a series of quoted texts, but I was present for few of these.

I was convinced by experience, however, that many of the poorer preachers I had heard covered too many topics in a single sermon. I was not convinced, either, that the more Scripture quoted meant the better sermon, for much of it probably passed undigested through the ears of the hearers. But I memorized and quoted Scripture, since I knew that was what it took to get many people's attention in our churches. I did, however, start using a text, though when preaching in Arkansas and Missouri I did not call it that, for fear of being charged with aping the denominations. I thought employing a text was good discipline, that it gave more focus to the sermon. I thought it created a more obvious commitment to the Scripture as the chief source of religious ideas. I also liked the idea of the text providing the subtopics for the sermon. I liked the sermons of Boyd Morgan and Andy Ritchie, which unfolded along these lines. To me, that seemed to be taking the Bible more seriously than working from logically predetermined subtopics.

I accepted the position as the chief interpreter of Scripture for the DeKalb congregation. How was I to fill this role? The questions I put to Scriptures would, in some measure, be the questions of the congregation. I was the one who decided which Scriptures the congregation was to take up and the manner in which they were to be interpreted. We needed to be clear about our focus and goals if we were going to be the people of the Book, as we professed. But in the final analysis, the most important questions are those the Scriptures put to us. How were we going to study Scripture in such a way that its questions to us were not ignored or sidetracked?

In the fall of 1949 my preaching, as well as my education, took a new turn. My explicit reason for staying in DeKalb, Illinois, was to preach for the young congregation Don Horn and I had started in the summer of 1948. The West Jefferson Street Church of Christ in Rockford, Illinois, had taken responsibility for the continuation of the work after Don and I returned to Harding in the fall of 1948. The preacher for the congregation, R. E. Van Tassel, an Indianan, was very persuasive in encouraging me to work with the congregation and attend Northern Illinois State Teachers College. Some time during the summer, I agreed to take up the new challenge. Early in the fall we arranged for a new meeting place where we could have night services as well as morning ones. This meant that now I preached two sermons a week, and they had to be new sermons each time, since the audience was the same. At Northern Illinois, I shifted from majoring in the sciences to speech and pedagogy. At that time, Northern was a state teachers college, and the only degree offered was a B. S. in Education. This meant that along with my speech major, I had to take enough education courses to constitute a major. When I graduated from Northern, not only did I receive a diploma denoting "B.S. in Education: Speech," but also a teaching certification in secondary education for the state of Illinois. All of these new experiences influenced the manner in which I studied and interpreted the Scriptures.

The new place of meeting was Kinnairy Hall, which belonged to an organized labor group. They used it for meetings, but also on Saturday nights for dances at which beer was served. The hall was on the second floor of a building on DeKalb's Main Street. It was dark, very plain, and tended to be unkept, but the rent was reasonable and it was available all day Sunday. Even though a janitor was supposed to clean up after Saturday nights, some Sunday mornings we had to go around picking up the beer bottles and putting away the organization's insignias. It was decided that the church in DeKalb could bear all the rental expenses as well as incidentals, such as additional hymnals and Bibles. The church in Rockford decided to contribute ten dollars per week toward my salary. Sometime in the summer the Northwest Church of Christ in Chicago heard that a church had started in DeKalb. They were unaware that such was the case, but were immediately interested because one of their new members, Franklin Schmidt, planned to attend Northern Illinois that fall. Since, as they thought, there was no church there, they had decided to provide ten dollars per week for transportation, so he could return to Northwest each Sunday. When they found out a church was meeting and that there would be a preacher, they decided to contribute the ten dollars per week to my salary. So, I was making the magnificent sum of twenty dollars per week. I paid ten dollars per week for a room with food privileges: I had a hotplate and I was entitled to use the kitchen refrigerator. Most of my regular outgo was taken care of. I didn't have to worry about college expenses, since books were inexpensive and I paid twenty-five dollars per quarter in tuition, or seventy-five dollars for the entire school year. I saved up enough through summer work to handle car expenses and other incidentals, including my church contribution of three dollars per week. I was preaching for minimal wages, but I had no second thoughts about it. In my home region, preachers with families were paid no more than two hundred dollars per month.

Sometime in the early fall we starting meeting for classes on Sunday morning at 10:00 A.M. and for worship at 11:00 A.M. These were standard times through most of the brotherhood. In the 1950s a movement was afoot throughout our churches to have a class and two preaching services on Sunday, and Bible study on Wednesday night. It was only that way that we could "march for the Master", a phrase popularized in a book of that title by Ira North. We had a few children, so we had a class for them. Fortunately, we had a room where they could meet. This meant that now I usually taught an adult class as well as preaching on Sunday morning and Sunday night. That was a big order for a young man who was not accustomed to saying very much, especially in public. How was I to fill all this pulpit time? I was committed to the Scripture being at the heart of it all. I spent considerable time reading the Scripture. I mostly read whole books, particularly from the New Testament, hoping to stumble upon sermon ideas, which I jotted down in a notebook. I also decided that I would not be able to come upon enough concepts in that way for both Sunday morning and Sunday night. I decided that on Sunday nights, I would preach through books of the Bible. I first tried a shorter book—as I recall, the book of James. After a time I had the courage to try I Corinthians, since it was one of my favorites. I liked the problems it addressed. I thought it enabled speaking about most of the inadequacies and controversies of the contemporary church. For the class I proposed studying the Gospel of Matthew, hoping that I would be able to put to work and share what I had learned under Andy T. Ritchie.

I recognized that I needed help interpreting the Scriptures. For one thing, I was unable, even by reading the books over and over, to generate the volume of creative material needed for all those sermons. Second, I recognized that when I wandered away from those parts of the Scripture which we had worked over so well—our canon-within-a-canon consisting of Acts, Ephesians, I and II Timothy, Titus, and, to a lesser degree James, I Corinthians, I and II Peter—I was often adrift. I knew that simple formulas such as commands, examples, and necessary inferences were not of much help in digesting and understanding the meaning of more difficult books, such as Romans. Since no religion or Bible courses of any sort were offered at Northern, I needed books and radio. At Harding I had bought *Halley's Handbook*. The *Handbook* introduced me to background and archaeological materials. It was not much, but at that stage every little bit helped. In the spring of 1949, I bought a set of Clark's commentaries. They were five volumes and covered the complete Bible. I knew they were dated, so I also bought a more modern one-volume commentary by

Jamison, Focett and Brown. These commentaries were authored by Methodists, but they were often quoted by our preachers. I did not buy *Johnson's Notes,* which so many of our older members used, a two-volume work on the New Testament. I probably should have bought it in self-defense, but I thought any items of interest in it would be reported by people who read it in class. Harding sold the Gospel Advocate commentary series on the New Testament. The reason I did not buy these, I am sure, was that they cost more than I thought I could afford. I had Young's *Complete Concordance to the Bible,* given me by my mother, as well as two King James Bibles, the kind which she ordered for neighbors and friends. These Bibles had several helps in the back, including outlines of biblical topics which cited numerous Scriptures, and a description of all the parables and miracles of Jesus, as well as his commandments and warnings. All of these were suggestive for sermons.

I also had two or three sermon outline books, including those by C. R. Nichol and L. L. Brigance, as well as Leroy Brownlow's *Why I am a Member of the Church of Christ*. I determined to avoid these outlines unless desperate, and even then I made various changes, deletions and additions. I was committed to developing my own insights from the text. My peers at Harding and my readings had encouraged me to take up a fresh exploration of Scripture, and to preach that on which I had a deep conviction. My upbringing rejected a show of emotion, as well as drama and flamboyance in any form. But I also rejected dry, pedantic, or argumentative sermons. My way of achieving deep sincerity and passion, which I considered admirable, was by preaching a sermon which was fully my own. In my opinion, I was not a ham of any sort. I was not good at taking someone else's material and preaching it with energy and passion. I even had trouble on that score with some of my own sermons. I did not seek startling or contrary ideas. I was quite content, even convicted, to work within the parameters of my heritage. But I wanted it to be a fresh manner of expression. As a preacher, I was never too popular with persons who wanted to hear the old run-of-the-mill ideas, spoken in the traditional vocabulary.

At Harding I had become a member of the Old Paths Book Club. Through this means I bought Alexander Campbell's *Christian Baptist*, the first ten volumes of the *Millennial Harbinger*, *Christianity Restored*, *The Christian System*, *Lard's Quarterlies*, and several volumes on individual subjects. I began to read in these volumes. I became convinced that I should know something of our heritage.

Another source of ideas, less doctrinal than inspirational, was the radio broadcasts from the Moody Bible Institute in Chicago (WMBI). There were several different types of programs. Late at night the predominant programming was inspirational music interlaced with (sometimes concomitant with) readings from Psalms, Job, and other poetic materials. Occasionally there were narratives about great missionaries, evangelists, and hymn writers, or testimonies from contemporaries. I also heard some expositions of Scripture, but these tended to be broadcast during the daytime, when I wasn't able to listen. Nothing more than an occasional illustration from Moody made its way into my sermons or teaching, but this material meant much to me in my personal life of faith. At times, like Elijah, I felt almost alone—estranged from both members of the congregation and my fellow students. I was in controversy with neither group, but they did not seem overtly spiritual, did not seem to see the Lord in the same way I did. I don't think I saw myself as better than they. In fact, I ran into a few students at intervarsity religious meetings whose faith in God and his work in the world seemed better grounded than mine. It's just that I seemed to bear a burden for God—as I understood him—that others did not bear.

One of the items I remember reading was Campbell's views on interpreting the Scriptures, found in *Christianity Restored*. The details of these ideas were new to me, but I recognized them as one of the sources of the meeting sermons which declared that we can all understand the Bible alike. Campbell maintained that we can understand the Bible alike if we have a proper method. He proposed that we read the Scripture just as we do any other document. In so doing, we determine who wrote a specific book, why they wrote it, and to whom they wrote it. We also needed to become familiar with the historical context. Campbell was especially interested in how we determine the meaning of words and literary allusions.

At that time I knew little about the history of biblical interpretation. I'm sure I didn't dwell upon Campbell's statement that he was dependent upon the German scholar Johann Ernesti and the American, Moses Stuart. These scholars meant nothing to me at the time. I was also unaware that his observations on style and literary devices came through Ernesti from standard medieval rhetorics, but this was to change.

Campbell's Hermeneutical Ancestry

The reformation produced a flowering of books on hermeneutics. Johann August Ernesti, the eighteenth century German scholar, cited nineteen Roman Catholic and twenty-three Protestant books on hermeneutics in 1761. Samuel Davidson, in 1808, published a history of interpretation in which he included a bibliography of some forty pages covering the category of hermeneutics.[1] This impressive succession of books set the style for instruction and works on hermeneutics which have prevailed since, especially so in conservative American circles.

The specific historical antecedent of Alexander Campbell's "Principles of Interpretation"[2] was the hermeneutic method of J. A. Ernesti, translated and elaborated upon by Moses Stuart (1780-1852), the foremost American biblical scholar of his day.[3] It was not atypical in the early nineteenth century for a translator to expand upon the work he translated, and Stuart did. It is the same Ernesti-Stuart tradition which serves as the progenitor of standard American hermeneutic books such as that of F. Milton Terry (1846-1914), *Biblical Hermeneutics* (1883). Terry taught at Garrett Biblical Institute, Evanston, Illinois, beginning in 1884. This heritage also influenced the best book among us in this mold, that by David R. Dungan.[4] The work by Ernesti picks up on most of the reformation themes. He declared that the Scripture must be interpreted grammatically by the same rules applied to other texts.

> Consequently, the observation of word usage is the special task of the grammarians, whose

> art is directed for the most part and chiefly to careful determination of what meaning a definite word had at a definite time, the usage of the word by a definite author, and, finally, the relation of the word to a definite form of speech. Therefore the literal sense is also called the grammatical, for the word literalis is the Latin translation of grammaticus [Greek, "knowing one's letters"]. No less properly it is also called the historical [sense], for it is contained, as other [historical] facts, in testimonies and authoritative records.
>
> Therefore, apart from the grammatical sense there is none other, and this the grammarians transmit. For those who, on the one hand, assume a grammatical, and, on the other, a logical, sense, have not comprehended the role of the grammatical sense; and [this] sense, [furthermore] is not changed by any use whatever of any discipline, or in the investigation of the sense of things. Otherwise, it would be no less manifold than the things themselves.[5]

The standard approach in hermeneutics texts of the nineteenth century was to reject mystical and allegorical interpretation in favor of the literal. The rest of the hermeneutic method contained what is, in essence, instruction in literary analysis, drawing heavily upon classical rhetoric and its heirs. It is no accident that the earlier hermeneutics books were produced by persons with training in rhetoric. Ernesti himself was a professor of rhetoric in Leipzig before being granted a professorship in theology and New Testament.[6] The work of Mickelsen in this century follows the traditional pattern. His first section is on basic principles, with a short history of interpretation. The second part is on general hermeneutics which concerns historical and cultural perspectives. The third part is on special hermeneutics and discusses the various literary types and rhetorical figures. Mickelsen may have adapted these characteristics more to the Scriptures than some in the tradition. He closed with advice on the actual practice of hermeneutics.

A Common Understanding?

It occurred to me that Campbell was much more dedicated than we to a grammatico-historical-literary interpretation of Scripture. In the meeting sermons we got as far as saying you have to determine author, purpose, and readers. We also charged that it helps to know the words in the original Greek, especially passages having to do with baptism. But other than that, preachers tended to offer the common-sense observation that, "of course we can understand the Bible alike." If we understand the Bible at all we understand it alike. If we understand it in two different ways then one of us understands it and the other doesn't.

Perhaps this claim is justified, but it is also possible that neither understands. Perhaps neither of us has valid insight into the original setting or meaning of the words. Indeed, in some cases it is impossible for us to understand some things, almost two thousand years after the writing of the words. Who among us can be certain of the identity of the "lawless one" in II Thessalonians 2:3? Sometimes too, it is claimed by biblical writers themselves that a text has more than one meaning: for example, "out of Israel have I called my son" (Matthew 2:15, cf. Hosea

11:1, then Exodus 2, 4:22), or Paul in Galatians, where he discusses the story of Hagar and Sarah (Galatians 4:21-31, cf. Genesis 16, 21).

For the on-going life of a Bible-reading church, the most important hermeneutical rules are those involving grammatico-historical-literary insights. Alexander Campbell, J. S. Lamar, and David Dungan were committed to these aspects of hermeneutics. We have found commands, examples, and necessary inferences helpful only in regard to certain specific actions: when and how often to observe the Lord's supper, the type, function, and qualifications of church officers, and how to maintain local church independence in the face of supra- or para-congregational structures, to mention some of the issues where the tripartite rule has been applied by us.

At this stage I clearly followed the hermeneutic rule so dear to us as we inherited it from Alexander Campbell's famous "Sermon on the Law" (1816), even though only the historians among us ever heard of the sermon! I did little with the Old Testament, first of all because I knew little about it, but probably more so because I was convinced beyond the shadow of a doubt that persons being encouraged to deeper spirituality needed the New Testament, not the Old. After all, Jews live under the authority of the Old Testament, but Christians live under the New.

Northern Illinois State Teachers College

Enrollment at Northern went well. I was seen as something of an oddity, and perhaps for that reason, as more interesting and better accepted than at Harding. At Harding I was respected by those interested in preaching, associates in the science labs, and the girls who attended Andy's personal evangelism sessions, but I was not in any sense a man-about-campus. Above sixty percent of the students at Northern were from Chicago or its suburbs. The rest were from northern Illinois. I was one of the few from out of state, so I had a degree of notoriety for that reason. I was perceived to talk very differently, but it was a matter of interest for my hearers, rather than a disadvantage. For some reason the girls seemed particularly attracted, but I did not date, since I was very interested in a certain Wisconsin girl whom I went to see whenever I got the chance. The new atmosphere was good for my self-image and enabled me to progress as a person and communicator of the Gospel.

At Northern, the chair of the Speech Department took me on as a special project. He thought I talked strangely and inadequately. He proposed that I take every class he taught and I believe I did. In a course in oral interpretation he had the class vote on who did the best readings, and I usually came out on the low rung because of my poor diction and sing-song patterns. It did not help, either, that I was tied up in knots with stage fright. The low vote did not help my self-esteem, but I determined to do better. Toward the end of the semester I still ranked toward the bottom, but I was voted the most improved. The chair, William V. O'Connell, thought I was particularly adept at reading popular folk poetry, such as that of Sam Foss, who wrote, "It takes a heap of living in a house to make it home," and "A House by the Side of the Road." He admired the creativity with which I selected the poems for my recital, and insisted that I read the project over the campus radio station during the time allotted for programming geared toward the farm community around DeKalb. I was the only one in class he put on the air. I think he thought it would benefit me more than it would the radio audience. When leadership roles were assigned in class, he always gave me one. In the acting class I was appointed director of a one-act play, even though several in my group had experience in directing. He believed that speech classes were to develop the personality of students rather than to highlight the stars among us. At commencement, perhaps as the result of his recommendation, I was asked to read part of Carl Sandburg's "Prairie."

As the result of my work in speech I improved considerably in the oral skills needful to an interpreter of the Gospel. I took a course in voice and diction in which I worked at length with recordings so as to change my vowel sounds toward a more standard midwestern sound. All the speech classes included oral projects, so I received much critique and experience. Another teacher who showed a special interest in me was Margaret Wood. She did her best to encourage a more dynamic delivery. She, however, also highlighted what she saw that was of value. She was so taken with a speech I gave on regional differences in meaning for the time designated as "evening" that she had me present it in another class and write it out so she could keep it.

As the result of these experiences I became a more effective interpreter of God's word. If God's word is dynamic, if the resurrection of Jesus Christ is the best news of the centuries, and if the story is so important that it is to be told with passion, then a public hermeneutic must ultimately include these oral and physical dimensions. Phillips Brooks declared that preaching is "proclaiming the truth through personality." Factors that contribute to a more dynamic personality, therefore, enhance the vocal and bodily interpretation of the Gospel.

In my senior year, as the result of my newly-gained confidence, I went out for debate. The debate coach, Paul Crawford, was of a different turn of mind. He believed in featuring the stars, and did not envision me as one of them. Still, I did quite well in debate. Despite my deficient communication skills I had considerable acumen at refutation and at ascertaining the crux of a question. When I began as a debater, I was the team's first speaker, due to inexperience. Before long my partner and I agreed that we should change positions. In the spring of the year my partner and I were selected by a local panel of judges to represent Northern in a national debate, winning out over Crawford's favorites. But that didn't matter to him. He thought the judges, who were the local professors, didn't know much about debate. He was interested in a smooth, polished delivery, and he overruled the judges' choice. Admittedly, one of the persons he picked for the finals was an outstanding debater. He was very bright, an excellent communicator, and had considerable debate experience in high school. The second person, however, was a lightweight in rebuttal and content, although very smooth in delivery. They did not make it past the first tournament.

True to my earlier years, I relished the clash of debate. I enjoyed digging out the most recent evidence which refuted older information utilized by less research-oriented debaters. I'm sure the debate experience gave me more confidence in preaching. But it also added to a conviction that our age-long interest in debating was appropriate. The data of Scripture was to be mustered so as to make the best case possible, I thought. The Scripture was the great reserve of evidence from which to disprove the contentions of those with opposing points of view. But I had no inclination to challenge anyone to a religious debate. I was neither a ham, a banty rooster, nor a rigid, black-and-white thinker.

I took most of my education courses with Professor Donald Berger. His doctorate was from Columbia University, where he had studied under John Dewey. Professor Berger was greatly admired by his students, but he was widely excoriated by his fellow education professors and others, especially by Dr. O'Connell, who did his best to talk me out of taking Berger. They saw him as the leader of a campus cult. Berger emphasized Dewey's conviction that learning takes place best in contexts in which the students themselves set the parameters. After World War II democracy and citizen involvement were key concepts. Berger argued that one of the last entities to be democratized in America was education. We therefore spent much time in class determining what we were going to study, what we hoped to learn, how we would proceed and afterward evaluate our progress. Berger seldom lectured unless we insisted on it. Most of the class time was taken up with individual and group reports and occasional field trips. Whether we learned much or not, we were deeply committed to the group, and put in more time there than in our other classes.

In later years I came to question the efficiency and the amount of learning in detailed matters, such as in tests and measurement, but Berger's courses were excellent for developing interpersonal skills and obtaining insights into group dynamics. These insights helped me orchestrate the decision-making involvement of as many church members as possible, and to utilize multiple persons in the nurturing functions of the church. Through experience, and because of my conviction about the priesthood of all believers, I became convinced that the entire local community of faith needed to have input into what Scripture was to be studied and how it was to be interpreted. I taught classes mostly by employing the discussion method, and we discussed at length what parts of the Bible we would study. I pushed men with inclination into teaching and—on occasion—preaching. I was convinced that the interpretation of Scripture in the body needed to draw from a larger pool of understanding than just my own. These courses helped me develop a perspective on community, that is, church involvement in hermeneutics. Of course, that was also the procedure in my home churches before the advent of full time preachers.

Controversies in Northern Illinois

During the summer of 1949 the West Jefferson Street church in Rockford acquired a new preacher. He was James P. Sanders, who was blind. He was then in his early forties and was a powerful preacher, both because of his communication skills and content. He was a graduate of Lipscomb and held a B.D. from Vanderbilt. He had studied on a Master of Theology at Yale Divinity School but had not completed it. I heard him speak several times in the fall of 1949. The Rockford congregation decided that DeKalb needed to hold a Gospel meeting. Since people in this region were not accustomed to that terminology, we followed the lead of the church in Madison and labeled it a series of special sermons. These were to run for a week, beginning on Sunday and ending on Friday. We printed brochures and distributed them in town and at Northern. We emphasized our undenominational posture. We rented the Masonic Lodge's main assembly hall, since we expected out-of-town visitors as well as those from DeKalb. Sanders had been preaching in Cincinnati, Ohio, and had spoken at various congregations and lectureships, promoting the Valparaiso Children's Home in Valparaiso, Indiana. He had built up a reputation because of his preaching skills and because he was blind. We had excellent attendance, averaging above a hundred each night. People came from Chicago, Rockford, and even some from Indiana. We also had a number of visitors from the community.

The DeKalb church members were engulfed and almost left out. They were blue-collar laborers who had migrated from Arkansas, Tennessee, and Kentucky. The visitors were middle management types, and the local visitors were natives of northern Illinois. Our members frequently did not know the Christians from the other places, many of whom knew each other. The outsiders seemed uncomfortable talking with the DeKalb residents. I think, too, the DeKalb members did not know what to make of Sanders' preaching. I thought it was excellent, comparable with the preaching of Andy Ritchie. It did not, however, sound much like typical meeting preaching of the time.

Sanders said all the right things about the plan of salvation, but he didn't stress it. He spoke on denominationalism and the contrasting ideal of being undenominational. He mentioned the formula from the early days of our movement—which I had not heard much—that we did not claim to be the only Christians, but Christians only. I thought he made excellent points, but some of our members had reservations. To them it implied that there might be Christians in denominations, and this they could not accept. One night we had a group of about fifteen visitors show up from an independent non-denominational church in DeKalb. Several such churches could be found in northern Illinois: they had no ecclesiastical ties, and identified theologically with Moody Bible Institute and Wheaton College. A leader of the group approached me afterward, when several had already left. He charged that our invitational brochure gave misleading information in its declaration that we were undenominational, since he had discovered by talking around that we were part of a brotherhood of churches. For him, "undenominational" meant complete independence from any group of churches.

In his preaching, Sanders cited passages calling for commitment, devotion and dedication. I suspect some of our members had never heard many of these Scriptures before. Sanders also preached with a great deal of passion, dwelling on the need for commitment from the heart. It was not enough to follow the right forms of worship and to know the plan of salvation better than anyone else, he preached: to simply trust in the proper forms was legalism. Andy Ritchie had said some of the same things, but he didn't normally use the word "legalism." Through Sanders' preaching, I received a first glimmer of the real message of the prophets. He did not mention the matter of prophetic fulfillment, but dwelt on those passages in which God declared that he desired mercy, not sacrifice. A favorite sermon of Sanders was based on Micah 6. To my knowledge, that was the first time I had heard an entire sermon based on a prophetic text. Micah 6:8 was the key passage: "He has told you, O Man, what is good; and what does the Lord require of you but to do justice, and to love kindness and to walk humbly with your God?" Sanders made his point in an especially forceful way. He charged that perhaps we had put the emphasis of early Christianity in the wrong place in focusing on the external structures of Christianity through what we called "the fundamentals." To restore the heart of Christianity, he held, we needed to emphasize internal commitment and compassion for the needy—especially homeless children. Another text he quoted often to make his point was Matthew 23:23: "Woe to you, scribes and Pharisees, hypocrites! For you tithe mint, dill, and cummin, and have neglected the weightier matters of the law: justice and mercy and faith. It is these you ought to have practiced without neglecting the others."

Sanders' preaching called for a new understanding of what it means to restore New Testament Christianity. He stressed that some items are more significant than others, and we hadn't been as concerned with justice and mercy as we should have been. I gladly granted his observation and felt no reason to object, but I didn't follow his conclusion that there was a fundamental core of Jesus' teaching that must be stressed, sometimes at the expense of minor details. I still followed the thinking of the preachers of my youth that we must preach the "whole oracles of God" (I Peter 4:11 KJV), which I understood to mean that everything in Scripture must be preached and receive the same weight, once the canon-within-a-canon—those Scriptures under which Christians are to live—has been determined. I did not find objectionable at all his assertion that we had not restored mercy—that was the rhetoric of my peers at Harding. We had not completely restored New Testament Christianity because we had not restored personal evangelism, missions, purity of life, and personal devotion. We would improve upon the failures of our fathers. We would try not to leave anything out. But to suggest that one or two aspects of Christianity stood higher than others—unless they were baptism and vocal music—was beyond our comprehension at that time. We were bound by what is now called a "flat "view of Scripture. In fact, this is a hermeneutical rule: that any single item found in Scripture is as important as any other item. I decided a few years later that the "everything is of equal importance" rule is not a biblical rule, according to Jesus (Matthew 23:23) and Paul (I Corinthians 15:1-9).

Sanders had problems with a few members at Rockford, but most of them grew spiritually by leaps and bounds under his ministry. When he arrived, the church had about one hundred-fifty in attendance. Soon the building would not seat all the people. They rented a school, sold their old building and set out to construct a larger one. Soon after changing to the school, their attendance reached two hundred-fifty. By the time they moved into their new building, some four hundred were in attendance. Such dramatic growth was unheard-of in the region in that time. Sanders had critics in other churches, perhaps partly out of jealously, but because of the feeling that he put down the traditional Church of Christ. Furthermore, his emphasis on children's homes, helping the poor, and social justice sounded more like the social gospel, than the true Gospel. The critics probably didn't know much about the social gospel movement earlier in the century, but they assumed that it distorted Christianity. Few Rockford members knew enough to differ, so they accepted Sanders' criticism without question. Sanders and his members stated that he preached, not the social gospel, but the Gospel of Jesus Christ. He quoted

Scriptures to establish the need to aid widows, orphans and the poor.

In the spring of 1950, there was a series of lectures for preachers at the church in Madison, with about ten different preachers speaking. They hoped to make the lectures an annual event. Sanders spoke on the Valparaiso Children's home, and the need for funds and left after speaking, since he did not feel he had the time to stay. I spoke later. I'm not sure of my topic, but I recall making a few remarks on Sander's emphasis. I stated that I thought he was quite right about the need to support children's homes. We had, in fact, been neglectful and needed to remedy the neglect. But sometimes when I heard Sanders speak, I stated, I received the distinct impression that he almost perceived this to be the entire Gospel, and neglected preaching on the fundamentals and the plan of salvation. I came down strong on that phrase in Jesus' statement in Matthew 23:23, "without neglecting the others."

I was in agreement with Sanders that if we embraced the heart of Christianity, we would be more concerned with caring for the children than with the arrangements by which it was done. To emphasize the propriety of the arrangements and avoid the care was real legalism. My statement was, of course, faithful to my hermeneutical rule that no one item in Scripture was to be stressed above another. Over another two years, criticism of Sanders and James A. Warren, who preached at Northwest in Chicago, accelerated. Sanders at that time decided the criticism was more than he cared to put up with, and resigned from the church, now called Kilbourne Avenue Church of Christ, in Rockford. He accepted a position with a Christian church (Disciples of Christ) in Anaconda, Montana. Later he preached in Sacramento, California. In the late seventies he told George Butterfield, a former student of mine at Abilene Christian who was preaching there, that he had abandoned ship too fast. He should have stuck it out since, even in the sixties, he thought he would have felt more at home among us than with the Disciples.

By the fall of 1950, certain members of the church in Iowa had been in contact for some time with a group of Christian Church people who operated a "School of Evangelism" in Ottumwa, Iowa. The president was Burton Barber. Those who had made the contact, particularly James Walter Nichols and Abe Lincoln, perceived that these people were much like us: they were conservative and very critical of the Christian Church. Their conservatism was more in the mode of Wheaton College: they opposed cosmetics, women cutting their hair, movies, and television, along with all the additional items that we opposed, such as creeds and mission societies. They were strong on tithing. As it turned out, they also had a different hermeneutic. In hopes of winning these people over, a debate was arranged between Burton Barber and G. K. Wallace.

James Walter Nichols had been an outstanding debater at Abilene Christian. Our schools in those years had strong debate teams, since we believed religiously in debate. I met James Walter early in the summer of 1949 at Madison, during the second campaign I worked in there. James Walter had been persuaded to lead the singing for the services. He had a lot of presence, and a good voice. I was impressed with him as a committed Christian. He grew up in Abilene, Texas, and his father had been a professor of Bible at Abilene Christian but had died at an early age of a heart attack. James had more dreams for the church in a day than most people had in a year. He envisioned winning over many conservative groups in Iowa. He had a radio program and later, he and James Willeford joined in broadcasting a program on three or four stations in the upper midwest. By 1951, Nichols had talked the elders of the South Fifth and Highland church in Abilene into launching a program on a major network. He then moved back to Abilene. He was good on the radio. He received several invitations to speak in various denominational churches which had conservative perspectives.

If anyone thought we were conservative legalists and that G. K. Wallace was a Pharisee of Pharisees, he should have been at the debate. G. K. Wallace came off smelling like a liberal because of his position on most of the items discussed. The debate focused on the use of instrumental music. Central to the arguments on both sides were commands, examples and necessary inferences. I probably heard these brought to bear more in those three days in Cedar Rapids than ever before or since. The hermeneutical difference between the two sides had to do with the Old Testament. Barber argued that certain items in place before the giving of the law of Moses remained sacrosanct, even for Christians. As an example, he mentioned Sabbath-keeping and tithing. He believed that Christians should make Sunday a day of rest, just as the Jews did Saturday. This was universal and for all time, since it went back to the beginning, he held. He likewise argued that the use of instrumental music in worship of God preceded the giving of the law and continued even past the Christian era, since musical instruments will be used in heaven. He agreed with the test of commands, examples and necessary inferences, but not with our typical dispensational divisions. It was there that the debate came to an impasse. My impression was that as the result of the debate and its careful delineation of differences over lifestyle, tithing, Sabbath keeping, and dispensational hermeneutics, two wings of our movement which had before respected each other at a distance learned to actively dislike each other. James Walter's hopes were dashed.

In the early 1950s controversy raged over the Chicago-area liberals. Early on, the best known was Robert Box, who preached for the Cornell Avenue congregation. He held a B.D. and was working on a Ph.D. in theology at the University of Chicago. He was a polished and effective radio preacher, and did not sound like the old-line Church of Christ. Since most members of the church in the Chicago area were transplants from rural communities in Arkansas, Missouri, Indiana, and Kentucky, this resulted in some discomfort in the churches. Box also sometimes quoted contemporary theologians such as Barth, Niebuhr and Tillich. He left Cornell Avenue to teach at Pepperdine, so by time the controversy really raged it centered upon James A. Warren, who preached for the largest congregation in the area, the Northwest Church of Christ. James P. Sanders had become Warren's companion, and they met periodically for theological discussions. I personally liked both Sanders and Warren very much, but tried to distance myself from them when attending area gatherings in Iowa and Wisconsin. The majority of Christians in northern Illinois either sympathized with Warren and Sanders or cared little for the controversy. But one smaller congregation particularly fanned the flames. They invited Foy E. Wallace, Jr., one-time editor of *The Gospel Advocate* and later champion of Texas right-wingers, to Chicago to set straight the "Warrenites." Not many

Warrenites showed up. I did not believe that Wallace adequately addressed the Chicago issues, but I was captivated with him as a speaker. He did not use the pulpit, but roamed freely with Bible in hand, without notes. He had a powerful voice, well modulated with much variety. He was a spellbinder of the old oratorical school, employing several of the traditional rhetorical devices. He spoke about an hour-and-a-half, and the audience seemed prepared to stay another hour if he had wished to continue. In fact, I was so intrigued that I wrote a critique for one of my speech classes which even impressed the professor with Wallace's variety of rhetorical skills.

Later that year J. D. Thomas, who had preceded Warren at Northwest, arrived to counter the Warren influence. Thomas had worked on a doctorate in New Testament at the University of Chicago and was now professor of Bible at Abilene Christian College. I went in to hear Thomas. He did not intend that session to be a head-on attack on Warren, but preached on grace and works and argued that salvation was by faith, "not by works lest anyone should boast." But Thomas taught that the person of faith who loves God does the works of God, not to be saved, but precisely because of God's prior love. His illustration was that of a nurse: a nurse cares for children in a hospital because she is paid, but she cares for her own children out of love. Thomas then published an article, printed in both the *Firm Foundation* and *Gospel Advocate,* in which he laid out twenty-five characteristics of liberals. A number of these characterized James A. Warren. There was a scare over liberalism elsewhere, but it mostly centered in Chicago and Los Angeles at Pepperdine. It was at that time that Bible professors with Ph.D.'s from major universities in biblical studies, church history, or theology were first beginning to appear in Christian colleges. Several of the older preachers—without a college degree in many cases—grew nervous. And in fact, well they should have, because these men harbingered a paradigm shift in the preacher training in the Christian colleges. A few of these university-trained professors were highly critical of traditional restorationist positions.

The furor surrounding Warren centered upon a mimeographed book of about eighty pages he authored, *The Heresy of Legalism.* The book charged that many preachers in the Churches of Christ were more concerned that the shell or blueprint of the church was perfectly structured than whether people had made a full commitment to God from their hearts. Furthermore, they were more concerned that an exact method be in place for helping widows and orphans and doing mission work than whether the work was undertaken. Warren identified this as legalism, and quoted many passages from the prophets and the rest of the Old Testament to establish that legalism is precisely counter to the messages of the prophets, Jesus, and Paul, and therefore a heresy. These were strong charges, eliciting much rancor from those who thought they were being singled out. Warren was very bright, and an excellent communicator. He had been a college debater at David Lipscomb. He was completing a B.D. at McCormick Theological Seminary, a Presbyterian seminary in Chicago. He could not refrain from satire, and his style probably created as much furor as anything else. He wrote that some members would refuse to enter heaven if, when they got there, they discovered that a few good Methodists had made it.

Warren held a meeting for us in DeKalb in the summer of 1951. He was a polished speaker, but somewhat out of his element among our blue-collar crowd. He confided to me that he had some problem speaking because he felt the audience was not identifying with his message. He explored certain views which, from our historical perspective, seemed far-out, and was greatly intrigued by Karl Barth. He preached a sermon on the devil and one on hell. He affirmed that evil did indeed exist in the world, but that the personification of a singular evil person in Satan was more mythical than in accordance with the Scriptures. He also argued that punishment for evil is actual, but basically takes place in this life, so that hell as an actual region is not required. Mrs. Thom, wife of a Rockford elder with whom I had become well-acquainted, surprised me by saying that she always had the feeling that neither Satan or hell were real, so she was relieved to hear an intelligent preacher declare so. Most of the members at DeKalb, however, wondered why we listened to ideas of this sort. A family with several married children had moved in, from Arkansas by way of Michigan. The patriarch of the clan was a sometime preacher. All of them were considerably disturbed. They didn't cause trouble immediately, but when I left in the fall, and Don Horn came to preach for the church and work on a masters at Wheaton College, they pulled out some of the members and started a new congregation in Sycamore, ten miles northeast of DeKalb. I was not upset by Warren's preaching, but I was not prepared to agree. Despite the different approach of Warren, we baptized two persons, including the husband of one of our most dedicated members.

Warren's theology called for a different

hermeneutic. He was not so interested in attacking the doctrines near and dear to people in Churches of Christ. Rather, in line with the neo-orthodox theologians under whom he studied—Joseph Haroutunian, for example—and in opposition to the modernists of a previous era—Shailer Mathews and Shirley Jackson Case, to name two—he revamped some of the basic doctrines of God, Christ, the Holy Spirit, Satan, heaven, hell, and others. His hermeneutic held that whatever seemed contrary to modern man, even though in Scripture, must be refurbished to fit modern understandings. To some extent, he incorporated Bultmann's demythologizing principle, but I doubt that he did so in accordance with Bultmann's overall existential program. Bultmann was not that well known in the United States in 1951. In the fall of 1951 Warren took a leave of absence from Northwest in order to be involved in an archaeological dig with G. Ernest Wright, a world-famous archaeologist, then a professor at McCormick, and later of Harvard, where I studied under him. While Warren was out in the field, his wife struck up acquaintance with a Presbyterian minister, divorced James and married the Presbyterian. She was about ten years younger than James, and her new husband younger still. Because of the criticism over liberalism and the embarrassment over the divorce, Warren resigned at Northwest and found a position as a Presbyterian minister, which was the most feasible confessional group for him as a graduate of a Presbyterian seminary.

Because of all the influences brought to bear on me from other preachers and trends in Churches of Christ, as well as the burden of interpreting the Scripture for the church at DeKalb, these were years of great development and change in my hermeneutic—my method and criteria for understanding the Bible. I was still, in many ways, close to many of the assumptions of my childhood. But seeds had been planted which, when they came to fruition, would require me to re-evaluate many of those assumptions.

---

[1] Samuel Davidson, *Sacred Hermeneutics Developed and Applied, Including A History of Biblical Interpretation from the Earliest of the Fathers to the Reformation* (Edinburgh: Thomas Clark, 1843). Davidson has an annotated bibliography on hermeneutics (677-718) which is helpful for the period covered.

[2] For details see "Principles of Interpretation," 34.

[3] Moses Stuart, *Elements of Interpretation, Translated from the Latin of J. A. Ernesti, and Accompanied by Notes and an Appendix Containing extracts from Morus, Beck and Keil* (Andover: Flagg & Gould, 1822) 2nd ed. London, 1822; 3rd ed., Andover, 1838; 4th ed., Andover and New York, 1842). Ernesti's work was titled *Institutio interpretis Novi Testament* (Leipsiae: Weidimann Reichium, 1775). On Stuart see, John H. Giltner, *Moses Stuart: The Father of Biblical Science in America* (Atlanta: Scholars Press, 1988).

[4] D. R. Dungan, *Hermeneutics* (Cincinnati: The Standard Publishing Company, n. d.)

[5] As quoted in Werner Georg Kümmel, *The New Testament: The History of the Investigation of Its Problems*, trans. S. McLean Gilmour and Howard C. Kee (Nashville: Abingdon Press, 1972) 60, 61.

[6] His books on rhetoric were: *Initia rhetorica* (Lipsiae: C. Fritsch, 1784), *Lexicon Technologie Graecorum Rhetoricae* (Lipsiae: C. Fritsch, 1795), and *Lexicon technologiae Latinorum rhetoricae* (Lipsiae: C. Fritsch, 1797).

5

Interpreting Texts: Iowa City, 1951-1954

The DeKalb experience was an influential one and I grew in many ways. In June of 1951, Dorothy and I were married. I also had decided to attend the University of Iowa in order to take a masters degree in speech. Sometime in my first year at Northern, I finally decided to forgo an agricultural major at Missouri. My interest in science lingered, however. I had worked for DeKalb Agricultural Association, which grew hybrid corn and hybrid chickens. Genetics, my speciality, was involved. The company employed a man with a Ph.D. in genetics. I talked with some of the men on the construction crew who knew him. They suggested that I talk with him, which I did, two or three times. He encouraged me to study genetics, but I finally decided on a new life goal.

I did not put aside the prospect that I might be a career preacher, but several of my close friends discouraged me. They said I could not really preach consistently good sermons, and I tended to agree with them. One of these was my roommate from

Northern, Franklin Schmidt. For him, James Warren was the ideal preacher, even though Franklin was far more theologically conservative than Warren. I decided that our future demanded better-trained preachers than those of my generation, and perhaps I could make a greater contribution by training preachers than by preaching. The Christian colleges were developing graduate programs in Bible at that time: Pepperdine led the way, launching a program in 1944. Harding and Abilene Christian entered the discussion stages and, within two years, each had commenced such a program. Since I had majored in speech I decided that I wanted to teach homiletics or preaching in one of the schools, preferably Harding. Somewhere I either heard or read that W. B. West, Jr.—then of Pepperdine, but who was to head the Harding program—stated that the person he would like to employ to teach homiletics would possess a B.D. and a Ph.D. in speech. As I anticipated what to do upon graduation from Northern, I decided that I either wanted to start work on a B.D. at McCormick, or begin a masters program in speech. Since I was getting married, I looked for a preacher's job, both for the experience and income.

Warren kept checking for me in the Chicago area, but no opening appeared. Some, including James Willeford, questioned whether I should go to McCormick. I discovered that the church in Iowa City was looking for a preacher, but they didn't want to pay anything on his salary, since they were saving for a church building. Willeford said he would help me raise money. I went to Iowa City to look over the situation, preach, and talk to the speech department at the University of Iowa. It seemed that it would work out. Iowa was appealing because Margaret Wood had taken her doctorate there and my first speech teacher at Harding, Bill Skillman, received an Iowa Master of Fine Arts. Also I knew that Fred Barton and Rex Kyker, who taught at Abilene Christian, went there. Iowa was reported to be one of the top speech schools in the nation. The interviews went well. I agreed that we would move there in late August. James Willeford managed to raise a salary of thirty dollars per week from three members of the church in Haleyville, Alabama. That was not much, but Dorothy planned to work. I could continue to seek employment in summers, if need be.

We arrived in Iowa City in late August 1951. It seemed like a great opportunity to study speech in a premier graduate program and preach for a body of believers in a university community. I had certain long-range goals in mind, but scant actual agenda as how to prepare for teaching preachers to preach, other than obtaining a B.D. (now an M.Div.) and a Ph.D. in speech. Since I planned to preach during my graduate studies, it seemed preferable to obtain the B.D. first. It didn't end up that way. We weren't too concerned, since in our view, if the Lord wanted me to train preachers he would open up appropriate doors. The activities of these years did little to evoke new patterns of biblical interpretation, but in many ways they widened and deepened patterns already established, and laid foundations for developments to come. The focus of my education made it more and more clear to me that documents must be understood in the light of their contexts.

The Church in Iowa City

The Church of Christ was launched in Iowa City in the late 1930s through the efforts of graduate students—mostly those in speech, theatre, and history. It flourished, especially after World War II, because of returning veterans, and usually averaged forty to fifty members. What was most remarkable, however, was not so much the number, but the percentage of them who were committed, outstanding leaders. These included such persons as Fred Barton, later dean of the Graduate School at Abilene Christian University, Elton Abernathy, longtime chair of the Speech Department at Southwest Texas State in San Marcos, Thomas Rouse of the history faculty at Texas Tech in Lubbock, and Olin Petty, professor of education at Duke University. All of these men were married with families, except Petty. The membership did not include anyone employed at the university. In addition, there were six or seven families who were permanent residents of Iowa City. None of these last contributed much to the public leadership of the congregation, but they functioned in other ways. An older woman whose husband was not a member served as the treasurer. The family which provided the long-range stability was the Doyle O'Rear family. When we first arrived, Doyle drove for Watkins Trucking, then later started his own trucking firm. This meant that he was not always there on Sunday. Still, his wife Marie and their children were regular attendees, as was also her sister Lucille, when she was not at work as a waitress. Doyle's brother's family attended. This extended family had moved to Iowa City from near Kansas City, Missouri. Ethel Williams, originally from Indiana, who had twin daughters, attended faithfully, but her husband was not a member. When we arrived, the congregation was in something of a down time because there were not many graduate students, but it soon started to pick up again. The congregation in Iowa City was much more diverse in education, employment and income than that in DeKalb.

In September 1951, the Iowa City congregation met for classes and a worship service only on Sunday morning, in a relatively small room in the Iowa Memorial Union. We paid a nominal fee to cover janitorial services. It was clean and light, and was adequately located for university students without being inconvenient for others, since parking was available. After a few weeks I encouraged the congregation to hold night services. Some members thought it was a good idea and some didn't. It required considerable negotiating with the Memorial Union administrator to secure night privileges. We had to agree that if another university organization required the room we would relinquish it for that specific night.

Hermeneutics: an Inventory

It may be helpful here to sum up my perspectives on hermeneutics in the fall of 1951. My outlooks admittedly were eclectic, with certain incongruities, but held together by the variety of materials found in the Scriptures. Most ingrained was that from my earliest experiences: I still believed that the Bible was basically a book of factual insights on God and his expectations for humans, and that its interpretation was best secured by detailed analysis of discrete—separate, self-contained—entities. At this stage I thought little about the narrative or story features of the Scriptures. I agreed that Christians are nurtured best by the New Testament rather than the Old, because they live under the authority of the New Testament. Because of the influence of Andy Ritchie, I had enlarged my vision to include the whole New Testament canon. In theory, this embraced even the book of Revelation, but not in practice (I have always been schizophrenic about studying Revelation in the church and have never taught it there, though I have covered it as one of various books in a graduate course in New Testament theology). My emphasis on the Gospels was new. I considered that commands, examples, and necessary inferences were helpful in determining specifics actions of the church but I did not preach many sermons in which I referred specifically to the triad. I had increased the topics for discussion in the churches from those having to do with puzzles and controversies, the plan of salvation, the first principles, and the identity of the church to include commitment of the heart, personal evangelism, devotion, prayer time, and concern for orphans and the needy. This meant that in some measure, the Psalms and prophets had entered my hermeneutic parameters. I justified including these Old Testament materials on the grounds that they were all contained in Scriptures and we must cover more of the message in Scripture, not less. I therefore held to a hermeneutic which encompassed understanding, application, and inner commitment. To understand Scripture, I increasingly came to believe, required knowing as much as possible about the languages, historical backgrounds, and literary features—in that order—of the books of the Bible. But I had also become more and more convinced that the personality, image, and adaptability of the proclaimer contributed immeasurably to biblical interpretation or hermeneutics.

I experienced the most growth in regard to grammatico-historical-literary interpretation and the image of the proclaimer while in Iowa City. An appreciation of the former requires an in-depth look at my graduate education at the University of Iowa. I will therefore take that up later, after some comments on the significance of the image of the proclaimer.

The Image of the Preacher

In a large sense, hermeneutics constitutes a theory about how one person explains or communicates a text to another. Much hermeneutical theory has focused on the text and the preunderstanding of the person doing the explicating. But the preunderstanding of the hearer may be as important or more so than that of the proclaimer.

Through my studies in speech I became convinced that optimal communication occurs when a mutual bond of understanding forms between the speaker and the audience. At Northern Illinois, my debate colleague and I discovered early on that winning debates had as much to do with knowing the qualities expected by the judge and adapting to them as it did with actual forensic skill and knowledge. In most tournaments, we knew after having received the schedule who our judges would be. If a prospective judge had critiqued us before, we tried to take into account her evaluations. If we did not know anything about a specific judge we asked around among the debaters about his preferences. We were not always capable of adapting enough to please each judge, but the attempt improved our ratings and, in some cases, won the debate.

Through my preaching and debating experience I was quite convinced that to be a dynamic interpreter of God's word required analysis of and adaptation to those with whom I communicated. That meant that I had to get to know them, to become a part of their lives. The initiative for this process, in my opinion, was on my shoulders. I knew if I chose to preach in upper midwest regions to better educated and more cosmopolitan persons than those with whom I grew up, that certain changes were required. A critical component of communication is the role, image, or personal characteristics of the speaker as perceived by the auditors. Ancient rhetoricians, such as Aristotle, discussed the speaker's image under the category of *ethos,* or character. *Ethos* constituted one of the three forms of proof, along with *logos* and *pathos*.

I was therefore determined to learn as much as feasible about the members of the congregation in Iowa City in order to advance the prospect that my explanations of Scripture could be understood, appropriated, and incorporated into their lives. It was also important, in my opinion, that my approaches be compatible with their outlooks and preferences, and these could best be learned through personal interaction. I also thought it important that they get to know Dorothy and me, to make it clear that we had our problems too, so that my exhortations would not come off as holier-than-thou. We also hoped, through personal contacts, that people would come to believe that we liked them personally even though we might differ with some of their actions and decisions.

I concluded early on that preaching in Iowa City would be more demanding than in DeKalb, both because of the diversity in the congregation, and the higher expectations for content. In DeKalb I could essentially be a rural Missourian and please most of the congregation. My roommate and fellow DeKalb member Franklin Schmidt, who grew up in Chicago and enjoyed a degree of sophistication, took me on as a special project, dedicating himself to eradicating my country ways and Ozark forms of expression. He did this in an acceptable, often witty manner. After Dorothy and I were married, she carried on the personal improvement project by pointing out southern Missourianisms which might not make sense in Iowa. But she, too, was a rural person, having spent most of her life on dairy farms in southern Wisconsin.

We had two ways to get to know people. First, we visited in their homes. I had done that in DeKalb, but not altogether systematically. I usually went if someone said, "come see us." That expression is typical in rural communities of the border states. It didn't mean that people really expected you to visit, but if you were so inclined, you were welcomed. The invitation was unconditional; no day or time was specified. So, in DeKalb, I would often drop by a week or two after the informal invitation was offered. At that time I was unmarried and not in a position to make reciprocal invitations, except to single males, since seven of us shared three sleeping rooms. But now I was married to a wife who liked to cook and invite others over to eat.

My first thinking about a ministry of personal, private contacts came through purchasing a book about Richard Baxter, a sixteenth-century English Puritan minister. I think I may have read the book before moving to Iowa City, but not carefully. Now I read it meticulously, with great interest. I had no model for a ministry of systematic visitation. Our preachers in southern Missouri spent their time evangelizing during meetings, or launching new congregations by preaching on Sunday afternoon or earlier Sunday morning while the class(es) were going on at the home congregation. They did little visiting among the members, though they went to a home if invited for a meal. To visit members was presumed to be a pastoral duty, and we wanted to separate the role of a preacher from that of a pastor. The pastor was the same as an elder, so if anyone was expected to visit members in their home it was the elders. But the elders did little visiting. We indeed were not involved in the "pastor system" whoever the pastor(s) might be!

Pastoral visits in homes has a long history in American Christianity, but in the twentieth century has become something of a lost art. Based on the model provided by Baxter and other Puritans, early American Puritan preachers, such as Cotton Mather, as recorded in his autobiography, made periodic visits at each member's home. The visit was far from a social one. Its specific purpose was to investigate the spiritual climate of the home and the fervor of each member. Encouragement was offered, but far more often the outcome was a reprimand and a charge to devote more time to prayer and Scripture reading, or whatever was needed. Often, matters of non-attendance, drunkenness, mistreatment of animals, or complaints from the neighbors entered the conversations. It would seem that the visits were an occasion to be dreaded rather than cherished. I wanted to avoid the harshness of the Puritan visits, but I wasn't interested in a purely social call, either. The first visit was mostly to get to know the members and let them ask any questions they might have. In subsequent visits I raised certain matters which pertained to the life of the congregation, such as the biblical materials studied, the sermon topics, classes for children, night services, and whether, in their opinion, it was feasible to buy lots for a building. In this manner I got to know the outlooks of the members and when I applied points in the sermon or called for involvement, I could speak in specifics, though in such a manner as to avoid embarrassment. Though I still fell short in certain communication skills, such as standard vocal intonations and dynamic delivery, I achieved a measure of success in attaining a credible image with the members. They became increasingly open to whatever recommendations I made. My hermeneutic principle—interpreting the Word through concrete insight into the lives of members—apparently achieved its ends. As to teaching and preaching responsibilities, I had it easy, compared with DeKalb, since one of the members, Olin Petty, an education professor at Duke who was finishing his doctorate at Iowa, taught the Sunday morning class for a time. Further, we did not have night services then. Graduate student members continued to teach the class most of the time I was there. When we started night services I occasionally was able to persuade one of the graduate students to preach.

My own approach followed much the same pattern as in DeKalb: topical sermons in the morning and expository sermons at night. I don't recall that I improved much on the quality of the commentaries I consulted. The University of Iowa had a school of religion which was founded in 1924, one of the first schools of religion in a state university. At that time it was totally funded by private gifts. The curriculum was in transition because of the appointment of a new director, Robert Michaelson. During my time, no graduate courses were offered in Scripture. The university library possessed a fairly good religious collection, compared with Northern Illinois. Some commentaries were available, but I don't recall checking many out. I did not know much about biblical scholars and their contributions, so I had little background for evaluating commentaries. I did know about the International Critical Commentaries and used them some.

The Iowa City congregation had saved money to buy lots for a building. There was not enough to buy near the University, at least in an area where a church would be permitted to build. Toward spring I noticed an advertisement in the Iowa City paper for two lots on the east side of town. They could be purchased for the amount of money the church had saved, with some left over. The major drawback was that the train tracks were at the rear of the property, but this was also a blessing, since that made them less desirable for residential purposes. Before we purchased the lots we checked with the city to see whether we would be permitted to build a church building. Some of the neighbors had qualms, but the city decided we could go ahead, and we purchased the lots. I proposed that we start with the basement. Encouraged by James Willeford and Abe Lincoln, who had worked with James Walter Nichols in Cedar Rapids, I told the congregation that I would make a trip to Tennessee, Alabama, Arkansas, Texas, and Oklahoma, in order to raise funds. I was not eminently successful at fundraising, but I secured enough so that we could proceed with the basement. The members did the work, along with a few persons from the congregation in Cedar Rapids who were professional home builders. Albert Gee and a member from Toddville essentially donated the equipment and expertise to excavate and landscape. In late fall, 1953, we met in our own building, which was quite adequate in size. We typically had forty to fifty in attendance, having grown from about twenty when we arrived because of new graduate student families as well as a few residential members who had moved into the area.

The University of Iowa

Graduate studies at the university contributed to my growing insights into the interpretation of documents, but not so much specifically of the Scriptures. I learned about Christendom—its history and the contemporary theological scene. All of these contributed directly and indirectly to my preaching and teaching. The work on my dissertation, "A Rhetorical Analysis of Representative Homilies of Basil the Great" and the courses I took contributing to it, raised a number of crucial issues regarding hermeneutics. Basil was a representative of the Antiochian school of interpretation, as contrasted with that of Origen.

The first semester, I took ten hours at the University, which kept me busy. I had made it at Northern without in-depth study, though I put in many hours on writing projects and keeping a log. We called it "busy work." Now, though, I was determined to learn as much as I could. My courses were "The History and Criticism of American Oratory," with A. Craig Baird, the grand old man of Iowa speech studies whose students occupied most of the major positions in state universities, "The History of Rhetorical Theory" under Orville Hitchcock, and "Experimental Phonetics" with James Curtis.

Graduate work in speech began in America in the early part of this century. Masters of Arts in Public Speaking were granted at the University of Iowa in 1902, 1903, and 1904, but most of the graduate degrees were given after 1920.[1] The University of Wisconsin speech department granted its first M.A. in 1920 and the first Ph.D. in speech in 1922. The first speech Ph.D. granted at Cornell University was in 1926. The first Ph.D.'s at Iowa were granted in 1930.

The method of A. Craig Baird is worthy of special attention. A. Craig Baird was one of the founders of the modern American speech studies which were launched at the turn of the century. Some of the professors were mostly interested in delivery —"elocution" as some called it. Baird, however, was interested in ideas, arguments, and invention. He considered persons only interested in performance and execution as neo-sophists.[2] Baird insisted that the speech critic focus as much on historical and social settings as on form and argument. Speech criticism began with the authentication of the text, which meant an exploration of all the channels available which might provide insight into the history of the specific document under consideration. The major undertaking of the critic, however, was to leave no stone unturned in the effort to reconstruct the social, political, and theological context in which the speech took place. This meant that the critic had to be, if possible, a better historian in regard to this specific speech than the historians themselves. Baird's book, co-authored with Lester Thonssen, was the bible of American speech criticism for almost three decades.[3]

Rhetorical criticism is today a rapidly-accelerating form of biblical criticism, but little interest in it existed in those days, either among speech or biblical scholars. biblical scholars, under the influence of various forms of historical and literary criticism, were dedicated to the same reconstruction that Baird proposed, though they tended to be little concerned with rhetorical proofs and arrangement. At various times in history, however, rhetorical analysis, hermeneutics, and biblical criticism have been overlapping, if not identical, disciplines. As representative historical samples, one may mention Philip Melancthon (1497-1560) who published *Institutiones rhetoricae* (1521) and *Elementa rhetorices* (1531)[4], and J. C. G. Ernesti, especially his *Initia rhetorica,* and his lexica of technical rhetorical terms, in both Greek and Latin.[5] Some of the studies at the turn of this century were by Johannes Weiss, E. W. Bullinger, Eduard König, Rudolf Bultmann, and Eduard Norden.[6] Now, at the end of the twentieth century, another surge of interest in rhetoric by biblical critics has emerged.

The next year, Dr. Baird was away from Iowa City as a visiting professor at Southern Illinois University. I therefore approached Dr. Hitchcock about doing a thesis involving questionnaires and interviews, seeking to discover how churchmen in Iowa City and Cedar Rapids prepared sermons. In the end, thirty-seven ministers were interviewed. The results were somewhat predictable, though different religious traditions approached the matter differently. Presbyterian ministers, for example, usually wrote their sermons in full, while ministers of the free church traditions only prepared outlines. Most ministers did considerable reading for preparation, especially in commentaries. My thesis was completed in three months and I was awarded the M.A. in June 1953.

The question at stake, once it was clear that the M.A. was forthcoming, was where to attend seminary. I had learned from Dr. Baird that Princeton Theological probably had the best program in homiletics, so I set out to determine if it was possible to work on a B.D. there. I thought perhaps I could teach speech in a high school near Princeton and attend the seminary part-time. The seminary informed me, however, that it would not be possible to work on a B.D. part-time. I read in the *Christian Chronicle* about a new congregation being planted in the first major suburban planned community, Levittown, Pennsylvania. At spring break, Dorothy and I decided to make a quick trip to the Princeton area to see if we could find a church situation in which I could work. We had hoped to be part of a team for the new congregation in Levittown, but the minister made clear that he was not interested in a team. We returned to Iowa City without any hopes of a position which would enable us to go to Princeton.

When we arrived back in Iowa City with the news that it didn't work out at Princeton, Dr. Hitchcock soon informed me that if I was interested I would be offered a graduate assistantship teaching "Communication Skills." We didn't have to think it over too long: the congregation was glad for us to preach for another year, the income from teaching and preaching was at least adequate for our growing family, and in another year and a summer I could complete most of the course work for the Ph.D., since I had taken extra courses in working for the masters. The Communication Skills course was somewhat unique at the University of Iowa.[7] Writing, or English composition, and speech were combined into one course, which the student took for a full year. The teachers were either from Speech or English, both full-time and graduate assistants. While I was not thrilled to teach writing, I saw this as an exciting opportunity, since there were weekly meetings of the staff to discuss and prepare upcoming tasks for the course. This was a premier program and much energy was put into it. By this time I had already taught my first university class. In the fall of 1952, one section of Public Speaking did not have a teacher. The public speaking course was taught for transfer students who had taken English composition elsewhere without the speech component. Dr. Hitchcock asked if I would teach it and I readily agreed, since the experience and extra income would both be helpful. The failure to work out something in Princeton was the second time seminary training was postponed. I was disappointed, but everything fell in place so quickly in Iowa City that little time existed for regrets. Who knew, at that stage, what God had in mind? I had trusted him to date, and the outcome had been auspicious, demonstrating to me that "God moves in a mysterious way, his wonders to perform."

Once the decision was made to stay in Iowa City, the question became what topic to propose for my Ph.D. dissertation. This was important because it would help determine what courses I should take to complete my program. Still anticipating seminary, I started taking Greek in 1952. Iowa had an excellent classics program. I took beginning Greek from the departmental chairman, Gerald Else, who had taken his doctorate at Harvard. Else, who published a major work on Aristotle's poetics, went on from Iowa to chair the department at the University of Michigan. Most of my Greek was classical, but I took one course in which we read the New Testament.

The study of Greek began to influence my interpretation of the New Testament and enabled me to understand new aspects of the commentaries. But I was careful not to drop Greek words and phrases into my sermons simply to try to make an impression, as I had heard debaters and some of my peers do. I had good teachers, and I was well aware that simply knowing Greek words and grammar did not resolve all the difficulties in translating or interpreting a text.

My earliest formal introduction to a critical approach to Scripture occured in a course on philosophy in literature. The professor who taught philosophy in literature had theological training and was fairly knowledgeable about biblical criticism—more so than I. I remember reading Lucretius's *On the Nature of Things*, Augustine's *Confessions*, and Job. I think we read additional documents but I don't recall now what they were. I was greatly interested in Lucretius because of his view of the atomic nature of reality. I didn't agree with him at a number of points, especially in his concepts of the gods and the afterlife, but I could identify with his vision of reality because of my scientific training. I had a difficult time with the *Confessions*. This was my first foray into Platonic philosophy. It ran counter to all my background, both theologically and scientifically. I was impressed by the devotional aspects, and it was mostly this I retained and appreciated.

In some odd ways it was the study of Job which gave me the greatest cause for alarm. Professor Turnbaugh offered standard critical conclusions on certain passages which challenged my preconceived interpretations. These were passages on which I had developed some great sermons, in my view, with the help of Moody,

McCartney or Spurgeon. If Turnbaugh was correct, these were improper texts for the sermon at hand. I had a difficult time thinking he was right. I wrote him off as a far-out liberal. Still, I discussed some of the passages with him. The one I remember particularly was Job 19:25, 26: "For I know that my redeemer lives, and that at the last he will stand upon the earth; and after my skin has been thus destroyed, then in my flesh I shall see God." Turnbaugh explained that though this passage has been given a Christological interpretation in the history of Christianity—even by Handel in *The Messiah*—the author of Job probably had in mind a human who was to arrive within his lifetime as his vindicator. I could not accept this. For me, the text obviously implied a Christological interpretation and that was, therefore, the only one possible. Turnbaugh was patient to explain why the passage was viewed in this way. He did not, however, address the larger issue of whether the proper interpretation of an Old Testament text must be Christological. Isaiah 7:14, for example, is certainly employed that way by Matthew (1:23). But is double, triple or a different sort of fulfillment possible? I didn't have the framework of preunderstanding at that time which permitted admitting the possibility of multiple fulfillment which, in fact, might possibly be the biblical way to interpret certain texts. I disagreed with Turnbaugh, in person and on the exams. Turnbaugh wrote comments and gave me an acceptable grade.

While I had to work hard and put in long hours, everything was falling in place, perhaps even better than I could have hoped. I desired, like most of my fellow graduate students, to complete my course work, then secure a teaching position, so our family would be out from under the financial pressures. The outlook at Iowa about writing dissertations was that while it might be more convenient to stay in Iowa City and get everything completed quickly, full-time teaching experience and a longer time span contributed to the maturity of the dissertation.

Early in the fall of 1953, Dr. Hitchcock and I conferred over the dissertation. I had decided that I should write on an early Greek preacher because of my interest in the history of homiletics and my course work in Greek. The field was wide open since few speech persons took Greek. Only one or two speech dissertations had been written on the early Greek fathers. Hitchcock didn't know much about the Greek fathers. An obvious person to write on was Chrysostom, but a dissertation had already been written on him. Somewhere Hitchcock had read that the most influential Greek father was Athanasius. I toyed for some time with the pros and cons of centering in on Athanasius. I thought it best to write on a father whose upbringing was well-documented. I was still intrigued with the idea of discovering the factors in a person's life and education which contributed to his ability as a speaker. After examining the fathers and their writings, I decided that Basil the Great would be the best. First, he was a man of affairs: a bishop, not simply a theologian, which always appealed to speech persons. Second, because of the letters and sermons of his brother Gregory and of his good friend Gregory Nazianzus, much could be learned about his early life and education. Third, he was rhetorically trained—which was standard—but had taught rhetoric before committing his life to the church. Various studies had been completed on Basil, but none of the sort I envisioned. Hitchcock agreed, after consulting with Baird, that I should write on Basil. We agreed that I select the number of sermons I thought feasible to master and translate from the Greek. I finally settled on seventeen homilies. Nine of the sermons were a series on the Hexamera—Lenten sermons on Genesis. These had been translated into English. The other eight sermons were not translated into English.

Because of the Iowan conviction, which had become my own, that as much as possible needed to be learned about the context of the sermons, Dr. Hitchcock and I set out to design a course of study. First, I needed to see everything in the larger perspective, so I took Greek history and then Roman history from James Osmund, a relatively new professor who had received his doctorate at Yale. Osmund was not the most exciting lecturer, but on better days he was at least lucid. He seemed to have mastered the original documents and the secondary literature. I asked questions in class and afterward. He was not particularly outgoing, but welcomed questions. I wrote papers in both classes which provided backdrop for Basil and the fourth century A.D. These classes not only supplied insight into the world of Basil, but also to the world of the Old and New Testaments. I drew upon these backgrounds in my teaching and preaching.

Next, for an understanding of the fathers of the church, I arranged for a class in the Greek fathers—the patristics—with Professor Walsh. His approach was that I read and write. I did mostly survey, which was his suggestion. I read in two or three patrologies, then perused specific materials on certain persons such as Origen, Chrysostom, Basil, and Athanasius. This was a good exercise, but I was essentially self-educated since Walsh made few remarks. What I knew I knew, but I was not apprised of the gaps in my knowledge, nor did I have the benefit of batting around ideas with an expert. This is what I missed the most.

In fact, all of the people with whom I worked confessed knowing little about Basil or the fourth century. To have some assistance with the Greek I took two semesters of guided study under Else in which we read Basil. He thought that only classical Greek was up to the standard, and he expressly despised the Greek of the church fathers: he thought it was bastardized. Else was an Episcopalian, which should have whetted his appetite for the fathers, but he had almost no interest in them. While we worked he was completing his book on *The Poetics*. I think that work demanded all his extra time and energy, because he was not much interested in Basil's vocabulary and did almost no checking on his own. He spent most of his time faulting my inability to identify all the grammatical forms. That was in some measure helpful, but it meant that we focused on grammar rather that what Basil meant. Else made it clear to me that I would have to struggle alone with what Basil meant; it was of little interest to him.

I also took other courses in the school of religion which helped with the theological insights. Although unavailable to me, a course in Greek philosophy would have been very helpful. It is possible that one was not taught during that year, but even if it had been I suspect it would have been off-limits, as far as Hitchcock was concerned. I therefore had to learn whatever I knew of Greek philosophy on my own. It was clear to me after reading in Basil that he drew many of his concepts from the philosophers, both by way of agreement and disagreement. I took a course in the Renaissance and Reformation, taught by George Burkhart, a scholar of some note. His focus was on the social and political backgrounds. He was not theologically uninformed but he did not spend much time on the theological factors.

I took a course in John Calvin and Jonathan Edwards from Robert Michaelson who had just come that year from Yale to be director of the school of religion. There were two of us in class, the first two graduate students Michaelson had at Iowa. Michaelson ended his career in the same capacity at The University of California, Santa Barbara. This course certainly enhanced my understanding of Calvinistic theology, but contributed little to my work on Basil. I also took a course with Pangborn on contemporary theology. It was not that challenging for someone with suitable background, but since, as a restorationist, I knew very little about theology—contemporary or otherwise—it was an eye-opener and a good course. It was also helpful for its focus on how contemporary theologians came out on traditional topics and conclusions. This meant that many of the topics I would address in Basil were discussed. Because of the Iowa approach to rhetoric, it would be necessary for me to assess the effectiveness of Basil's ideas. One of the ways to do so—which, I decided later, was greatly flawed—was to ask how his ideas had stood the test of time. The contemporary theology course provided insight on such questions.

In 1953 and '54, several of us who had got to know each other through classes and teaching Communication Skills started meeting every morning at a coffee shop across from the speech offices. There were five: Ted Johnson who taught theatre at Western Colorado in Gunnison, Mal Sillars who ended his career at the University of Utah as dean and sometimes chair of speech, Bob Jeffrey who, after a few years, ended up as chair of speech at the University of Texas and then dean of the school of communication, and John Ostendorf, who had been around Iowa, both as an undergraduate and graduate student. He had worked under A. Craig Baird for some years as debate coach. He went to Wisconsin State at Black River Falls, but died not long after of a heart attack. I was the odd man out, since they were all interested in politics and writing dissertations on contemporary political campaigns. Still, they had been turned on by Rheinhold Niebuhr's political analysis, so they welcomed whatever insights I could offer which would help them understand Niebuhr. This meant that I had to start reading *Christian Century* and *Christianity and Crisis*. All of these colleagues were active church persons at that time. Ted was a Methodist, Jeffrey a Presbyterian, Sillars a Baptist, and Ostendorf a Roman Catholic.

We had some great conversations. That was a time of significant spiritual renewal among intellectuals. On the university campus this translated into an interest in theology. The news magazines were doing regular features on neo-orthodox theology: theologians such as Niebuhr, Tillich and Barth made the covers. Rather than being part of a persecuted minority, those interested in religion were the "in" group—as long as we could intellectualize about it. My little enclave was a great support group for one who had been an outsider during his earlier college years. I learned much from them about the current political scene which contributed to my work as a debate coach for the next five years. Because of these experiences and my accepted expertise I approached preaching with greater confidence. A preacher with confidence in God and in himself is always a greater blessing when the word is being interpreted. These discussions also added certain content features to my preaching, but I was careful not to mix preaching with politics. In my view, I had heard that done more than I cared to at Harding.

The consequence of the Iowa experience was coming to grips with our western heritage, which is also the backdrop of Christianity. I finally obtained a classical, liberal arts education, but in graduate school. It is difficult to interpret Christianity or the Scriptures without such an education. That is not to say that Scripture speaks only to persons with this education: in its inspiration and call to obedience it speaks to every person. But it is difficult to see how some can set themselves up as official interpreters without the broad exposure to historical and literary contexts provided by such an education. It is even more difficult to understand how such persons can claim, "Pay attention to me. I have the correct understanding. Dismiss everyone else!" Such would-be authority figures have many preunderstandings of which they are likely not aware. They probably have few of the necessary tools for scrutinizing their own presuppositions and critically comparing and aligning them with biblical presuppositions. Jesus has a term for such persons: "blind guides!" They should decline the role "guide" until they acquire the needed tools. It is one thing to do the best one can with the training and light God has provided in order to answer to God for oneself. It is another to display the shingle of "God's Official Interpreter" without proper training and tools. A question put by Job needs to continually haunt all of us: "Will you speak falsely for God, and speak deceitfully for him," (Job 13:7)?

In 1954, when I began thinking of a teaching position, I didn't cast my net wide. I wasn't being forced to move in order to survive, since I could stay on in Iowa City, preaching and teaching Communication Skills. The two salaries were not that much, but enough to get by. And since my parents now lived in Searcy, I kept up with developments at Harding. When I heard that a faculty couple, both of whom taught speech, were leaving to work on a doctorate, I wrote Evan Ulrey, the chairman, and received a letter in reply saying they would be making a decision in a month or so. I didn't really know Evan, since he was working on his doctorate at LSU when I was a student.

My parents had started talking of moving to Searcy when my sister went to Harding. Since there were four of us, they thought they might as well move to Searcy so we could attend Harding and live at home. My sister went summers and graduated in 1949, the year I moved to DeKalb. They put off the move, however, because Glenn and Owen were very active in sports at Thayer High School. Owen was an especially good basketball player, so the pressure was on to stay. His senior year, the team went to the state tournament and won two or three games before being eliminated. Finally in 1950, when Owen was a Harding freshman, they moved. We visited them once or twice a year.

Sometime after writing Ulrey, I noticed a story in the *Des Moines Register* which voiced opposition to farm subsidies. I wrote Dr. George Benson, president of Harding, sent him the article and expressed my approval. Dr. Benson was strongly opposed to large federal government and aid programs of all sorts. I had likewise grown up among people who opposed all government supports and welfare programs. We opposed Roosevelt's WPA, PWA and similar programs, because we felt they were a waste of money. Despite that, most of my relatives kept voting for Roosevelt. My insight into the Iowa farm situation led me to oppose this specific program. By this time I had come to believe, contrary to Dr. Benson's views, that the prophetic call for justice showed that some welfare programs, if administrated properly, were needed. I did not go into all my views in the letter to Benson, just those on the farm subsidy. I was not opposed to helping farmers, but this bill seemed to assist the larger farmers the most, and they were, in my assessment, the ones who least needed subsidies. Furthermore, the support system would increase consumer prices, and negatively impact markets and small farmers in third-world countries. Writing Dr. Benson helped me secure a position, but resulted in expectations on his part I didn't anticipate nor intend.

In the letter I also mentioned my interest in teaching at Harding. As a student I had talked with Benson on various occasions, and in later years had run into him when visiting Searcy. But he was not known for remembering people unless he had a specific interest in them, so there was no reason for him to remember me, though his secretary Margaret O'Bannion, who by this time was quite influential with Dr. Benson, did. A few weeks later I received a letter from Dean L. C. Sears, offering me a position with a respectable salary. I was to learn later that neither Ulrey nor Richard Walker, the other speech professor, wished to employ me, because they had someone else in mind. The offer was Benson's idea.

In late August 1954, I borrowed a small truck from Uncle Cleo for moving what little furniture and other items we possessed. Owen drove the truck from Alton, Missouri, to Iowa City. I preached my last sermon at the church. We said our goodbyes with a degree of sadness, both at church and to friends and professors at the University. We loaded our two girls in the car. Suzanne was almost two years old by this time, and Eloise, three months. We stopped in Thayer and visited grandparents and other relatives, then made our way to Searcy. We had arranged to buy a fairly new, two-bedroom house, just north of the College Church of Christ building. It cost the frightening sum of eight thousand dollars. My father was mainly responsible for our buying the house: he did not believe in paying rent if it could be avoided. He rented when he first went to Searcy, but built a new house as fast as he could. He loaned us the thousand-dollar down payment. As far as I was concerned the situation looked very good, but Dorothy was not so sure. In Iowa City we had been one hundred-fifty miles from her relatives. They visited often and we visited them. Her sister, Cleone Kiel, was a junior at Harding, which helped. But she was not sure she liked Searcy, especially the way the Harding wives dressed, and, in her opinion, the airs they put on; much too formal for her. So, she had a great deal of apprehension. It wasn't the last time her intuitions would prove well-founded.

---

[1] H. Clay Harshbarger, *Some Highlights of the Department of Speech & Dramatic Art* (Iowa City: The University of Iowa, 1976) 17, 18.

[2] Baird was a 1907 graduate of Wabash College in Indiana, a private liberal arts college of some note. From there he entered Union Theological Seminary in New York, receiving the B.D. in 1910. He studied under such scholars as Arthur Cushman McGiffert (1861-1933), who, as the result of studies in Germany, especially with Adolf Harnack (1851-1930), embraced the scientific historiography which came to the forefront both in Europe and America.

[3] Lester Thonssen and A. Craig Baird, *Speech Criticism: The Development of Standards for Rhetorical Appraisal* (New York: The Ronald Press Company, 1948).

[4] C. J. Classen, "Paulus und die Antike Rhetorik," *ZNW*, 82 (1991) 1-32.

[5] J. C. G. Ernesti, *Initia rhetorica* (Lipsiae: C. Fritsch, 1784), *Lexicon technologiae Graecorum rhetoricae* (Lipsiae: C. Fritsch, 1795) and *Lexicon technologiae Latinorum rhetoricae* (Lipsiae: C. Fritsch, 1797).

[6] See Duane F. Watson, "Rhetorical Criticism," *The International Standard Bible Encyclopedia* (Grand Rapids: Wm. B. Eerdmans, 1988) 4:181, 182. Also Watson's *Invention, Arrangement and Style Rhetorical Criticism of Jude and 2 Peter*, 1-8. Johannes Weiss, "Beiträge zur Paulinischen Rhetorik," in *Theologische Studien Bernhard Weiss dargebracht* (Göttingen: Vandenhoeck and Ruprecht,1897) 165-247; E. W. Bullinger, *Figures of Speech Used in the Bible* (London: Eyre and Spottiswoode, 1898); Eduard König, *Stilistik, Rhetorik, und Poetik in Bezug auf die biblische Literatur* (Leipzig: Theodor Weicher, 1900); Rudolf Bultmann, *Der Stil der paulinischen Predigt und die kynisch-stoische Diatribe* (Göttingen: Vandenhoeck and Ruprecht, 1910); Eduard Norden *Agnostos Theos* (Leipzig and Berlin: B. G. Teubner, 1913).

[7] Robert J. Conners, Lisa S. Ede, and Andrea A. Lunsford, *Essays on Classical Rhetoric, 8.* "The communications movement in American education began in 1944, when the first communications courses were taught at the State University of Iowa and at Michigan State University." 8.

6
Conventional Christian Interpreters: 1954-1959

I came to Harding to teach, which was fortunate, because I didn't have time to do much else. The standard teaching load was fifteen hours, or five three-hour courses. I was given a one-course reduction for directing debate—forensics, as we called it. Each of the two semesters at Harding I taught three required courses in beginning speech, along with argumentation and debate. In the required courses the students did not know in advance who their teacher would be. This was done by design, and students could not transfer to another teacher, even after they found out. I had a few unpleasantries with two or three students who insisted that they didn't want me as a teacher, but otherwise I got along fairly well. Much of what I tried to do was new to me and I was on edge much of the first semester. Since I was neither loquacious nor dramatic by nature, it was something of a struggle for both the students and me.

Debate, however, went better. Ulrey had been directing debate, but he had not yet finished his dissertation. He was given a lighter teaching load that year so he could get it finished. Also because of his dissertation, he had not put much energy into debate. I decided I wasn't going to get much done on my dissertation anyway, so I plunged into debate and recruited whomever I could. I spent considerable personal time with the debaters and they did very well, perhaps better than Harding had ever previously done in debate.

Teaching speech and directing debate at Harding contributed to the additional elaboration of my insights into interpreting Scriptures at two points. First, because of a 1952 summer experience selling hospitalization insurance for an Iowa company—National Benefit, now American Republic—I gave much thought to the difference between persuasion and manipulation, and I incorporated these insights into my classes. Various persons, at that time in our movement, vigorously promoted personal evangelism. Books circulated which took their evangelistic models from sales technique. After being introduced to sales devices—especially those of one particular supervisor—I decided that much selling technique is mere manipulation—placing people in situations where they are too embarrassed to back down or say "no"—rather than persuading them on the basis of principles. The latter I considered ethical persuasion, a needful part of teaching the Gospel. But the former I viewed as manipulation, and therefore highly suspect from a Christian perspective. I therefore came to question the vaidity of the analogy between bringing persons to Christ and selling a product like insurance.

The National Benefit Insurance Company had a guaranteed minimum salary which was more than I could make doing most other things, so in the summer of 1952, while still a graduate student, I sold insurance. The company also offered a bonus if one sold more than ten policies per week. The approach was to blitz a particular county, selling hospitalization insurance to farmers. A crew of six to ten agents worked the county until it was canvassed. About three weeks before we commenced the blitz a full-page ad was placed in all the county weeklies, announcing that we would be calling. We then arrived at the door with a copy of the advertisement in hand, saying that we had come to explain our hospitalization plan. The strategy was good: we were rarely refused entry. The sales weren't as simple, however. That was in the early days of hospital insurance and it was not easy to convince people of the need.

We first worked Keokuk County, and Sigourney was the county seat. I was not imminently successful but I stuck it out. I usually sold my ten policies per week, but not much more. Toward the end I had an especially good week and sold twenty policies. I did not enjoy selling but I thought it might be a valuable experience and help me better relate to people, which I thought very important in preaching. I loved the Iowa countryside and felt at home talking with farmers. But I dreaded pressuring people to close a sale and I avoided the closing devices as much as possible.

One of my managers could sell a policy to just about anyone because he had a whole series of ways to psychologically entrap them. He enjoyed manipulation. Not only did I have doubts about the ethics of what he was doing, I concluded that he was not a productive salesman. He often spent two hours or more completing a sale. For him that was a half day's work and he frittered away the rest of the time. He had ways of playing the wife off against the husband so that each would look bad in the eyes of the other if they rejected his argument. For example, he might ask the husband, "What would happen to your wife if you injured your arm in a corn picker?" Then he would turn to the wife and query, "How can your husband manage the house, the children, and the farm, all at the same time, should you become hospitalized?"

He especially relished manipulative tricks. After a period of conversation and explanation, rather than asking them if they were interested, he took out an enrollment form and started asking questions in order to fill out the form. Though he carried pens, he did not take his out. He asked the residents if they had a pen or pencil. Few people would admit to being without writing devices. Once the pen was brought, he asked their name and its proper spelling and filled that in on the form. If they were hesitant to give the name he would depict a few more catastrophic scenarios. He might also explain that the purpose was not to commit to take the policy, but for information in case they wanted it later. Halfway through he might drop his pencil or pen. He would make no effort to pick it up. Instead, he waited for the prospects to pick it up for him. He did that, he said, to soften them. The moment of truth came when he asked the person to sign the enrollment. If a person had agreed to everything so far, they tended to be embarrassed not to sign, even though they might not want the policy or feel they had been "suckered" into it. He rationalized that even if people were being manipulated, it was for their own good, because the likelihood was that on some occasion they would need hospitalization insurance.

I decided that manipulation was an unethical form of persuasion, even if it might be for the benefit of the person manipulated. Honorific persuasion, by contrast, expends all its efforts to show a person how the proposal is compatible with her commitments and needs. No tricks are involved, and if she decides to act, it is at her own volition. The same is true of preaching. I therefore rejected the sales model for the one who interprets the word of God as a hermeneutic method contrary to Christian ethics. It sounds quite counter to Paul's principle: "For our appeal does not spring from deceit or impure motives or trickery," (I Thessalonians 2:3), "For we are not peddlers of God's word like so many, but in Christ we speak as persons of sincerity, as persons sent from God and standing in his presence" (II Corinthians 2:17). Not all methods of persuasion or hermeneutical models are compatible with the word of God. I argued that our movement needed to be more sensitive to hermeneutics that are biblical in method and intent, and reject the ones that distort the very heart of the faith.

Because of these experiences, I carried similar views into my debate classes. I thought, and still think, that college debating is a very important experience which teaches participants to locate the crucial issues, to think on their feet, to marshall arguments and evidence, and to employ effective modes of refutation. It provides experience, enhances delivery, and provides feedback for improvement from colleagues and judges. But certain approaches to and perspectives on debate may ignore Christian values. Debating is not conducive to inspiration and devotion. Jesus debated very little: he spoke more often in parables and aphorisms. In the Old Testament, much Scripture is narrative—story—and not so much argument. Despite the contention of certain debate proponents—and there were many among us at that time, including J. D. Bales—it was not clear to me that Christians are commissioned to debate, or, at least, to seek out debates. Jesus debated with the scribes and Pharisees, but he did not seek to do so—it was their idea. Peter's charge, "Always be ready to make your defense to anyone who demands from you an accounting for the hope that is in you" (I Peter 3:15) does not imply debate. Rather, it simply challenges one to supply reasons for faith in Jesus Christ when called upon. I had long talks with Alan Highers, now a judge in western Tennessee and editor of the *Spiritual Sword*, who was then a student in the Harding Academy and aspired to be the best-known debater in the brotherhood. I challenged him to consider whether Scripture itself lends support to the conclusion that the best way to interpret the Bible is through debate. Is not another model—a teller of stories and parables, perhaps, or an encourager such as Barnabas (Acts 4:36, 9:27)—better? I also shared with him my observations on the Barber-Wallace debate; how James Walter Nichols had hoped the debate would bring the two groups together, but which resulted in their being driven farther apart.

The Church in Monticello, Arkansas

I was interested in preaching because of my commitment to tell the Gospel story and my desire to keep a hand in for the experience. I still aspired, at some time in the future, to spend my time teaching speech and homiletics to prospective preachers. My brother Owen heard that the church in Star City was looking for someone to preach two Sundays a month. Star City was south of Pine Bluff, about one hundred twenty-five miles southeast of Searcy. The church was perceived as small by Arkansas standards, with forty to fifty in attendance. I didn't object to the size, so I went. After the service two men introduced themselves. They said they had heard I was coming and they would like for me to come the next Sunday to Monticello, another twenty-five miles south. They were interested in employing someone to preach every Sunday. They had never heard of me, but they perceived that since I taught at Harding I might be qualified for the job. I agreed to go, since I preferred to preach regularly at the same place. That first Sunday they negotiated with me to come regularly. They would pay me fifty dollars a week for preaching Sunday morning and Sunday night. About twenty dollars of that would be considered car expense, since the round trip would amount to three hundred miles. Harding still had classes on Saturday, but not Monday. So, even though it was after midnight when I returned to Searcy, I did not have to worry about classes the next day.

Monticello and I were a good match. It was a college town, the home of Arkansas A. & M., later to become the University of Arkansas at Monticello.

Several of the members were college students, others worked for the university, and there was a professor or two, but they weren't prominent in the leadership. Most of the members had not grown up in Churches of Christ, and did not require old-line preaching. I did not change topics or style from Iowa City days, but I continued to prepare new sermons. My illustrations, however, were drawn more from that region. I continued the practice of getting to know the members of the congregation by visiting in their homes. It took awhile, since there were about one hundred-fifty of them and I could only visit on Sundays. I was invited to lunch and dinner each Sunday by a different family. Dorothy and the two girls often went along, which added to the growing relationship. In the afternoons I visited members who were probably not in a position to invite us for a meal, in order to get to know them also.

A few comments on the written interpretation of the Word are appropriate here. The first fall in DeKalb, I had decided a church bulletin would help. The members were indifferent one way or the other. I traded my portable typewriter for a standard and purchased a used mimeograph machine with my own money. I decided to continue the practice at Monticello.

My peers at Harding were sometimes critical of bulletins, especially those with quoted materials which may or may not have had local application. I agreed with them, and decided the bulletin I would turn out would provide information about the congregation and the members. I would almost never print quoted material. The material would be specifically for our members, not for a mailing list of people elsewhere. In addition to announcements I wrote commentaries on Scripture we were studying, either in the Bible class or the sermon. I always employed 8 1/2 X 14 paper, which meant that most Sundays I had space for a three hundred- to four hundred-word essay or sermonette. I considered this good discipline for me and, hopefully, helpful to the members. By writing, I was required to argue more cogently, to chose words more carefully, and in some cases, to check out information and ideas for accuracy. I hoped to attain a readable style. At one time, my ideal was the *Reader's Digest*. It was also the standard for James P. Sanders. He read it regularly in Braille. At this stage the *Reader's Digest* model was appropriate, since it encouraged liveliness and narrativity. That style was more likely to captivate bulletin readers. Later, however, I opted for more substance than the *Digest* model permitted. I still, however, sought readability. Lack of enthusiasm and vivacity tended to be the downside of my preaching. I worked on these, but with diminishing returns. To compensate, I spent much time searching for apt illustrations, and a clear and animated style. To some degree, I succeeded with both, and writing contributed to my success. In the interpretation of the Word, writing is crucial, since it encourages careful exposition.

One of our regrets about leaving Harding after one year was the termination of the association with the congregation in Monticello. They treated us very well. I probably did some of my best preaching there, because of their constant encouragement. I felt comfortable, even when I took positions that ran counter to our traditions. For several weeks we had a box in the back of the building in which people could place questions which would be answered on Sunday night in the sermons. People were not required to sign their names, but in various cases I surmised who asked the questions. A month or so after we started, this question showed up: "Will you please preach on the fundamentals of the Gospel?" The next Sunday night I preached on I Corinthians 15:3: "I handed on to you as of first importance what I in turn had received, that Christ died for our sins in accordance with the Scriptures, and that he was buried, and that he was raised on the third day in accordance with the Scriptures." I suspected who wrote the question: an older woman who had complained in the class—in a nice way—that the preaching wasn't focusing as much on the fundamentals as it should. In the sermon, I argued that we should consult Paul in order to determine the fundamentals of the gospel. After the service was over this woman came up to me and said, "You knew what I meant, but you did not preach on those fundamentals." I said, "Yes, I knew what you meant, but whose fundamentals should we prefer: yours, or Paul's?" She took it well. She said she got my point, but she still thought I should preach on the plan of salvation and the identity, worship, and organization of the church. I said, "You have accepted this in a good spirit, so will I." I preached on her "fundamentals," but in a manner which I thought more biblical than the traditional way. I think she had mixed feelings about the results.

Because of this and similar experiences, it had become clear to me that we had imposed an extra-biblical hermeneutical principle on the Scriptures by identifying certain topics as the fundamentals of the Gospel according to our assessment, rather than using the criteria of the writers of the New Testament. I had concluded by continual reexamination of the text that the core of the Gospel in the New Testament had more to do with what God had done for humankind through Christ than with the response expected of man. In our preaching of the Gospel, though, the human response had become the focus, resulting in a different spin—and a non-biblical emphasis in the message.

Politics and Religion at Harding

Relations with the faculty at Harding were congenial. Ulrey was kind, though distant and not too complimentary of my few successes. I got along well with Richard Walker, the other speech teacher, but we didn't strike up a friendship. Don and Pat Sime became our close friends. We had first met Don and Pat in Trenton, New Jersey, when we went to assess the prospect for attending Princeton Theological Seminary, where he was completing a B.D. The Simes liked to fish, so I went with them to the Red River a few times. He occasionally preached at Star City, so we often rode down together. Don was in the Bible department. Harding had initiated the M.A. degree the year before we arrived. W. B. West, Jr. had been brought from Pepperdine to head the program. Jack Lewis arrived the year I did, and Jimmy Allen, a classmate of mine from 1948-49, was teaching undergraduates. The faculty sometimes played tag football, and I played with Allen, Clifton Ganus, James Atteberry, James Burrow, Richard Walker, Ken Davis, and many others. Andy T. Ritchie, Jr. was away for the year, working on a master's at Scaritt College in Nashville.

About a month after classes commenced, an unexpected turn of affairs occurred. I was asked to meet with Dr. Benson in his office. He handed me a pamphlet which he said I should read. If I agreed with it he wanted me to make a statement about it in chapel, distribute it and encourage students to read it. I read the pamphlet. I don't remember now exactly what it said but it was on the subject of the federal budget and the means of reducing it. I read it and was in general agreement, but I thought some of the arguments were specious, some of it misinformed, and certain facts inaccurate or misused. It especially denounced welfare programs, some of which I thought desirable in providing for the needy. It was clear that my letter to Dr. Benson about the farm programs had created certain anticipations on his part. I had some tough decisions to make. He apparently planned for me to be a special associate to promote his political programs. I was honored, but could not in good conscience accept such an assignment, because I had so many reservations about his views on government and the manner in which he grounded these views in Scripture. I went back the next day and told him I would be pleased to do as he requested, but I had reservations about certain statements in the pamphlet, which I pointed out. He said, "All right, go ahead," but it was clear he was not too pleased. That was the last request of that sort I received.

It was a bad year for someone in my position. That year the national debate topic was "Resolved: that the United States Government Recognize Communist China." For a time, the topic caused a furor. Certain politically conservative schools, such as the University of Omaha, refused to debate the topic. The official United States policy was adamant against recognition, as were most senators and representatives. This was the McCarthy era and it was dangerous for any public official to come out affirmatively on this topic. In the opinion of many persons this was not a topic open to discussion. Some high-level discussion of the matter went on at Harding. Dr. Benson asked me my opinion before the meeting. I told him I opposed recognition, but I thought it was a debatable topic. It might be that the best way to know what was going on in Peking was recognize the government and openly oppose it in official ways. Dr. Benson considered himself an expert on China, having spent most of the 1920s as a missionary in Canton. Many of his conservative views on government resulted from his observations of the takeover in China. He didn't say much in response to my remarks, other than that he would "let me know." A few days later he called me into his office and said he thought we should debate, but we should do our best to see that the official government position was upheld. If we had a choice of which side to debate, we should always opt for the negative. I told him that in most the tournaments we had to debate an equal number of times on each side. I respected him for his decision. I was afraid it would go the other way, since other college presidents less adamant than he had closed down their debate programs, rather than risk having to take the affirmative side of the question. I think, however, he hoped I would show more enthusiasm for a strong anti-communist line.

My interpretations of Scripture led me to different conclusions on governmental policy than those of Dr. Benson. I was by no means a Niebuhrian but I appreciated several of his positions. Niebuhr himself had by this time become an active critic of Communism. I was probably as anti-communist as Benson, but I was not of the opinion that there was a conspiracy in the United States to the extent alleged by Joseph McCarthy. I believed that on constitutional and biblical grounds, persons should be assumed innocent until proven guilty. I was not, however of Benson's opinion that Christians should adopt the destruction of communism as a major priority. After all, during New Testament times the Roman government practiced polytheism and even atheism, but Paul did not argue for its destruction. Paul, rather, commanded obedience (Romans 13).

In my early years at Harding I was persuaded by Ritchie and Bales that pacifism was the proper Christian position. David Lipscomb had set the course, holding that human government is a rule of evil persons by evil persons. Christians should not involve themselves in civil government, but should give all their allegiance and efforts to the kingdom of God. Before World War II, Benson's 1954 position was, at best, a minority one at Harding. But by the early 1950s Benson had won over James D. Bales and William Font Mattox. Ritchie was sent away, ostensibly to pursue a graduate degree, but also, I think, to defuse his power. To George Benson must go some of the credit for leading Churches of Christ away from detachment from government to active involvement.[1] Benson accepted the first part of Lipscomb's view—that government was evil—referring to the early 1950s government which he viewed as dominated by big-time spenders and legislators who were soft on communism. But he differed in his belief that Christians and others should arise and divest the government of its power.[2]

In 1954, as the result of my introduction to international affairs through forensic activities, I was only a quasi-pacifist, deeply concerned about the erosion of freedoms in the world. Some of my strongest objections to Benson's views had to do with labor rights and welfare legislation. It was clear to me that free enterprise, for Benson, justified the exploitation of laborers in order to generate as much profit as possible for the employer. I could understand how one with little regard for God or Scripture could justify these privileges, but it seemed counter to all the teachings of Scripture to pay minimally and inequitably, or to prevent workers from seeking changes conducive to safer working conditions.

I also questioned Benson's approach to unemployment, the poor, and the parentless. Benson believed that the government should not be involved in these matters at all. To trim the budget—a legitimate enterprise, I thought—he proposed cutting all the social welfare programs. The problem was that these items were a miniscule part of the budget at that time, and cutting them out would accomplish little. The best way to cut the budget, I thought, was to cut military spending. Benson thought the military might be able to operate on less money, but he wasn't for meaningful cuts. I didn't object to private support for the needy, since the prophets called for it. But Benson never showed much interest in private benevolence to replace governmental support. His main concern was to get the federal government out of it. I was by no means a "social gospeler," but I did think that the government had as much business, if the prophets were to be believed, relieving the cries of the hungry, as in creating unnecessary military buildups. Isaiah's charge to the nation of Israel was, "Learn to do good, seek justice, rescue the oppressed, defend the orphan, plead for the widow" (1:17). With James P. Sanders, I had come to believe that our hermeneutical rules about the Old Testament had led us to deny some of the basic biblical teachings about public and private responsibilities toward those without privilege.

We had no theatre professor in 1954-55. The decision was for each of the three speech teachers to direct a play, and mine was to be last. This was because I would be through with debate by the time we were into the thick of the play. I struggled over what to produce, since I was not too familiar with theatre repertoire. I wanted to do something current, but that posed difficulties because of the inclusion of moral outlooks with which I did not agree. In fact, I could not, in good conscience, direct some of the plays I had seen at Harding. At first, a play called "Barefoot in Athens" appealed to me. I could draw upon my classical background. It was basically about Socrates. But the more I thought about the play, the more I concluded it would not go over, since not that many people at Harding knew much about ancient Greece. I decided, too, that the play was not particularly powerful.

Since I had worked on early American sermons and read a good deal of Jonathan Edwards and his time, I became interested in Arthur Miller's "The Crucible," set during the witch trials in New England. I was attracted to it because of its religious setting. For me, it offered a forum to challenge the religious witch hunts Harding had experienced at the hands Foy E. Wallace, Jr., and his cohorts in regard to premillennialism. Such efforts had been soundly criticized a few years earlier, but I was aware that the play was a tract for the times. It was overtly anti-McCarthyist, but artfully so: one had to bring his own insights and views on McCarthyism to the play. I was also aware that Arthur Miller had been accused of being a Communist, but many others in theatre had likewise been accused. I discussed the play with Evan Ulrey. I think he read it. I planned to cut various scenes dealing with immorality, and I indicated these in the copy I provided. He said he did not see any problem with me directing it. Both he and I were naive.

When the play was publicly announced I received a visit from J.D. Bales. He asked why I had decided to produce it. I gave him my reasons, but he was not impressed. He asked if I knew that Miller was a communist, and mentioned talking with Dr. Benson about the possibility of calling off the play. I told him I didn't mind for myself, but I felt that to do so would be unfair to the students who had put so much time into rehearsals. I was later informed that the play would go on. Bales, however, insisted that I must have had much communist pressure put on me to produce it. When I told him I was not contacted by anyone, he replied that I was, nevertheless, a communist dupe. It was obvious by the next week that my credibility had declined considerably with those who either suspected or affirmed the great communist conspiracy. A number of faculty and several students at Harding were of that frame of mind.

Dean Sears assumed that Benson had informed me that my contract would not be renewed. When I told Sears such was not the case, he was very apologetic and told me he would be pleased to write an outstanding recommendation so I could find another job. I think he was very sincere and he did as he promised. Evan Ulrey, in contrast, berated my teaching and said I dressed shoddily. I was as much hurt by his charges as anything else. I did not talk with Benson, but I doubted that what Ulrey told me had much to do with the decision to release me. Why he felt called upon to be so critical puzzled me, but I remembered that Ulrey didn't want me as a professor to begin with. Some ten years later, after he had been engaged in a battle with Benson, he apologized, and said that I had handled it very well under difficult circumstances. My parents were very upset, since they were admirers of Benson. They felt that I was at fault and had embarrassed both myself and them. They saw it differently a few years later, though, when Dr. Benson terminated my mother from a position at Harding Academy.

I returned to Iowa that summer to work on my dissertation. I was told I could teach at Iowa again for the coming year and the church would be glad to have me preach. But I explored the prospects for teaching. It appeared that two situations were possible: Doane College in Crete, Nebraska, and the University of Dubuque. I interviewed at Doane and was impressed with their offer, but I deferred acceptance until I could interview at Dubuque. The offer at Dubuque was not quite as good, but it was closer to Iowa City and only sixty miles from Dorothy's parents. Another major consideration was that the Dubuque Presbyterian Theological Seminary was connected with the University. It provided a library which would be of much help as I worked on the homilies of Basil the Great. I decided to go to Dubuque.

The University of Dubuque was a congenial place. It was founded in 1852 and had great traditions. Among the Presbyterians it was considered moderately conservative, both theologically and in regard to student rules. It was not politically conservative, unlike a few of the more than forty small Presbyterian liberal arts colleges—Grove City College in Pennsylvania, for example.

The students in the seminary ran the spectrum from fundamentalist to liberal, but were predominantly moderate. Critical biblical scholarship was the norm, but not such as to upset the fundamentalist students. The full-time seminary professors were all Presbyterians since the seminary was controlled by the General Assembly of the Presbyterian Church. Some relatively well-known scholars taught there. When I arrived, Marcus Barth, son of Karl Barth, was a professor. Other internationally known scholars were Arthur Cochrane, Robert Healy, Charles Carlston, and Donald Bloesch, who was just beginning his career. The seminary was founded in 1901 and had about one hundred twenty students.

The college of the University had four hundred fifty students. It was a mix between high achievers and mediocre students. The majority of the faculty were either Presbyterian or Methodist, with a few Baptists and an occasional person from the Church of Christ. Jack Boyd, later of Abilene Christian, was choir director there for a time in the 1960s. The balance of Methodists and Presbyterians was by design: the school sought and secured funds from private Methodist sources over the years. The regulations for the college students were not too much different from those at Harding: the rules prohibited alcohol consumption and smoking in buildings, provided curfews for both men and women, had restrictions in regard to visiting in rooms, and eschewed public displays of affection. Dances, however, were sponsored on campus. We lived next door to the president, in a house provided by the university for which we paid thirty-five dollars monthly rent, heating and water included. The pay was the same as at Harding, but the housing made it a somewhat better situation. President

Gaylord Couchman and his wife were very approachable but not by way of seeking friendship. He had been a Presbyterian minister before becoming president. The dean, Leo Nussbaum, grew up a Mennonite in Indiana but had become a Presbyterian. We struck up a friendship and even kept their cat for a year while he was on leave as a Fulbright lecturer in India. He was later dean at Austin College in Sherman, Texas, and ended his career as president of Coe College in Cedar Rapids, Iowa.

John Knox Coit, son of a Georgia Presbyterian minister, soon became my best friend. John took his doctorate in philosophy at New York University, writing on Reinhold Niebuhr. He was also knowledgeable in theology. We often discussed ancient philosophy as it impinged upon Basil's sermons, as well as theological topics, both ancient and modern. He was an excellent source for bibliography in philosophy and theology. Unfortunately, he did not know much about patristics, and the seminary had no professor who specialized in patristics. Charles Carlston was of considerable help in New Testament matters.

Dorothy and I felt warmly welcomed at Dubuque. She later took a couple of classes and enjoyed them. At times, when I buried myself in the dissertation, she packed the girls in the car and went to Blanchardville to visit her parents for a day or two, or sometimes a week. We loved both the Iowa summers and winters. In winter, the girls and I sledded around our house and on campus. A place for ice skating was erected in a nearby park and I took the girls there to skate while I sat and watched. In summers we went on picnics to Eagle Point Park, high on a bluff above the Mississippi. We could look down and see the barges laced together on the river, pushed by a tug. At the upper end of the park we could view the locks and see the boats going through. Some of the barges were so long they had to unleash them and take them through half at a time. In the fall there were colorful maples, especially to the north, along the river. In spring the balmy weather signaled the return of flowers and the planting of corn, the perennial Iowa crop. The commonly repeated cliches in regard to the corn, were: "Knee high by the fourth of July," and "On a warm summer night, if you go out in the middle of the corn field, you can hear it growing."

I was well received on campus as a teacher, a religious person, and a director of forensics. We had two speech teachers and I was chairman. I focused on public speaking, debate, and speech correction. The other professor taught theatre, oral interpretation, and directed the plays. We both taught several sections of speech fundamentals. We offered a speech major and graduated a few students each year. Our forensic team did especially well after the first year. The second year we took four teams to the Bradley tournament in Peoria, Illinois. Each team debated four times and we won thirteen of sixteen debates, with one team going undefeated.

The first year the seminary was without a speech teacher, so I served as the speech critic for the homiletics course. The homiletics professor was a Presbyterian minister named Kenneth Berger, a converted Jew who sometimes made interesting remarks about his early years. He was essentially blind, so my remarks on students' gestures and visual clues were crucial. He had not been trained in homiletics, but had read a few books on the subject. He had several ideas of his own which grew out of his experience and were helpful. I also taught public speaking and radio and television speaking for ministers. Here was my first and only time ever to be a professor of preaching in a ministerial training situation, even though this is what I aspired to be from about 1950 to 1964. God moves in mysterious ways.

In the course of my four years teaching at Dubuque I heard several student sermons, attended seminary chapel, attended the college chapel which met twice a week, and heard Presbyterian sermons on various special occasions. I served for two or three years on the chapel committee, so I heard various behind-the-scenes reflections on the sermons. What impressed me most about Presbyterian sermons was that they focused much more explicitly on the biblical text than the sermons I had heard in Churches of Christ to date. That destroyed one of my biases, namely, that we were the only religious group around who really preached the Bible. The Presbyterians did not quote as much from the Bible as we, and in that sense we may have put more Bible into sermons. But their preaching, going back to Calvin himself, was basically exposition of the selected texts. Every sermon had at least two texts, one from the Old Testament and one from the New. This was a second difference I noted: much more preaching focused on the Old Testament. I found this refreshing, because I heard sermons on Old Testament materials with which I was not familiar. This, too, went back to Calvin, who divided the covenants differently than we. He began the covenant of grace, not with the coming of Jesus Christ, but with the promise of God to Abraham. He therefore spoke of the older covenant of grace, that is, the Old Testament, and the newer covenant, the New Testament. For persons of the reformed heritage, therefore, Christians are nurtured by the Old Testament as much as the New. I didn't hear too many sermons emphasizing particular Presbyterian doctrines and this was intentional, since the student body was mixed, including several Roman Catholics, despite the fact that there were two Roman Catholic Colleges in town: Clark and Loras.

My experience at Dubuque did change certain ways of thinking about the Scripture and its interpretation. In the first place I saw the need to highlight Scripture more in sermons by undertaking a serious explanation of a specific text. In this manner Scriptures would be employed in context, rather than without context —the usual practice of those who preach topically, quoting a series Scriptures in order to bolster their arguments. Sometimes, in fact, such extra-contextual preaching cites biblical texts having little to do with what the speaker's argument presupposes. If we are to be a people of the book and live under it, then we must let the Scripture judge our presuppositions, rather than using it willy-nilly to give support to preconceived notions. Living under the judgment of the Word is much more likely to happen in textual preaching. Preachers can stand under the text and still preach topically if they do their homework and avoid using Scripture out of context. But serious textual preaching has built-in safeguards that encourage the preacher to set forth what the text really means rather than what the preacher hopes it means. Furthermore, one is more likely to declare the whole counsel of God by developing texts from his Word, rather than topical sermons which refute some "false doctrine" heard or observed by the preacher. What makes anyone think that a proper diet for God's people consists of exposing the inadequacies of religious perspectives—whether external or internal? Rather, what is needed is a recitation of the mighty acts of God, a call to a life of discipline and devotion, and a proclamation of the empowerment of the Holy Spirit. "For the kingdom of God is not food and drink but righteousness and peace and joy in the Holy Spirit" (Romans 14:17). This is not to say that I thought Presbyterians had all the good traits and we only the bad. They too, had their favorite Scriptures, their canons-within-a-canon, which skewed the biblical faith.

The second question I began to raise was the way in which we had essentially ruled out the Old Testament as the word of God for Christians. An incident which happened at the church in Dubuque is illustrative of this attitude. In a Wednesday night adult class we studied I and II Kings. When we got to II Kings 2:23-25, we reflected upon the story of Elisha and the boys who derided him, as "baldhead," whereupon Elisha cursed them in the name of the Lord and two female bears came out of the woods and mauled (the KJV translates it "killed") forty-two boys. We puzzled over whether this outcome was worthy either of God or his prophet. Finally, an older member who was visiting for a few months from Tennessee said, "Let's not worry about it even though it is troublesome. After all, it is in the Old Testament." For him, the Old Testament was God's word in a different, inferior sense, as compared with the New. It occurred to me that when we did study the Old Testament, it actually spoke to and nourished the church, despite our theology to the contrary. I remembered I Timothy 3:16, 17: "All Scripture is inspired by God and is useful for teaching, for reproof, for correction, and for training in righteousness, so that everyone who belongs to God may be proficient, equipped for every good work." That Scripture, it dawned on me, is explicitly about the Old Testament, not the New. It is a charge to Christians who live under the Old Testament. Our hermeneutic in regard to the Old Testament required revision. It was a few years, however, until I had a clearer vision of how we might depict the authority of the Old Testament for Christians.

The Church of Christ in Dubuque

The Church of Christ in Dubuque was founded in June 1955, two months before we arrived in August. When it appeared that we might be moving to Dubuque, I contracted the preacher, Jerry Loutenzenhizer, and discussed with him our coming. He and his wife Pat were cordial, but somewhat reserved. It may have been that they didn't want to get their hopes up, in case we didn't come. Later we found out that Jerry was not one to show great enthusiasm on any matter. He, too, had been raised in a German family where exhibitionism was discouraged. But it seemed that he also had some reservations about where I was coming from, since, at that time, he was somewhat new in the faith and a stickler for the traditions with which he was familiar. I think he may have been apprehensive that, because of my preaching experience and education, I might be overly critical. I understood how those fears might be warranted and tried to encourage him and stay in the background.

The church in Dubuque was started because of the uncle of one of the members, an elder of a church in Compton, California. That congregation trained Jerry Loutenzenhizer, moved the Loutenzenhizers to Dubuque and fully supported them. They also sent their preacher, Hugh I. Shira, to Dubuque to preach in a gospel meeting, which was advertised in the *Dubuque Telegraph-Herald.* The result was that two or three other families were discovered, one of whom was a medical doctor from Ohio named John Moberly, who was from a conservative Christian Church background. His wife Juanita was from a Kentucky family of long standing in the Restoration Movement. Another member family owned a jewelry store in Lancaster, Wisconsin, thirty-five miles north. A single man, Germaine (Jim) Lockwood, who had worked as an engineer for Chrysler and who held an M.S. from their institute, was stationed at the Savanna Army Depot, several miles down the Mississippi. The Loutenzenhizers had also learned that the Bill Totty family was moving to Dubuque. Bill was the son of W.L. Totty, long-time preacher for the Garfield Avenue congregation in Indianapolis, which at that time had a membership of above six hundred and was the largest Church of Christ in the state of Indiana. He had taken a position with a loan company whose headquarters were in Dubuque. So, by time we were all there in late September, there were twenty to twenty-five of us. We met on Sunday mornings in a church building which was used by other people. We met Sunday nights and Wednesday nights in homes, moving from place to place.

The church did well under the circumstances. Soon two couples in their late forties had moved to Savanna to work at the Savanna Ordinance Depot.

They had been members in Alabama. Because of the presence of the Tottys, the Garfield Avenue church in Indianapolis became interested in the work. They encouraged us to build a building and proposed that if we would buy a lot they would give us enough for a down payment on a building and we could secure a bank loan for the rest. We located a lot which, though too small to provide any parking, was in an excellent location on the corner of the major east-west highway, U. S. 20, and the major avenue, University, which meandered around the rim of the city. The Tottys knew some builders from Portland, Tennessee, who came to do the construction. My father-in-law and brother-in-law did the electrical work. We were able to construct the building at a very reasonable cost.

About the time we initiated the building plans, the Loutenzenhizers moved to Marshalltown, Iowa. There was no deep friction in the congregation, but certain tensions had begun to build. With Jerry gone, I was asked to preach. I was more seasoned now and with my work in homiletics and debate I was especially capable of presenting sermons people could at least follow. Also, on occasion, I could generate a bit of fire. I talked with Couchman and Nussbaum about preaching full-time. They said they didn't mind me filling in on an interim arrangement, but I should not become the permanent minister. Noble Robinson liked me because I took so little pay—ten dollars per week. But then, he thought I should have not have taken anything. He didn't know, of course, that I was contributing more than that each week. Students and professors from the university frequently came to hear me preach. Donald Bloesch, with whom I had become fairly well-acquainted, came to hear me a few times on

Sunday night. I was somewhat puzzled as to why, since he was more evangelical than most of the university professors as well as the Presbyterian churches in town. He could easily have located an independent evangelical church to attend. I think perhaps he was trying to determine what our fellowship was really about.

By this time, through talking with seminary professors, I became better acquainted with some of the major biblical commentators of the twentieth century. I frequently checked commentaries out of the library. I seldom quoted the commentators, however. That was not typical in a tradition which only quoted the Bible and works more than a hundred years old, such as Henry, Clark, Barnes, Johnson, Lipscomb, Thayer, and McGarvey. I pursued my standard ways of visiting, and published a bulletin.

Within a year we employed a preacher: Harding Lowry, from Winchester, Kentucky. He had been a high school principal, and had preached regularly but not full-time. He was aggressive and, in general, Bill Totty's type of man. He came with great confidence that he could cope with every situation and build a large congregation. He was a hard worker, but tended to spin his wheels because he had almost no insight into or interest in the cultural differences between Kentucky and Iowa. Whatever the value of our fellowship's interpretation of the Scripture, we had essentially no hermeneutic rules for translating the message into the lives of people of different backgrounds until we became more culturally diverse as a people. At that time, we had few clues that communication is culturally conditioned and that we needed to "become all things to all men." In fact, we characterized efforts to adapt preaching to different audiences as "soft" preaching. The preacher should tell it like it is, we insisted, which implied, of course, that Arkansas-Texas-Tennessee-style preaching was God's own style!

Lowry's gaffes ran the gamut from the very simple to the very complex. For example, he argued that the major step we could take to draw outsiders to the building would be to have air conditioning. This in a region where air conditioning might be needed three Sundays out of the year. In Kentucky, it was no doubt the case that some people attended church because of air conditioning. At that time, people in the upper midwest resisted air conditioning. In Kentucky it was also standard for the men of the congregation to gather in front of the building, do their smoking, greet attendees, and decide on last-minute arrangements as to who did what. Lowry encouraged a similar strategy in Dubuque, even though this practice was unknown in Iowa, where people made their way to their seats as soon as possible. The result was that in winter, since we had a small vestibule, visitors had difficulty getting in the door, since they were embarrassed to push their way through. I made some remarks about this and other matters, but Lowry couldn't see my point and I didn't get support from other quarters. I think he decided I was a troublemaker, if not a liberal.

Lowry represented what I perceived to be a new and increasing breed of preachers. He was an educated person, having a master's degree in educational administration. He, however, had almost no biblical training, in the classical grammatico-historical-literary sense. He was a modern, kindly person, and though he held to traditional positions, did not preach the old hellfire-

and-brimstone sermons against denominational error.

I was brought up to believe that we in the Churches of Christ were unafraid of the truth, which should have freed us to read and listen to anyone. That should also have enabled us to be critical, as well as appreciative, of our heritage. It seemed to be Lowry's perspective, though, that we had all the truth we needed: we had cornered the market. What we needed to do, he thought, was to find suitable channels for attractive marketing of the truth we possessed. He felt threatened when additional knowledge or insight entered our discussions.

Before Lowry came to Dubuque, the members, upon learning that I knew something of the history of our movement, asked me to speak on that history on Sunday nights for a month. Even though Lowry had arrived in the meantime and had preached for a month or so, it was agreed that I go ahead. He probably had reservations, but apparently felt that he should not object, being new on the scene. He therefore encouraged members to attend and bring outsiders. The Sunday night attendance almost doubled. The first night I spoke on the four wings of our movement's beginnings: the James O'Kelly-Methodist Virginians, the Abner Jones-Elias Smith-Baptist New Englanders, the Barton W. Stone-Presbyterian Ohioans and Kentuckians, and the Thomas and Alexander Campbell-Presbyterian Pennsylvanians. I made no effort to glorify these early leaders or to make them conform to our views on Christianity and the church. I had heard it said by people such as Mattox that our forefathers were forthright and honest, but sometimes wrong. Our difference as a movement lay in the inbuilt principle that our perspectives and approaches are always subject to change as we learn more about God through his Word.

Lowry apparently hadn't heard the views of some of these forefathers who welcomed Holy Spirit conversion, quarterly communion, and associations of preachers. His alarm surfaced in his remarks after the presentation. In effect, he attempted to disassociate us from our own history, and argued that we now stood upon the Bible and in the truth, whatever our forefathers believed. He tried to make it clear that the Churches of Christ in the 1950s were what New Testament churches should be, no more and no less.

I continued with the study, but as the result of Lowry's anxiety, received only lukewarm appreciation from members of the congregation. It dawned on me that a new day had arrived, in which our preachers were more interested in "marching for the Master" than in searching for truth, whatever the source. We were approaching what I considered an unfortunate new era, in which some among us feared new insights, either about our past or from the Scripture. We were moving toward a hermeneutic which held scriptural interpretation valid only when it supported positions which we currently held.

Basil, Homiletics, and Hermeneutics

Most of my thoughts about hermeneutics centered in my dissertation, since that was the project which demanded all my extra time in those years. I worked on it especially hard during vacations and in the summer. I could not do much during the school year because of the teaching load, committee tasks and various other responsibilities. I sometimes despaired ever finishing, but I persisted. It always seemed, as a semester wound down, that it took me a week to regain the prospective I had enjoyed when I had to leave off. I felt like Sisyphus: never quite getting the stone to the top, and standing discouraged as it rolled back down the hill. It took me about two years to complete the translations, though I did other work at the same time, such as reading philosophy and theology.

The matter of interest here is Basil's hermeneutics. Basil, because of his training, was familiar with the classical manner of interpreting Homer's poems. An honored tradition had developed of interpreting documents, not so much according to the meaning of the document's words or any insight into the context of the time, but according to views of the later period. A literal sense was recognized—that the words, grammar, and etymology disclosed meaning. But this literal meaning came to be perceived as an inferior understanding of a text. It was thought both primitive and petty in philosophical and theological perspective. The deeper meaning of the text had to do, in ascending order, with morals, ethics, spirituality, and philosophy.

These approaches to interpretation had already influenced syncretistic forms of Judaism before the time of the New Testament. Allegory, of which this was a form, was, of course, not unknown to the Old Testament: the allegory of the vine (Isaiah 5:1-10), and the eagle (Ezekiel 17:1-10) serve as examples. These are not, however, allegories on previous texts, and allegory is not a major feature of the Old Testament. Paul undertook a lengthy allegory on the Genesis narrative of Sarah and Isaac, and Hagar and Ishmael (Galatians 4:21-31), and he certainly employed a use of the account which exceeded the literal one. No amount of spade work into the vocabulary, etymology, grammar, or history of Genesis could support, in a literal way, Paul's conclusions. Does Paul think that his allegorical employment of this text was endemic to—contained in—the text? Or does he view it as an allegory which is useful only for illustrative purposes? In other words, did he not really assume that his allegory was what the text meant? One suspects he did not. Another example is I Corinthians 10:3: "For they drank from the spiritual rock that followed them, and the rock was Christ."

A Hellenistic Jew by the name of Philo, a contemporary of Christ, borrowed heavily from the ways in which Homer was interpreted. A native of Alexandria, Philo hoped to reconcile the Old Testament with Greek philosophy which, in his case, meant a version of Platonism, best described as middle Platonism. Philo distinguished two forms of allegory: the physical, which has to do with God and nature, and the ethical, which has to do with human duties. For example, when Philo discussed the story of Moses and the burning bush (Exodus 3:1-6) his question was, what explanation can be given for the fact that the bush flamed but was not burned? How can an intelligent philosopher accept this as factual when it defies his experience? Not all ancients were gullible: they weighed and sifted stories of extraordinary magnitude and rejected those which seemed credulous. Philo offered an explanation which incorporated philosophical categories. He proposed that the bush be scrutinized from the standpoint of accidents and essence, a good Greek distinction. For example, the accidents of a rose bush are the height, the leaf style, and the color of the roses. The essence of the rose bush is that inner feature which all rose bushes share. Philo argued that it was the accidents of the bush that burned, but the essence did not, and therefore the bush was not consumed. To the objection that humans cannot separate accidents and essence and burn one and not the other, Philo answered that what is not possible for humans is possible for God. Philo's explanation is an interesting one. It offered a perspective from which a Hellenistic philosopher might, in good conscience, contemplate the story. We, however, I am sure, have severe reservations as to whether the text presupposed such sophistication, and in fact, whether the explanation is more believable than the direct meaning.

Origen (188-254 A.D.), also of Alexandria, developed an even more layered hermeneutic. In fact, he carried it so far that his method of hermeneutics was condemned by his contemporary bishops. Origen suggested a fourfold categorization: the literal, the moral or ethical, the spiritual or anagogical, and the allegorical. For example, the city of Jerusalem meant (1) literally, the actual Palestinian Jewish city, (2) allegorically, the church, (3) tropologically, the human soul, and (4) anagogically, the Christian's heavenly home.[3] At the lowest level is literal interpretation, suitable for those who are untrained and cannot fathom the higher levels—in other words, the ignorant multitudes. It is by rational activity that one enters into the presence of God. Interpretation, therefore, moves through the levels to the allegorical, which is the highest. The problem with such an approach is that any philosophical system could be plugged into the equation. In the final analysis, then, the original biblical presupposition always becomes the most primitive and undesirable one.

My basic objection is that the Scripture, for Origen and his ilk, serves as a springboard for whatever one wishes to embrace, rather than as a means of judging the ways of God and obedience to him. By this method Origin turned his back on the true reality of God. Biblically, the greatest reality is that God is one who acts lovingly on behalf of his people. His highest self-disclosure is not an idea, or a profound philosophical concept. Rather, God reveals himself through his acts in history. History is, therefore, not the lowest form of revelation, but the highest. Interpretation which struggles with the literal—the historical—is probing the most profound aspect of God.

Hermeneutical battles in the third and fourth century church pitted Alexandrian interpretation against the Antiochene. Alexandrian hermeneutics moved from the bodily, or literal level, upward to the spiritual. The Antiochene, in contrast, focused upon careful textual criticism and philological and historical studies. Though the Antiochenes were especially interested in the literal meaning of the text, they did not eschew spiritual meanings, just as the Alexandrians did not ignore textual and philological matters. In fact, Origen was a noted textual critic, and churchmen like Basil did not avoid Hellenized interpretations, despite certain contentions to the contrary.

Basil the Great (329-379) was born in Caesarea of Cappadocia. A rhetor, later churchman and bishop, Basil was born of wealthy parents who owned land in both Cappadocia and Pontus. He received his early education from his father, a noted teacher of rhetoric, his mother Emmelia, and his grandmother, Macrina. After his father's death he was educated in Caesarea (c. 345-47), and then Constantinople (c. 348-50) where he studied rhetoric and philosophy, probably under the famous rhetorician Libanius. In about 350 he joined his friend Gregory of Nazianzus in Athens, where he continued his studies of many subjects, pursuing rhetoric with Proehaeresius and Himerius. Leaving Athens about 355, Basil returned to Caesarea where he taught rhetoric for about two years. His interests turned more and more to religion. He embarked upon a journey to Egypt and other lands to visit renowned ascetics and monasteries. Upon returning he joined his mother and sister Macrina in a semi-monastic life at the family estate in Annesi in Pontus. He was active in the life of the church, establishing monasteries throughout the region. He was ordained a priest (c. 364), and after the death of Eusebius (c. 370) was elected bishop of Caesarea, with responsibility for most of Cappadocia. He was effective as a bishop, both in marshaling the people to benevolence, and in promoting doctrinal and political unity in the east, and between the east and west. Generally orthodox in views, he allied himself with Athanasius, Gregory Nazianzus, and his brother, Gregory of Nyssa, in opposing the Sabellians, the Arians, and the Anomians.

As a younger man, Basil, perhaps through the influence of Gregory Thaumaturgus, a friend of his family, became interested in Origen and, with Gregory of Nazianzus, compiled an anthology of his writings, which they titled *Philocalia*. But though Basil learned much from Origen he sometimes reacted against his biblical interpretation, leaning more toward the Antiochene school. In the last homily on the Hexaemera he stated, "And I hearing grass, think grass; and hearing plant, and a fish, a wild beast, and a domestic animal, and all things as the Scripture reveal, I take them as they are stated." Basil's exegetical skills are preserved in his sermons, of which forty-nine are extant: nine on the Hexaemera, seventeen on the Psalms, and twenty-four on miscellaneous subjects. In these sermons Basil, along with his Jewish and Christian predecessors, developed discourse unaccounted for in Greco-Roman rhetoric, since the structure and invention often were determined by the features of a privileged text—the Scriptures. In his exposition Basil drew upon the Scriptures, comparisons and contrasts with Greek philosophers, and common experiences.

The Antiochene school arose specifically as a reaction against the hermeneutics of Origen. It included the renowned Chrysostom, and the greatest exegete of the early church, Theodore of Mopsuestia. These men tried to take seriously the Semitic backgrounds of Scripture. Theodore, through his studies, decided, unlike Origen, that the message of Scripture is not the great ideas of a Platonic world vision, but rather a unified presentation of God's redemptive activity through time, which made it crucial to understand the Scripture in its historical context. Furthermore, prophetic utterances cannot be understood as independent messages. Rather, their meaning is disclosed through fulfillment in a later historical setting, the Antiochenes held.

From writing this dissertation I discovered not only the problems inherent in Origen's conceptual, non-historical approach to Scripture, I learned that, with all of us, the tendency is to interpret the Scriptures from the preunderstanding of our own era. We may fault Origen as much as we please for his efforts at Platonizing the Scriptures, but the major intellectual winds of his time wafted a Platonic dust over everything. So it has been down through history. When Aristotle was rediscovered in medieval times, exegetes proceeded to interpret the Scriptures with his presuppositions as a backdrop. The Reformation took up the renaissance emphasis on the recovery of ancient times and interpreted the Scripture from that perspective. In our own heritage, we were children of the Scottish Enlightenment which drew so heavily upon the British empiricism of John Locke. What I learned was that it is almost impossible for us not to interpret Scripture in the light of what the Germans call the *zeitgeist*—the spirit of the times. Rather than deny that we do so, we need to readily accept the fact that, in some measure, we all proceed as did Origen. Not that we situate allegorical interpretation as the highest good, but that we attempt to interpret the Scriptures according to the dictates of the prevailing philosophy of our times. Once we admit this, we may be freed to raise the question of how biblical presuppositions run counter to our own. The problem, of course, is that our assumptions are so much a part of us we do not even think to question them, and if we do realize we have such assumptions, we often presume them biblical. Once we admit that we, like humankind throughout the ages, have certain unconscious suppositions which are products solely of our place and time, we are finally in a position—if we are interested in doing so—to really live under the authority and judgment of the Scriptures.

One More Time Around: Plans for Seminary

My thoughts turned once again to seminary. I was now almost thirty. In Dubuque, two more children were born, Joel in 1956 and Adele in 1958. My family and most of my friends thought I had been in school long enough and that I was demented, with the size of our family, to even think about another graduate degree. But I had encouragement from friends in the theological faculty in Dubuque, and from Dr. Baird at Iowa. It was my view, and I think that of most people at the time, that the premier American seminary was Union Theological Seminary in New York. If I was able to attend seminary I might as well go for the best. Dr. Baird certainly approved, since that was his alma mater. He took special pains to see that they give me a good scholarship. I was not concerned, justifiably or not, if I would be accepted. The question was locating a position of some sort from which I could support my family.

I had two possibilities. One was to teach, and I explored that first. Through the placement services of the University of Iowa and the Speech Association of America I checked out every job opening within commuting distance of Union. Finally, I was asked to come to Chicago and interview with the president and dean of Paterson State in New Jersey. They had seen my credentials and seemed impressed with them. We had a long discussion about my interest in attending seminary, which, to them, seemed a waste of time. I did not get the job.

The second possibility was to work for a church. I thought it best, since I wanted to complete the program as rapidly as possible, to be an associate minister for some church, rather than the main preaching minister. I had met Alfred Palmer in Iowa, when he was preaching at Jefferson. He now preached on Staten Island, so I wrote and asked if he would welcome an associate. He said he would. The question now was raising the money for it. I thought I could raise the money, but the problem was finding the time, in view of completing the dissertation. Meanwhile, I was admitted to Union and given a full tuition scholarship.

About this time I read in the *Christian Chronicle* that Everett Ferguson was leaving Melrose, Massachusetts, where he had been an associate minister, and was going to Villanova, Pennsylvania, to be dean of Northeastern Christian Junior College, which was opening in the fall of 1959. He was completing a doctorate in church history at Harvard. I had never heard of Everett Ferguson before, but I decided to write him to see if the church there was looking for his replacement. I was not particularly interested in going to Harvard at that stage, but if I could find a job it would be more feasible than trying to raise money to work at Staten Island. Everett wrote back a nice letter, saying that the church there might consider a replacement, but the money wasn't that much. He had another suggestion. He proposed that I write the church in Natick, Massachusetts, which was looking for a preacher. Pat Harrell, their minister, was also going to Northeastern Christian as chair of the Bible department. He had taken a B.D. (STB) from Harvard and was completing a doctorate in theology from Boston University. I wrote the church at Natick and after a bit of correspondence they decided to employ me, sight unseen. In true Yankee fashion, they did not wish to waste money by having me come out for an interview. With the job came a three-bedroom house. The salary was four hundred dollars a month, which was somewhat standard at that time for churches of one hundred members or less. A factor in the decision was J. Harold Thomas, who was the first president of Northeastern. He had been involved in establishing the church in Natick, so they asked him about me. He said he had never met me, but had heard of me, possibly through John Patrick Fogarty, who had moved to Davenport, Iowa, from Bangor, Maine, and had worked with Harold. He told them they should employ me. Indeed, the Lord moves in mysterious ways, his wonders to perform. It is not always easy to obtain a position, even when recommended by friends. But in this case, it was at the recommendation of strangers!

I immediately applied to Harvard Divinity School. Everett suggested that I write Harold Forshey, who had been admitted to the B.D. program for that fall, and learn from him the details of applying at Harvard. I had met Harold, since he was a debater at Abilene Christian. He had come to Searcy in 1955, with Rex Kyker as his debate coach, and we had staged some Harding-Abilene Christian debates. The Abilene team then came to Arkansas for a tournament at Arkansas State in Conway. Harold was very helpful, but thought it would be impossible for me to be admitted to Harvard at this late date. He had had to wait a year to enter. I was not discouraged by that. A year to get acclimated to New England and the church would probably be good. Only a short time after applying, however, I was admitted and given a partial tuition scholarship. All the guys around Boston who were either going to Harvard or who had attended there were amazed.

Not knowing much about it, I was not that impressed. I tended to think that whatever God wanted would happen. I had placed it in his hands.

---

[1] See Michael W. Casey, *Saddlebags, City Streets & Cyberspace: A History of Preaching in the Churches of Christ* (Abilene: ACU Press, 1995) 91-99.

[2] See L. Edward Hicks, *Sometimes in the Wrong, But Never in Doubt: George S. Benson and the Education of the New Religious Right* (Knoxville: The University of Tennessee Press, 1994) 1-22.

[3] Karlfried Froelich, *Biblical Interpretation in the Early Church* (Philadelphia: Fortress Press, 1984) 28. Cf. John Cassian in Conferences XIV. 8, in about 420 A. D.

7
Larger Contexts for Interpretation: 1959-1962

In August 1959, Dorothy, Suzanne, and Eloise watched as I was hooded in commencement ceremonies at the Iowa Memorial Fieldhouse. Dorothy had typed the final draft of the dissertation. Dr. Hitchcock believed that one revised up the last minute, and I did. We had a large double desk. I revised on one side, Dorothy sat facing me, typing on the other side. Dorothy had to do an original and three carbon copies. By the rules, it was to be perfect copy. We turned out about thirty pages a day for over a week, working twelve to fifteen hours a day. This was only possible because we were in a foster parent program for unwed mothers in which a girl lived with us for the last two months of her pregnancy. Fortunately, the one at that time was very helpful and she managed to keep four children clothed, fed, and busy.

In early September 1959 Dorothy's brother Orville drove over in his Chevrolet station wagon from Blanchardville. We rented a twelve-foot U-Haul trailer and packed his wagon, the trailer, and the trunk of our Nash Ambassador. The church in Natick said they would give us three hundred dollars for moving expenses, which dictated that our move was a do-it-yourself affair. We said goodbye to whomever was around at the university and headed for Blanchardville, where we spent the night. Dorothy's father, in particular, thought this relocation to Massachusetts was the worst of moves. Not only was I going back to poverty wages just as I received my Ph.D., but I was taking his daughter and his grandchildren off to a far country. It didn't help that he had overheard a conversation in which I mentioned that I was approached about a position at Eastern Illinois University which would double the Dubuque salary. After some tears all around, we got in the cars the next morning and headed east. Orville and his wife Fern volunteered to go with us because they had been interested in visiting New England for some time. They now had a reason.

We drove up to the preacher's house the day after Labor Day. I went to John Hamilton's home, according to instructions, for the key to our house and information. He was very helpful, but definitely a Bostonian. I had not met many, so I knew right away that we might face a bit of culture shock. We also knew we were in a different world when the neighbor, a fireman, drove up as we were starting to unload. He said, "Let me park my car in the garage and I will help you," but with the short, nasal "a" characteristic of New Englanders, it sounded a little to my midwestern ears like he had said, "let me pack my cat in the grash." Nevertheless, we got settled in. The house was comfortable and we were pleased with it because it was roomy, light and airy. It had a partial, unfinished basement which was an excellent place for my desk and therefore became a "study." In the summer it was cool, and warm in the winter because the furnace was there, which also kept it dry. Members of the congregation loved the house because of the large fieldstone fire place in the living room, the internal beveled-glass doors, and a tremendous oak tree in the back yard which was something of a community monument. We weren't as impressed with the fireplace, the glass, or the tree, but we didn't say anything since it was apparent that we had some things to learn about New Englanders. We discovered later that older, primitive house features, such as the fireplace, were highly prized. We just thought it looked rather crude. We liked the glass doors, but we thought a problem might develop should the kids break them. We soon found out, though, that what should have worried us the most was the tree. The cutting of an ancient tree could make headlines in the *Boston Globe*. A couple of the kids climbed into the large oak one day and a neighbor from below came up and told them to climb down, since they might damage the tree.

The next day John Hamilton took me to see the church building. They had mentioned their new building, of which they were very proud and had sent a picture. On the outside it looked very modern: stucco and wood with nice vertical lines. But on going inside I was in for something of a shock. Once inside the entryway, I could look into the unfinished upper portion. Various items were stacked all over, including unattached opera seats lying about in disarray. It was dark, like going into an unlighted warehouse. I was aware that the upstairs was unfinished, but I was unprepared for the scene that loomed before me on the way to basement. At minimum, I thought, a temporary screen of some sort, blocking off the disorder, would give a much better first appearance. The basement also looked only partially finished and rather junky, with items stacked here and there. It was something of a shock. How could people speak in such glowing terms of facilities of this sort? But again, I had something to learn about New Englanders.

We arrived about three weeks before classes began at Harvard. I pledged myself that I would visit in the home of every member of the congregation. I did this for two reasons. First, I needed some grasp of the specific problems faced by the church members if I was to be for them an effective interpreter of the Word. Second, I was somewhat reluctant to receive full-time pay for preaching and at the same time be a full-time student. Through the years I had heard much criticism of ministers who did that. I soon found out it was no problem for the people in Natick. I obtained a church directory from John Hamilton, bought a good, detailed map of the region, and, without making any announcement in church, set out to visit. Dorothy went with me part of the time. Most of the members were amazed that we showed up at their house. They said that Pat Harrell had preached at Natick six years and had never visited them. We learned as time went on that Pat and Nancy, his wife, were something of recluses. The members were also shocked that we had been able to find where they lived. Places were very difficult to locate. Streets curved a great deal because of the many lakes and ponds (in the Midwest we would have called them all lakes) and many roads were dead ends. However, I was something of a map freak, which most New Englanders are not, and we managed to find everyone.

We loved the area. Though eastern New England is densely populated, one does not notice it because of all the trees. Even new developments retain the trees, rather than bulldozing them. It was like living in a small town but having all the shopping conveniences of a large city. We soon discovered, visiting in people's homes, why the haphazard appearance of the church building didn't bother the natives. In fact, a few homes had magazines and newspapers stacked high all over and the host had difficulty arranging places to sit. It also did not take us long to find out why New England was perceived in the midwest as a paradise for antique hunters: New Englanders never threw anything away, so an estate sale there is always an event in the antique world.

I have gone into some detail about our culture shock and the readjusting we had to do. It's important to get some sense of this, because we moved to Natick to interpret the Gospel of Jesus Christ to these people who were different in so many ways from those with whom we had grown up. I myself had learned to adjust in Arkansas, Illinois, and Iowa. I knew New England would be different still, but I was somewhat amazed at the extent of the difference. I think I would have been much better prepared had I visited in advance. As a result, I do not recommend accepting a preaching position sight unseen. I knew we were in for some rough sledding, but I had longed for and waited a long time to obtain a B.D., so I wasn't about to back out at this stage, however great my inner turmoil. I was also convinced that whatever the circumstances, the mission remained: to take seriously the call of Jesus Christ, even in the new circumstances. We were required to be different, whatever the cost, but Christians are always strangers in a foreign land. If they honestly faced the Gospel, these people would have to change, too. But I needed to make sure, when I proclaimed the need for change, that the call came from the Gospel, not from my midwestern upbringing. As is true with everyone, my upbringing was so ingrained that I took its norms to be those of the entire world. It is difficult, even for culturally sensitive Christians, to envision how someone might grow up under circumstances entirely different from theirs and still, without changing culture, be good Christians.

The Church of Christ in Natick

The congregation in Natick commenced in 1943, in the midst of World War II. Unlike other congregations in the Boston area, the reason was not the influx of service persons and industrial workers moving in from the midwest, south, and southwest. After having read an advertisement, John Hamilton started attending the Church of Christ in Brookline, where J. Harold Thomas was preaching. Soon he, Louise, his wife, and June, his daughter, were baptized. A decision was shortly made to hold services on Sunday afternoon in an abandoned building which had been a hose house for the Natick fire department. The building was used for various community functions, including scout meetings. John was a long-time scoutmaster. He secured the building and J. Harold Thomas came out on Sunday afternoons to preach. Later, Tom Paine, who preached occasionally, started coming out on Sunday morning. The Hamiltons knew several people, John and June were both encouragers, and soon several persons had been baptized. In the summer of 1947 a group from Harding came with Andy Ritchie, Jr., held a vacation Bible school, and Andy preached. In that group was my sister Nedra and Bob Gilliam, later professor at Harding, then Pepperdine.

The real growth began with the arrival of John Franklin. John was the sort who believed that what a preacher needs the most is a good pair of shoes. He walked up and down the streets in the vicinity of the building, visiting, teaching, and baptizing. Seven or eight years later, when I duplicated his actions, people still remembered John Franklin. I was always greeted warmly when I said I was minister for the Church of Christ because they remembered John with considerable affection. In his time the church had above a hundred in attendance if all the children, of whom there were many, were counted. At that time about eighty percent of the members, including most of the leaders, were New England natives. The rest were either military or technology workers for some of the firms located on the famous Highway 128. Most of these were well-educated, one man holding a Ph.D. in physics from M.I.T. One of the members was a woman M.D., before there were many such in America, and was director of medical services at Wellesley College.

Though we liked several of the people and most of them readily accepted us, we felt that they needed a challenge to convert their faith into action. Pat Harrell, my predecessor, received part of his income from a church in the southwest. This church wished to discontinue the support when he left. We were informed that we should raise money to make up the difference. The church could pay more, but they wanted to save it to finish their building. People like John Hamilton were of the opinion that the church should not borrow money, and in New England in those days, loans for a church were difficult to secure even if a congregation desired to do so. In late August I visited with some churches in Memphis about support. We stayed with the Don Simes family, since he was then teaching at the Harding Graduate School in Memphis.

When we arrived in Natick, it soon became our conclusion that if people gave as they should, the church could both pay the salary and move ahead fairly rapidly on the building. I agreed to receive less salary than Pat, though the amount was what they had mentioned in offering the job, if they would take up this challenge. I wrote the churches considering support and told them it was not needed. The business meetings of the congregation were open to all members, women often being in the majority. When I made this proposal in a business meeting about a month later, one of the women objected, saying that the congregation there did not believe in asking people for money and that she was uncomfortable with the congregation being requested to increase its giving level. That upset me a bit, but in what I hoped was a nice way, I responded, "Perhaps you don't believe in asking members here, but you aren't hesitant to ask members elsewhere to support your work. These congregations I have been approaching for support have a much higher ratio of giving per member and they are no more capable to give that amount than you." That took her aback. Fortunately a few members said they thought I was right and the church accepted my proposal.

We were willing to grant New Englanders some differences, but we did not believe that regional difference justified spiritual indifference. We were told in correspondence before coming that the church had about eighty members, but on any given Sunday the attendance was fifty to sixty. It was true that New Englanders went out of town on weekends more than in the midwest—to the Cape, New Hampshire, or Maine—and that regular church attendance was not as typical in the region as in Missouri or Iowa. Nevertheless, we had good evidence that some failed to come even when they were in town. We did what we could to encourage them, though not so much from the pulpit. I preached on commitment, but not so much on giving, attendance, or other outwardly-visible actions that have traditionally been used as indicators of commitment. My experience had been constant harping on the specifics was counterproductive, often driving people away from the assembly. In the assembly of God's people the attitude should be that it is a real joy to be present. The attendance Sunday night and Wednesday night seemed to us appalling, about one-third of the congregation. New England, again, was different from the midwest. Churches of other groups in New England did not even have services at these times. We granted that some people had to drive several miles commuting to work and some of our members had to drive twenty miles to get to the building, but we felt that attendance could be much better. What bothered us most was that the children's classes on Sunday morning were poorly attended. Only about half the children of members were attending the classes.

We brought up the matter in a business meeting. I suggested that we close in some available space with walls, create two new classrooms and make an effort to get as many to attend as possible. The objections came rapidly: the space was needed for receptions and showers! I raised the question as to whether that was the chief reason for the church to exist. In the churches where I grew up, no attention was paid to such matters. If someone had suggested that members of the church should prepare the building for weddings and showers, it would be pointed out straight away that the church was not a social institution, but a religious one. Its responsibility was to preach the Gospel. We worked out what I thought a suitable solution, which indicates how we sought to adjust to these new circumstances: we closed in the space with doors on tracks which allowed them to be removed. The design was created by Albert Smith, a draftsman, and executed by his father, a carpenter. All of us were pleased: we started the two new classes, pushed for attendance, and in a matter of a few weeks were reporting eighty for classes, whereas before we averaged forty or less.

The other matter concerned the building, which we addressed about a year later. It became clear to me that the reason the building wasn't finished was that the carpenters connected with the congregation talked about doing it, but tended always to put it off. They didn't get around to doing it themselves but they couldn't bear to see someone else do it. I learned that this was a New England trait. I was sensitive enough to know that one should not attack it head-on, but seek out a viable solution, which usually came about through talking with certain people in the congregation who would like to see something done, but were not in the leadership. The leadership, in fact, was the problem. Good advice came from members who respected the leaders and who knew them well enough to know what might be proposed to meet their approval. In the first place, we had to address the money problem. I proposed that we find the money to complete the building from among the church members. We would make official notes payable to a member who loaned a given amount. The old-line leaders in the congregation opposed this move, but acquiesced when the majority thought it could be done. We had a period during which we asked for commitments, and were soon promised enough money. Very little of it came from the older leadership, however, even though they were able. A few who loaned considerable amounts were less able, but lived frugally. We thought that the leaders had money because of their life styles, but perhaps the fact was that they were just keeping their heads above the water while meeting bills.

The next question was, with whom should we contract the construction? It was clear that we dare not suggest someone without church connections. An older women, a native of Natick and a charter member of the church, had a son-in-law who was an excellent carpenter. Neither he nor his wife were members, though their daughters were. As a carpenter he was well-respected by the established leaders. The carpenter's son-in-law, who was from Texas and a very active member, found out from him that he would be interested in working on the building with his crew. Soon arrangements were made and, two years after we arrived, the building was finished, money owed only to the members, and my salary was always paid on time.

As a preacher I was respected as an interpreter of the Word, translating it into life. As a public proclaimer, however, I didn't do as well. I did shorten my sermons. Some complained that I did not put as much into them as Pat and I did not disagree. I had wanted a theological education, but that was yet to come. After a time those sort of comments ceased. I'm sure that as I studied, my sermons became more substantial. Perhaps members came to recognize a new hermeneutic, one which sought to put ideas into action. What the church really needed at that stage was someone who could take the lead in translating commitment into reality. Later I was able to inject far more of the Scripture. I also drew on church history and on the novels I read for course work. My life mostly consisted of reading books and writing papers. I also read in the history of our movement. I preached much more from the complete Scriptures than formerly, especially increasing the Old Testament content of my sermons.

My first year at Harvard, I took a seminary course synthesizing psychiatry and religion. We focused on counseling, and it was well that I did, for soon I was involved in counseling persons with a number of different problems. I had never done this much before, since in the southwest and midwest, our preachers were mostly expected to preach. In New England, however, ministers were counselors, perhaps more than they were preachers, especially so in the denominations. That had not yet fully influenced our New England churches, but at Natick, since the members were not from our traditional background, much more was expected, especially from someone who seemed so available. I counseled with a woman who had been to psychiatrists and in a state hospital for a time. One night when she was worse than usual, her husband brought me to see her. We sat silently for a time, then I asked her if she would like to move back to Deer Island, in Canada where they previously lived. She said she would. Her husband said, "All right, we will." They started making arrangements to move. The woman improved steadily. I counseled couples with marriage problems, some of whom were in the congregation and some just in the neighborhood. I counseled a family with a son who was mentally handicapped. I did wedding ceremonies and a few funerals. I managed to get far more involved in people's lives than I intended, but it occurred to me that Jesus got involved in people's lives. His hermeneutic was to translate the love of God into the lives of the persons with whom he came in contact. "No one has ever seen God. It is God the only Son, who is close to the Father's heart who has made him known." That was, in a sense, a new hermeneutic for the people of Jesus's world. It was also new for ministers in our churches at that point in time. And, after all, doesn't hermeneutics have to do with the interpretation of Scripture? Because of all the work load in counseling, working on the building, and going to school full time, I began to suffer some symptoms of burnout.

Theological Education in the Churches of Christ

The fifties marked a socioeconomic sea change in Churches of Christ. At the close of World War II it appeared that we might be on the verge of moving across the tracks and out of cultural isolation. By the late 1950s that was no longer a prospect but a reality. Across the United States we planted congregations and built attractive buildings in the residential areas and sprawling suburbs of all the cities in the regions of our strength. We expanded church planting into all the states. Our major colleges were accredited by regional accrediting associations. We had increasing numbers of missionaries at work on all the inhabited continents. Our journals were doing well. *The Christian Chronicle* encouraged our rising self image and expansiveness. We announced our newly-gained status by featuring city wide meetings in major auditoriums, and through a national radio program, *The Herald of Truth*, started in 1953. This new era perhaps culminated in our exhibit at the New York World's Fair in 1964-65—for us, a creative and victorious announcement of our arrival. In fact, according to certain outside observers, ours was the best of the religious exhibits at the fair.

The surge of GI education after World War II deeply impacted the membership of Churches of Christ. Many persons, both male and female, graduated from college in the late forties. Myriads became public school teachers and helped address the needs of the baby-boom generation. Numerous others went on to graduate schools, several with a goal of returning to teach in the rapidly expanding Christian colleges. Among those seeking graduate education were persons in theological and biblical studies. By 1960 Jack Lewis, LeMoine Lewis, and Everett Ferguson had their Ph.D.'s from Harvard, J. D. Thomas from the University of Chicago, where Don Sime also had completed course work, Joe Sanders and Pat Harrell at Boston University, and W. B. West, Frank Pack, and J. P. Sanders from the University of Southern California. Others were studying at Princeton, Vanderbilt, Southwestern Baptist, Southern Methodist, the University of Iowa, and Southern Baptist Theological Seminary. The trickle of people working on doctorates in religion in the 1940s grew to a steady stream in the 1960s. One of the unusual phenomena in the Churches of Christ in the last half century has been the percentage of those who attended professional and graduate schools and who later ascended to the highest attainments in their respective fields.

At that time several persons from the Churches of Christ were attending Harvard. Those working on doctorates were Abraham J. Malherbe, now Buckingham Professor Emeritus of New Testament at Yale, Roy Ward, professor at Miami University (Ohio), and Don McGaughey, who took his B.D. at Harvard, but was working on the Ph.D. in New Testament at Boston University. McGaughey was minister of the church in Brookline, and Ward his associate. The year I started the B.D. program Harold Forshey, now at Miami, entered. He worked with a black congregation in Roxbury. The following year Harold Vanderpool, who teaches medical ethics at the University of Texas Medical School in Galveston, and William Martin, who teaches sociology at Rice University, began studies at Harvard. I talked the congregation into giving someone a bit of financial help to do some teaching, occasional preaching, and helping in other ways. The first year, Harold and Natalie Vanderpool drove out from Cambridge. Harold had taken a beginning speech course from me at Harding in the fall of 1954. Malherbe left Harvard the next year to teach at Abilene Christian. He had been preaching for the Lexington congregation, so Vanderpool preached there for a time. My last year Jim (J.J.M.) Roberts and Genie Lou came from Abilene. He came to work for the congregation and was my successor. Roberts received both his B.D. and Ph.D. in Old Testament at Harvard and is now Green Professor of Old Testament at Princeton. Also coming that year was Derwood Smith, now Professor of New Testament at Cleveland State/Western Reserve. Our families got together periodically for meals and we were a very congenial group of colleagues, sometimes eating lunch together at the divinity school.

Harvard Divinity School

Harvard Divinity School was an exciting place to take up studies in 1959. While I had preferred Union Theological Seminary; in retrospect, I must say that Harvard was the much better choice. We know little in advance about career outcomes. For that reason, it is wise to turn these decisions over to Management at the Highest Level.

Harvard was the best place to be, first, because of the contingent of students from the Churches of Christ. Second, there were also several evangelicals. Earlier, a large number of evangelical leaders took Ph.D.'s at Harvard, including Edward Carnell, George Eldon Ladd, and Kenneth S. Kantzner. Some of our friends were Robert Kraft and Eldon Epp, both of whom had graduated from Wheaton College. Mark A. Noll has written at length on evangelical biblical scholars and noted the coterie of evangelicals working on Ph.D.'s at Harvard in the 1940s.[1] He advanced various reasons. I mentioned some of Noll's explanations to LeMoine Lewis, who was at Harvard during that period. He mused, "Actually, the reason was simple. The school was, in effect, a Unitarian school. They had plenty of scholarship money, but few Unitarian candidates. Harvard, compared with most doctoral programs, offered great scholarships. That was the main attraction."

But perhaps best of all, Nathan Pusey, then president of Harvard, had decreed a renewal of the seminary along ecumenical and neo-orthodox lines. While some may not see this as important, it was actually a considerable retrenchment, at least, among the newly appointed Harvard faculty, from early twentieth century liberalism. The contrast was perhaps greatest in Old Testament studies. Both of the major Old Testament scholars had written their dissertations under William F. Albright at The Johns Hopkins University—G. Ernest Wright and Frank Cross. Though Albright was not exactly a conservative—in regard to the documentary hypothesis, for example—he was widely admired and quoted by evangelicals. About this time Joe Schubert was taking courses at Vanderbilt Divinity School. In an Old Testament class he was surprised to hear the professor speak of that "hotbed of conservatism in Old Testament at Harvard Divinity School."

At Harvard no specific courses were required, except for one in speech. A final comprehensive exam made it crucial to take appropriate courses in all the areas because the exams were demanding. I indicated an interest in church history so I was assigned to George Williams as my advisor. He was either on sabbatical or leave most of my first two years, so I sometimes counseled with Robert Slater, who taught world religions. Actually, I sought out most of my advice from the "lunch group" of students mentioned above. I was very interested in church history, but also in theology. I hoped to lay a solid foundation in biblical studies, but I decided that since so many members of the church took Ph.D.'s in Old or New Testament, that some of us should specialize in other areas. The first semester I took Introduction to the Old Testament from Frank Cross, in which we moved from the Pentateuch into the histories, Philosophy of Religion from John Wild, a course in ministry from Samuel Miller, the school's dean, and History of Religions, coordinated and mostly taught by Arthur Darby Nock. The second semester I continued Old Testament introduction, the second half taught by G. Ernest Wright. History of Religions was, likewise, a full year course. I took Introduction to the New Testament under Amos Wilder, brother of the famous playwright, Thornton Wilder (at Dubuque I had directed Act Two of Thornton Wilder's famous play, "Our Town"). I also took a course in Christian ethics under James Luther Adams.

It was particularly in the courses of G. Ernest Wright and John Wild that certain new insights and changes in my thinking occurred. These had to do with God, the way he relates to his world, and the manner in which he reveals himself to humankind. In the end, these insights impinged upon an understanding of the Scripture, which, in turn, resulted in an emended hermeneutics.

To this point several different forces had shaped my understanding of God, the universe, man, and revelation, producing, in some cases, disparate, if not antithetical, presuppositions. For example, in the Scriptures, God is always at work in his world, sometimes behind the scenes in long-range developments, but at other times in the forefront, as at the Red Sea. But in my upbringing, reinforced by scientific education, God had receded from the world, and continued only the long-range influences. This was what providence was all about, I thought. But God had ceased to act in special situations, I believed: the age of miracles was past. But if this was so, it occurred to me at various times that prayer was a strange exercise and the basic presumptions of the biblical faith no longer were in effect in our world. Since God no longer acted, how could he be present? He was evident in our time, so most of us in the Churches of Christ believed, only in Scripture, not in action. He had provided instructions and directions on his concepts and will for man in Scripture. God's plain will in our time was his law, which provided for man a manner of coping in his world. God no longer needed to act, it was supposed. His good intentions for humankind came about through law-keeping. Scriptures contained the thoughts and laws of God, and we believed any useful hermeneutic should be designed to pinpoint as accurately as possible the expectations of God for humankind in the world and in the church.

G. Ernest Wright was a lecturer with great charisma when in good form, which was often. He was very personable, often inviting students to dinner at his home in Lexington. He was also very respected academically, since he had published a few seminal books and several scholarly articles of various sorts in journals and *festschriften*. At that time the biblical theology movement was in full swing, especially in America. Wright was at the forefront, with his books *The Old Testament Against Its Environment* and *God Who Acts: Old Testament Theology as Recital*.

In the first book, Wright argued that though some similarities existed between the faith of Israel and the surrounding faiths, what stood out were certain distinctive features, including belief in a single God who spoke for social justice through the prophets and acted powerfully to establish love and justice in history. Not only was the faith of Israel different from the religions of Assyria, Babylonia, Egypt and Canaan, but also from the Greco-Roman religions. In a later book, *Theology and The Old Testament*, published in 1964, Wright also argued that Hebrew faith was different from the forms of Christianity spawned by Hellenistic thought and philosophy. The major difference centered in the great love of Yahweh, who acted mightily in history for his people. In theology influenced by the great Greek philosophers, Plato and Aristotle, God was the one with great ideas, which in turn produced forms and essences, giving the world its permanent features as a place which functions through natural laws and is amenable to reason. The chief work of the theologian is, therefore, rational: to reason so as to apprehend the regularities, or ontologies. I began to sense certain problems with this world view as I worked on Basil. It became clear to me that he borrowed several of his basic assumptions from Plato, rather than from the Scriptures. Was there a clash between the world view of "Jews who demanded signs" and the "Greeks who desired wisdom" (I Corinthians 1:22)? Wright thought there was. At the same time, Wright's book fought on another front against those who located the action of God only in Jesus, a Jesus who responds immediately to every whim and wish of the true believer. Wright identified this trend as Christomonism.

In the small monograph *God Who Acts*, Wright developed the point of view that the God of Israel is not so much concerned with reason, profound thoughts, and passive contemplation, and is not principally a God who provides true reflections and just laws and stands apart from the created universe. Instead, he is a God continually at work in his creation; who acts lovingly for his people in their historical existence. In this work Wright, somewhat unguardedly, located revelation in the acts of God rather than in his words. The basic revelation from God is in what he does, Wright argued. The words in Scripture having to do with revelation are those which describe what God has done. According to Wright, the verbal description, with its attendant interpretation, is secondary to the action itself. He sometimes seems to say that all the descriptions are human and subject to human perspectives. It is the action itself which, in the final analysis, is truly divine. Wright therefore envisioned the salvific acts of God as the central affirmation permeating the Old Testament and flowing over into the New. The recognition of God's actions are the core of worship: worship is a recital of the mighty acts of God (I Samuel 12:1-18, Micah 6:1-8).

In his lectures, Wright developed a series of corollaries from this central affirmation about Israel's faith. First, the Old Testament has a core, a central focus. It is not a two-dimensional handbook of God's rules and regulations. Instead, the whole work revolves around God's mighty acts. Second, the proper interpretation of the Old Testament involves identifying these powerful acts and ascertaining their significance in the life of God and for humankind. Third, God's actions are motivated by his love. God chose Israel, not because of any intrinsic merits, but because he loved her (Deuteronomy 7:7-11). God's laws are therefore not some impersonal, arbitrary set of rules, like speed limits, or mathematical laws that reflect the physical nature of things in the universe. Rather, they frame a proper response to God's prior loving acts. For example, the sympathetic treatment of aliens living in the midst of Israel is a law, but it is grounded in God's prior loving action toward Israel. According to Leviticus 19:34, "The alien who resides with you shall be to you as the citizen among you; you shall love the alien as yourself, for you were aliens in the land of Egypt... (19:36). By their continual evocation of this phrase— "I am the Lord your God, who brought you out of Egypt"—God's laws call upon his people to emulate his gracious actions.

Fourth, the 1954 studies of George Mendenhall of the University of Michigan provided new insight into the call and election of Israel, corroborating Wright's proposal that the loving acts of God have priority in time over any giving of laws. Earlier, in his article on the "Faith of Israel" in *The Interpreter's Bible* (ed. George Buttrick, vol. 1), published prior to Mendenhall's comparison of the Mosaic covenant with the Hittite suzerainty treaties, Wright had argued that before God ever presumed to hand on to his people a set of laws, he blessed them mightily at the Red Sea and in the wilderness. It was then, and only then, that he called them into a covenant relationship and set out his ten basic stipulations. God's proffer of the covenant is grounded in his love, and the laws are the stipulations of the covenant. Therefore, the laws of God are grounded in the love of God. The scenario of the Hittite treaties was that of a Hittite suzerain who befriends a small state on his border, protecting it against the advance of some major power from the east—the Assyrians, perhaps. Following upon this benevolent act—not before—he draws up a covenant to the benefit of the small power. In setting out the covenant he identifies himself, his action on behalf of the smaller country, sets forth his expectations (laws), suggests arrangements for the storage and periodical reading of the covenant, and identifies a series of deities as witnesses. Finally, he proposes blessings attendant to keeping the stipulations and curses for ignoring them. All these elements are discovered in the Mosaic covenant, especially as set forth in the book of Deuteronomy. In Deuteronomy 5, in the presentation of the decalogue, God identified himself, "I am Yahweh," (5:6), then set out his prior loving acts: "...who brought you out of the land of Egypt, out of the house of slavery." This makes it clear that the laws of God are not natural laws inherent in the universe. Rather, they are God's laws and are not designed merely to keep humankind from self-destruction. They propose that humans relate to each other just as, in prior acts, God has related to them.

Fifth, Wright proposed that the prophets were not liberals who turned their backs on the ways of the fathers, as depicted by Wellhausen and the modernists at the turn of the century. Rather, they sought the old paths. They were indeed creative about the manner in which the old actions applied to situations in their time, but they were not despisers of the old. They had a hermeneutic in which criteria for judging the current scene were drawn from the past. These criteria were based not so much on a set of laws as on the loving characteristics of God as shown in his actions on behalf of humankind. An example is Jeremiah as he reflected on Judah's current unfaithfulness. He utilized the powerful metaphor of a bridegroom and bride on their honeymoon, depicting the wilderness time of Israel as God's honeymoon with his people (Jeremiah 2:2,3). The wilderness was a great demonstration of God's love. "...in the wilderness you saw how the Lord your God carried you, just as one carries a child" (Deuteronomy 1:31). The problem was that Israel acted unfaithfully, despite this great show of love: "All who ate of it were held guilty" (Jeremiah 2:3). In the next several chapters Jeremiah went on to show that, just as in the beginning of the covenant relationship, so Israel was still the unfaithful bride, seeking out lovers from among the gods of the surrounding nations.

The past mighty actions of God, therefore, form a catalog or canon of God's activities. They inject a measuring device, a yardstick, by which current happenings are weighed and judged. In the Old Testament itself, then, canon is not so much a set of documents to be properly authenticated, nor is it primarily a set of authoritative propositions or laws. Rather, it is a catalog of the loving actions of God which, in turn, serve as a standard by which the unfolding of his works in human history may be ascertained. In the Old Testament there are several catalogues of this sort: Deuteronomy 26:5-11, Joshua 24:1-15, Nehemiah 9:1-31, and Psalms 78, 105, 106, and 136, for example. Frank Cross once made the point that God does not have to bring his people through the Red Sea again in each generation. The Exodus was a once-for-all event. It was not just for that generation, but all future generations. The future generations recall it and appropriate it through the celebration of the Passover (Exodus 13:14-16). "Not with our ancestors did the Lord make this covenant, but with us, who are all of us here alive today" (Deuteronomy 5:3). The great past actions of God are recited, in order that God's activity on the current scene may be appropriately discerned by God's people. This is most clear in Psalm 136. God's steadfast love is first affirmed (1-3). God's work is never passive, nor merely verbal. It is always active. It is shown through the wonders of creation (4-9). It is shown in the historical victory of Israel, first in Egypt and at the sea (10-15), then in the wilderness and conquest (16-22). God did not leave his people homeless with no base of operations. He gave them a land. These great actions of Yahweh are in the past in once sense, but in another they are contemporary. They are the means whereby to locate God's presence, even here and now. The close of the canon, that is, the closing down of the catalog, by no means inferred the cessation of God's action. Rather, they, through their salient features, provided the very basis for identifying God's work on the current scene (23-26). He "rescued us from our foes...who gives food to all flesh."

We turn now to the crucial question: is Wright correct? If we should decide to reject his perspective in regard to either the Old or New Testament, we should do so on the grounds of whether it is supported by the biblical witness. I was brought up to view the Scripture as God's handbook of rules and private channel of information. By reading the Scripture one can find the answers to all puzzles and determine God's expectations or laws pertaining to human decisions of every kind. We have supposed this is the case. Are we willing, or able, to weigh our ingrained presuppositions in the light of Scripture? Sometimes we are unwilling.

In 1967 I published a series of articles on the covenant in the Old Testament in the *Firm Foundation*. I carried on a correspondence at some length with Robert Taylor over certain aspects of it. The discussion finally came down to his conclusion that I was wrong in my analysis of the command-example-necessary inference hermeneutic. I wrote back and asked that he establish this hermeneutic out of Scripture: he adamantly declined. He charged that if I did not accept this hermeneutic I was the same as an infidel and he must decline further correspondence. I hadn't said I rejected it, however. I asked him to show me that it was biblical. I suppose that either he thought he couldn't substantiate it by Scripture or else he was unwilling to try.

I came to believe that, in fact, the Old Testament as a whole did revolve about the mighty acts of God and their interpretation. Unlike Wright, I would not assign the interpretation of these acts a secondary role: the opening of the Red Sea did not disclose its own meaning. The raw event may have been a freak accident of nature; no more, no less. Only because of the interpretation of the event—also an act of God—do we confess that it was Yahweh, coming to the rescue of his people (Exodus 15:1-5), who parted the sea. The Scripture is a report on the mighty actions of God and what they mean. Scripture discloses an act-interpretation event. "I am the Lord your God who brought you out of the land of Egypt" (Deuteronomy 5:6). The law of God which follows is based on God's prior love and its concrete form.

> Remember that you were a slave in the land of Egypt, and the Lord your God brought you out from there with a mighty hand and an outstretched arm: therefore the Lord your God commanded you to keep the Sabbath day (Deuteronomy 5:15).

The proper interpretation of Scripture, therefore, first identifies God's loving action for his people and his profession of why he acted. Only then does the focus shift to the manner in which God's action is to be translated into human action.

> When an alien resides with you in your land, you shall not oppress the alien. The alien who resides with you shall be to you as the citizen among you; you shall love the alien as yourself, for you were aliens in the land of Egypt. You shall keep all my statutes and all my ordinances, and observe them: I am the Lord (Leviticus 19:33, 34).

G. Ernest Wright had a great love for the Old Testament, especially the prophets. He highlighted in their words the struggle of the God who is one—Yahweh—with humans in history and of his compassion for the lowly and downtrodden. But Wright, unlike the earlier liberals, did not locate the prophets at the highest evolutionary point in the development of ethical monotheism. He believed that God-as-one and his concern for the needy was at least pre-prophetic and could be traced back to the era of Moses, if not earlier. Neither was Wright mostly concerned with ethics and little with God: he did not stress ethics as such. Ethics were the natural outcome of a discussion of God. He argued that love for God as a response to his love resulted in ethical action. He presented a God who loved his people and who wanted them to treat one another in love, just as he had.

Wright's study of the prophets was a much different perspective than that of S.A. Bell. It seemed to me that Bell had slight and uncertain evidence on which to pin down his concern—ascertaining

Christological ramifications in the prophets. With Wright, history became the focal point. God's loving actions took place in the history of Israel, his people. The rapidly accelerating archaeological finds in the near and middle east added insight to historical developments and made such study very exciting. New materials provided concrete insights, clarifying many incidents that before were incomprehensible. More and more, it was obvious to me that the Old Testament, especially in its theology, was an authoritative word for the church of Jesus Christ. God is the Father of the Lord Jesus Christ. He is known first and foremost through what he did for Israel in the Old Testament. Wright's book, *The Old Testament and Theology* made clear how impoverished is any theology which focuses on Christ only. The Old Testament is indispensable for the proper view of God, he held. Wright's emphasis on the message of the Old Testament as couched in a recital of God's mighty acts renewed my interest in Scripture as story, and in preaching as "telling the old, old story." In various ways I was leaving the parameters of my grandfather, father, and my scientific training, and reverting to the beginnings encouraged by my mother.

A second set of reflections set these new insights into the Old Testament into a larger context. While in Dubuque, I read theologians who incorporated into their theological reflections new understandings in the sciences. In the past, the universe was visualized as a closed system held in place by the laws of nature. The pendulum served as the analogy for the world of Isaac Newton: the pendulum is in motion, but its position at any point in time can be carefully mapped. It abides by the regular, unchangeable laws of nature. Such a universe is fully rational and beautiful in its regularity and order. Should God decide to act in such a world, even he is forced to deal with the natural laws before he can do anything. In other words, he has to momentarily interrupt the laws of nature in order to do one of his special works. That was how theologians of the era defined a miracle: as a violation of the laws of nature. In a real sense, therefore, even God was subject to nature's laws, even if only to the necessity of suspending them from time to time. That was the outlook of the Deists. It essentially became the vision of our forefathers. From this position on nature, and under the conviction that God had elected not to interrupt nature's laws since the biblical age, we in Churches of Christ were in a position to refute any and all who claimed a special work of the Holy Spirit: a miracle, or the ability to heal.

With the coming of atomic energy and exploration of sub-atomic particles, however, scientists like the German physicist, Werner Heisenberg (1901-1976) suggested that at such minute levels, the universe is not at all like a pendulum. He realized that, though we can predict with some statistical accuracy where a series of sub-atomic particles will be, we cannot pinpoint the exact location of a specific particle. Statistical tables had to be substituted for pendulums. Heisenberg labeled this perspective "the indeterminacy principle." While he did not maintain that the principle applied to the larger features of the universe, that prospect was raised by the theologians.

They asked, is it possible that the universe is not, after all, bound in chains by natural law? The Hebrews writer suggested, in contrast to natural laws, the faithfulness of Christ to the universe as manifested by his sustenance of it: the universe is regular because Christ is faithful. It appears to have within itself natural (i. e. regular) laws because we can calculate its regularity—the rising and setting of the sun and the high and low tides, for example. "He sustains all things by his powerful word" (Hebrews 1:3). Nature's predictability then becomes, not an impersonal law, but the result of God's covenant: "If any of you could break my covenant with the night, so that day and night would not come at their appointed time, only then could my covenant with my servant David be broken..." (Jeremiah 33:20). If the order in the universe is the result of God's constant sustaining power, then a loving act of God on behalf of an individual or church does not entail a change in the "laws of nature." God need only redirect his sustaining power. Contrary to our forefathers' affirmations, such an understanding would imply that the world, rather than being under the constraints of impersonal laws implanted by an absent God, is instead being constantly maintained by him, because of his steadfast love.

I worked on the relation of God and nature in at least two classes. One was the Philosophy of Religion, taught by John Wild, and the other the History of Medieval Christianity, taught by Heiko Obermann. John Wild was like a man without a country among the philosophers at Harvard. The Harvard philosophy department, almost to a professor, was committed to logical positivism or some version of British analytical philosophy. These professors asserted with those like the British philosopher, A. J. Ayer, that there is no reality exterior to the natural world. As a young American in pre-Hitler Germany, Wild had studied under Edmund Husserl, the father of phenomenology. He also had some contact with Martin Heidegger, who was influenced by Husserl. Another designation for this philosophical tradition—especially in France, among philosophers such as Jean Paul Sartre and Merleau Ponty—was existentialism. Wild had later reacted against these earlier influences and had became something of a neo-Thomist. By the fall of 1959, he had once again become interested in the existentialists, though he faulted them at certain points. A few years later I asked Henry Johnstone, Jr., my philosopher friend at Penn State, what he thought of Wild. He responded, "Oh, he has held so many philosophical positions, what can one think?"

Wild, like Wright, was a dynamic lecturer. In Philosophy of Religion we read Thomas Aquinas, Blaise Pascal, Hume's *Dialogues*, Ludwig Feuerbach, and a book by John McQuarrie which related the thought of Martin Heidegger and Rudolf Bultmann. I appreciated Wild because he did not hesitate to share his faith and tell you where he stood, if asked. I found him, to my surprise, fairly conservative, from a traditional Christian perspective: he was Episcopalian. Wild's critique of Aquinas—some indication that he had moved away from neo-Thomism—was that Aquinas's universe was "bound in chains."

I learned much in the course, especially about existentialism. I discovered, though I knew something about existentialism already through discussions with John Knox Coit at Dubuque, that existentialism was embraced both by philosophers who believed and philosophers who were atheists. I also discovered that Soren Kierkegaard, often attacked in the later 1960s by our preachers, was as orthodox and evangelical as may be found, in respect to basic Christian doctrines. These preachers were right, however, in perceiving Kierkegaard as an enemy of an empirical, rational world, and a religion grounded in public logic rather than in individual decision—subjectivism, as designated by Kierkegaard. Wild favored a universe in which God acted. Though he thought there was much to learn from Bultmann's phenomenological analysis of certain categories such as faith, the resurrection, salvation, and others, he did not buy into certain of Bultmann's presuppositions. On one occasion a student pointed out to Wild that Bultmann held that all the causes in this world are initiated in this world, which in turn ruled out special acts of God and miracles. He asked Wild if he agreed. Wild conceded that he did not agree with Bultmann at that point. He believed that God could and did whatever in his world he wished. Nevertheless, he wanted it perfectly clear that he thought Bultmann's analysis of categories of faith were a great contribution.

I decided to write my paper on the medieval dispute over nominalism, realism, and conceptualism. Those who are not philosophers or church historians will begin to tune out about here, but hold on! I'm not going to explain the intricacies of that dispute. Taking up this subject got me into the quarrels of the various religious orders of medieval times. We also studied the orders and their disputes in a class on medieval history. The study of these disputes was very influential in developing my thinking about God and the world, as I was reminded again in the fall of 1990. Pepperdine has an international program with facilities in Heidelberg, London, and Florence, and arrangements with Ibaraki Christian College in Japan. We teach thirty to fifty of our own students in each of these locations. In the fall of 1990 it was my privilege to teach in the London program. In our course, Religion and Culture, I taught the history of the English church. That forced me to renew once again the battles of the orders during medieval times. The conflict had to do with how God's universe is to be conceived, and pitted the Augustinians and the Franciscans against the Dominicans and, much later, the Jesuits. The question at stake was: What sort of a world is it in which we live and how does God relate to it?

The Augustinians were named in honor of Augustine, who basically viewed human reality as under the constant and watchful eye of God. He saw history as moving toward the city of God because of God's constant involvement in it. Not only did God work in history but in the thoughts of men, especially when they came to true insights and solutions. The Franciscans were founded by Francis of Assisi (1182-1226), who viewed not only humankind, but also animals, as under the constant care of God: St. Francis was famous, as you probably remember, for preaching to the birds. In fact, early ecological measures were introduced by the Franciscans, who reprimanded the destruction of wildlife, as evidenced in England by the demise of a species of ducks. For the Franciscans, the smiling face of God's love could be seen in all things physical. For this reason they rejected the concept of mechanical natural laws. This natural law approach held that the physical universe was impersonal, cold, and unrelenting in lawfulness and order. The world the Franciscans occupied was warm, and each day was a time for anticipating God's new actions on behalf of his creatures. Whatever regularity is to be found in the world is the result of God's steadfast love, they held. He does not forsake the constant needs of his creatures. That is why the Franciscans tended toward nominalism. They perceived the essences of the realists as restrictions on the actions of God in the world.

The Dominicans, in contrast, drank deeply from the teachings of Thomas Aquinas, who, in turn, was influenced by Aristotle and also, of course, by Augustine and the Scriptures. Thomas, much like Aristotle, thought that the universe operated according to its own laws. He argued that, in fact, reason itself must conclude that the universe has always been and is eternal, thereby agreeing with Aristotle. But Aquinas rejected an eternal universe on the grounds of revelation. It is only through revelation, he argued, that one knows differently than reason would dictate. In Aristotle's view, God is not creator: the physical universe has always been, just as God has always been, and God has only an impersonal relationship to the world. He is the unmoved mover, the one who supplies constant motion to reality, but otherwise he is not concerned or involved. Instead he is involved in self-contemplation. In Aristotle's view, there is no such thing as divine providence, because God has no interest in the physical universe or humankind. The universe runs on its own, according to its laws. Thomas, in contrast, argued that by revelation we believe that God created the universe *ex nihilo*—from nothing. He also believed that God works through the laws of the universe. He held that the universe is orderly and lawful because of the natural laws built within. God has no need, and, in fact, does not interfere with the due course of the laws of nature (which is why John Wild charged that the universe of Thomas Aquinas is bound in chains). The Dominicans followed Thomas. They were very aggressive and came into conflict with the Augustinians and Franciscans. The only higher education in that era was supplied by the various orders through their newly-founded universities in England and on the continent. So the battles of the orders were also the battles of the universities.

In struggling through this material I kept asking the question: who had the better case, from a biblical perspective? One thing I have never been is a dilettante. The pragmatic disposition of my father has forever distanced me from learning simply in order to know something. I have always felt compelled to raise the question of application. What are the ramifications? It is obvious that if I followed the inclinations of my upbringing that I should go with the Dominicans, even though there was a difference: they were rationalists in a deductive, syllogistic sense of the word. Our British empirical background, in fact, reacted against that tradition. Alexander Campbell, for example, can be found attacking Aristotle on more than one occasion because Aristotle, or at least the Aristotelian tradition, was so deductive in its thought. Those who had learned from Bacon and Locke definitely preferred the inductive and the empirical. Perhaps that is one reason why I instinctively shied away from the Dominicans.

By now, however, I think the major reason was biblical. If the core of the message of the Scripture is that God is one who reaches out and touches his universe, who, as the result of his relentless love, is always acting on behalf of his people, then one is compelled to align with the Franciscans, for that was their perspective on reality. The indeterminacy principle in physics paved the way for my changed perception. I was not, nor am I yet, prepared to see every act claimed on behalf of God as being from him. Even in Scripture people are held up as models who retain a healthy skepticism about unusual events claimed for God—Gideon, for example, who, when the angel appeared to him, wanted to know how he could be sure the angel was from God. Indeed, when told to battle the Midianites and that God would give him the victory, he had the audacity to suggest that he needed signs—proof—that it was really God speaking. As a result, he proposed the test of the fleece and the dew (Judges 6, 7).

Now, for the first time, a series of perceptions fell in place for me. There was a paradigm shift in my perception of reality, and not just in mine, but in that of several of my contemporaries, even those who had little insight into the intellectual battles among the medieval schools. This shift has had far-reaching ramifications, as we can see in the emergence of the charismatic movement and the openness of many in our heritage to perceive the actions of God in today's world. Those who maintain the old Baconian, Lockean views among us charge that their assumptions are the same as those in the Scripture. They accuse the people on the other side of the shift as having been deeply influenced by existentialism, with justification, in some cases. In my case, though, it is not the result of existentialism—though I was studying it at the same time—but rather the result of making a decision on these medieval battles, as well as my view that the biblical God is one who continues to act in history. I propose that those who cling to the Baconian-Lockean model of reality on the grounds that it is "biblical" need to examine afresh the witness of Scripture. I think if they are willing and able to do this that there is only one place at which they can come out. I think they, too, will take up this new, warmer vision of reality on the grounds that it is, after all, more biblical.

Preacher's Meetings, New Testament Theology and Hermeneutics

In the late 1950s the preachers within an eighty-mile radius of Boston met monthly for fellowship and scholarly discussion, one of the few groups in my experience to meet for the latter purpose. Some of the men involved in our meetings, in addition to those pursuing graduate degrees, were Cecil Allmon and Robert Lawrence of Worcester, James Jarrett of Warwick, Rhode Island, Morris Thurman of North Eastern, Norman Gipson of Melrose, C. M. Tuttleton of Providence, Rhode Island, Charles Chandler and Decker Clark of Keene, New Hampshire, Mickey Blake of Chicopee Falls, Jay Carver of Littleton, Tom Finder of New Bedford, and occasionally Claude Danley of Pittsfield. With the approximately ten persons attending either Harvard or Boston University the meetings ran ordinarily between twelve and twenty people.

I began to see, especially through the presentations of Abe Malherbe, that in the New Testament as well as the Old, the rules or expectations for humans are not merely detached laws—as in, "Do it or else!" Rather, the action God expects of humans is action which he himself has already undertaken on behalf of humans. Jesus himself was baptized in order "to fulfill all righteousness" (Matthew 3:15). He in turn commanded his disciples to go forth teaching, and those who heard gladly, he commanded to be baptized.

> "Go therefore and make disciples of all nations, baptizing them in the name of the Father and the Son and the Holy Spirit, and teaching them to obey everything that I have commanded you" (Matthew 28:19, 20).

Jesus declared to the disciples, "Love your enemies and pray for those who persecute you" (Matthew 5:44). But it wasn't simply a rule Jesus pulled out of the air in order to exercise his authority, even though he said, "All authority in heaven and earth has been given to me" (Matthew 28:18). Notwithstanding assertions I have heard to the contrary, Jesus by no means intended his disciples to have the attitude of the Light Brigade: "Ours is not to reason why/ Ours is but to do, or die." Instead, he gave the reasons. If we love our enemies we are acting like God has already acted: "...for he makes his sun rise on the evil and on the good, and sends rain on the righteous and on the unrighteous" (Matthew 5:45). Believers are to give because they have already received from God: "As you have received, freely give (Matthew 10:8). Paul commended giving because Christ had already given.

> I do not say this as a command, but I am testing the genuineness of your love against the earnestness of others. For you know the generous act of our Lord Jesus Christ, that though he was rich, yet for your sakes he became poor, so that by his poverty you might become rich (II Corinthians 8:8, 9).

In the same way, believers are to love each other, do nothing from selfish ambition or conceit, be humble, and look out for the interest of others. That is a tall order, but God, in Christ, has already done the same.

> Let this same mind be in you that was in Christ Jesus, who, though he was in the form of God, did not regard equality with God as something to be exploited, but emptied himself, taking the form of a slave, being born in human likeness. And being found in human form, he humbled himself and became obedient to the point of death—even death on a cross. (Philippians 2:6-8).

The Hebrews writer likewise employed the prior example of Jesus as a grounds for endurance in the face of persecution.

> Consider him who endured such hostility against himself from sinners, so that you may not grow weary or lose heart. In your struggle against sin you have not yet resisted to the point of shedding your blood (Hebrews 12:3, 4).

If we are seeking a method of hermeneutics which comes from the New Testament, we might do no better than to first ask who God is and what he has done, then base what we are to do on God's prior action. That is the proposed ground of action in much of the New Testament. What is it that we are authorized to do in the church? What God has already done! What is it we are authorized to do as Christians? What Christ has already done! A member in State College, Pennsylvania, once said to me, soon after I arrived, "We haven't been given any reasons for being baptized. We are baptized simply because God said to be baptized." I responded, "But Paul gave reasons." Indeed, by our baptism we emulate the death, burial and resurrection of Jesus Christ. We are baptized to disclose what he has already done on our behalf, and to indicate that we accept his death and resurrection as the mode of our own life (Romans 6:3, 4). Another way to state this hermeneutic rule is that the narrative of Christ's life sets the stage for the narrative of our life. By beginning with the narrative of God's salvific acts, or, in the words of Robert Milligan, *The Scheme of Redemption*,[2] we are provided a far more profoundly biblical perspective for focusing on commands, examples, and inferences. The old, old story is not a page from the textbooks of logic. It is a page, rather, from the life of the living God, who so loved the world that he gave his only son. Why is it that we think hermeneutics begins with the rules of logic, rather than with the actions of the living God? Perhaps, because we have reformulated life and its rules according to an enlightenment-influenced, logistic, scientific vision, rather than according to the biblical model in which God loves and gives himself up on behalf of the beloved. Why is it that certain religious leaders among us keep saying that they have not been influenced by anything but the Bible, when their vision of God, the world, and his expectations for humans runs counter to the Bible itself?

Another enterprise which drew the New England churches together was Camp Ganderbrook. Soon after I arrived I was approached by Jay Carver, who was the preacher at Littleton, to promote the camp among the members at Natick. I was pleased to do so because of interest in outdoor recreation and belief in the value of Christian camps. I was also willing because our oldest daughters would soon be of the age for camping. Camp Ganderbrook drew support from most of the New England churches. It was initially located in Jackman, near the Canadian border, but the year before I arrived it had moved to Raymond, Maine, near Lake Sebago, about thirty miles from Portland. A commercial camp had been purchased which had adequate facilities, but which were generally in a deteriorating condition. When the term at Harvard ended in early June, I was pleased to help clean up the grounds and do repairs on the buildings. I also contributed a week of teaching at the camp. I was elected to the board and assigned the task of writing the new by-laws for the camp organization. My expertise was based on teaching Robert's Rules of Order in discussion and debate for several years. I believed that in camps such as Ganderbrook, Christianity was being concretely interpreted for young lives.

I grew through reading the theologians in Harvard classes. I explored in great depth the significant theological topics which were largely ignored in our fellowship's circles: God, Christ, the Holy Spirit, the Trinity, and the atonement. It was through these studies that I came to see how Christian theology has, through the centuries, developed a catalogue, a canon of subjects from which to put questions to the Scriptures. These were much different from the questions explored in our movement. Which of these two canons were to be preferred? My instinct was to turn to the Scripture itself to reflect on what topics are portrayed as central. As I thought about it, I was surprised that we, who profess to settle all matters by the Bible, had not seriously questioned whether the topics or issues to which we assigned such importance were that important in the Scripture itself.

The theologians varied as to how these topics unfolded. I learned that the typical order was first, to raise questions of how people know about God—whether from the world about, through revelation, or through Scripture. Then there is the question of how one enters into a relationship with God—whether by reason or faith. After these matters are settled, the theologians take up the substance of theology—God, Christ, and the Holy Spirit, as well as their interrelationships, that is, the nature of the Trinity. They follow that with the way God works in the world—through creation, in salvation, in the church and its unity, and in bringing history to its end; eschatology, in other words. A standard set of topics might therefore be structured along the following lines:

1. Faith
2. Revelation
3. Scripture
4. God
5. Christ: Savior and Salvation
6. Holy Spirit
7. Man: Sin and Evil
8. Creation
9. Church
10. Worship and Sacraments
11. Ethics and Morality
12. Ecumenics
13. Eschatology

These standard topics commenced with Origen and came to be known by the Latin term, *Regula Fidei*. I was not convinced that these were necessarily the crucial topics by biblical standards. They seemed influenced by the Hellenistic mind since the question, how do we know what we know? preceded the question, what do we know? Or, to put it philosophically, epistemology preceded ontology. Paul Tillich held that theological method proceeds through correlation—through questions and answers. He held that in Christian theology, culture raises the questions and revelation provides the answers. For Tillich, Scripture is included under the topic of revelation, but revelation is not limited to Scripture. I had to admit that Tillich was right, in that this is the way theology happens, even theology in the Churches of Christ, as I think I have shown in these pages. Our fellowship has rarely hesitated to embrace extra-biblical sources when doing so corroborated a position we already held. But I questioned whether that is the way it should be. For people committed to *Sola Scriptura*—to the Bible alone, it would seem that not only the answers, but the questions, should come from Scripture.

I received the degree of *Scientia Theologicum Baccalaureae* (S.T.B) in June 1992, in Harvard Yard. I had for some time been trying to decide what to do after finishing. I wanted to teach, especially homiletics, so I made contacts with our schools. Harding Graduate School did not have a teacher of preaching, but I received no encouragement from W. B. West, Jr., the dean, even though by his standards, I had the proper credentials. Abe Malherbe proposed that I continue at Harvard, pursuing a Th.M., focusing on theology, and I gave this consideration. The church at Natick would have been pleased for me to stay on, but I was somewhat burned out, both from preaching and going to school full-time. I therefore decided to see if I could secure a position teaching speech. At about the same time I heard from Dr. Robert T. Oliver at Pennsylvania State University, and Dr. Ray H. Sandefur at the University of Akron, both requesting that I come to their campuses for an interview. The Akron position paid better, but the Penn State position offered more potential in working with doctoral candidates.

We visited Penn State first. Oliver had asked George Gurganus, who was completing his doctorate there, about me. George knew Dorothy and I were coming so he arranged for us to stay with his wife, Irene, since he had gone to Japan in an effort to collect the final data for his dissertation. I didn't know George well, but as I remember, I had met him in debate circles. He had earlier taught speech at Freed-Hardeman.

Dr. Oliver was congenial. We liked the mountain and sylvan setting of the region. The church seemed up-and-coming, despite certain rifts. Happy Valley, as some called it, was a good place for raising children. All systems seemed "go." Dr. Oliver spoke optimistically about making an offer, which he said he would send in a letter. The rank and salary in the official offer, when it came, was less than he had mentioned, but after agonizing over it, we decided to move to State College. We did not interview at the University of Akron.

---

[1] Mark A. Knoll, *Between Faith & Criticism: Evangelicals, Scholarship, and the Bible in America* (San Francisco: Harper & Row, 1986).

[2] Robert Milligan, *An Exposition and Defence of the Scheme of Redemption* (Cincinnati: Carroll Publishing, 1868). Milligan was a well-known second generation Restoration Movement leader.

8
The Word in the Church and in the Academy: Pennsylvania, 1962-1967

When I reminded Oliver that the salary was not what he mentioned, he apologized and said he would give me teaching assignments in adult education short courses that would provide additional income. The first was in the middle of the summer of 1962. That assignment enabled us to take a trip to State College and look for a house. The weather was great and the kids enjoyed it. Joel mentioned that it was so quiet. In Natick we lived near the Massachusetts Turnpike, and when the wind was right we were in the flight path for Logan Field, so we had a constant hum in the air, both day and night.

The church situation in State College took an unexpected turn. I was invited to lunch by one of the longtime members, Crumbaker Jenkins—commonly called Crum. When I arrived, two other members were there with him. One was a visiting professor from Long Beach State, Ottis Castleberry. Castleberry received his Ph.D. from Penn State, and had talked Oliver into exchanging summer teaching responsibilities. After a few pleasantries, Castleberry informed me that I could help with recent problems that had developed in the church at State College. A few men who had recently arrived at Penn State as professors had taken the leadership away from Crum and were aggressively pushing in new and undesirable directions, he said. The purpose of the luncheon was to enlist me on Crum's side. Perhaps I should have been taken by surprise, but wasn't. As yet I had not been in a congregation in which leadership struggles were absent. I thanked Ottis for the information, but informed the three present in no uncertain terms that I would not make up my mind in advance. I told them that in my experience, when there are rifts, no one side has a monopoly on Christian actions or positions. If I thought Crum's situation warranted it, I would support him. Ottis assured me that it did. In my view, Ottis and Crum already had a strike against them in that they set out to recruit me—a Christian should not try to stack the cards in advance, I thought. We must be prepared to suffer injustice for a time, if necessary, but proceed in the confidence that right will eventually win out. I have tried to let God take care of inequities directed against me, and in my experience he has more than adequately justified such confidence. "Beloved, never avenge yourselves, but leave room for the wrath of God; for it is written, 'Vengeance is mine, I will repay, says the Lord'" (Romans 12:19).

State College was in an isolated region of central Pennsylvania. The jibe was that "Penn State is in the middle of the state and inaccessible from all points." At that time, no major roads went in or out, though in a few years, Interstate 80 opened ten miles to the north, running east into New York City and west to Cleveland, Ohio. Robert Oliver told those who mentioned the isolation that we were twenty-five minutes from the Phillipsburg airport, and therefore twenty-five hours from any place in the world. Penn State had 25,000 students on the University Park campus, as it was called. An additional 25,000 lived in State College and its surroundings. Almost all of these were either professors and their families, the secretarial and maintenance staffs for the university, or employees of a few local high-tech, "brainware" industries. The industries employed graduate students in physics, mathematics and engineering, and some of the part-time professors. The shopping was minimal: as yet, no malls existed.

The Church

We felt warmly received by the members of the church. We were soon immersed in various activities. The preacher was John Barton, his wife was Mary and their daughter was named Cynthia. John grew up in Florida and Mary in Missouri. She was of a large family that had produced several preachers, including her brother, Earl Edwards, with whom I spent a bit of time in Florence, Italy, where he was a missionary. John and Mary were later longtime employees of Northeastern Christian

College—he as Vice President—and more recently, of Freed-Hardeman. They had been in State College about a year. He was a graduate of David Lipscomb, and they had moved from Athens, Alabama, where they had taught at Athens Bible School. He was aware of currents in the church at large and about these we had many discussions. He was interested in taking graduate work at the university, probably in speech. He was later to write his master's thesis under my direction.

The most active families in the congregation, with a few exceptions, were those of professors at the university, most of these from the College of Agriculture, although two were in physics, one of whom was not actually a member. I was at that time the only professor in liberal arts in the church there. The congregation was founded in the early 1930s, and the organizer was the wife of Phil Rice, a physics professor. She was the daughter of a well-known preacher, J. T. Hines. Mrs. Rice had been dead some years when we arrived. In 1936, James D. Willeford came to Penn State to preach and to finish his undergraduate degree. He was perceived by the congregation as a good preacher, but since he did not pursue his degree as actively as Mrs. Rice preferred, she had him fired. The church had expanded in State College, principally through the ministry of Pres Higginbotham. Pres was not the greatest in the pulpit, but he was a people person. He expended most of his energy teaching people one-on-one, and had led several families to Christ. Most of these members lived in outlying towns. Many of them worked for the university in secretarial or maintenance jobs. While these people did not provide leadership, some of the women taught children's classes.

When we arrived in 1962, a recent influx of university professors and graduate students had changed the complexion of the congregation, and the rifts in the congregation were essentially along town-gown lines. Crum Jenkins was the self-designated leader of the town group. He had the Balfour Jewelry franchise for a large region of Pennsylvania and did very well financially, since he sold class rings and other jewelry to Penn State students and had a field representative selling rings in high schools across the region. He was an aggressive promoter of the church and a heavy contributor. He professed popularism, downplayed education, and ridiculed the antics of professors, especially their religious and political liberalism. He never backed away from battles with professors, in the community or in the church. He had had a number of skirmishes in the past with graduate students at Penn State, most of whom were either in speech or psychology. Many of these students had departed from the faith, so I understood and sympathized with his "holding the fort" mentality. But it may have been that had he taken a different approach—encouraging, rather than attacking—fewer may have departed. We did not lose any students in the five years we were there, but an undergraduate or two quit attending regularly. Crum was very hospitable and a genuine encourager until someone expressed an opinion different from his, at which point he became an aggressive opponent. When I arrived, his main problem was that the only people in the congregation he could muster to his cause were those converted by Pres Higginbotham. They mostly came on Sunday morning and then not regularly. The Sunday night and Wednesday night crowds were families of the university professors and graduate students.

The church situation was interesting, to say the least. Large egos characterized the leadership, all around. I respected John Barton, who did what he could to encourage a Christ-like spirit. Though lacking graduate training in biblical studies, he believed in consulting good commentaries and books, and asked me frequently about what to read. He did what he could to keep the disputants in check. In fact, the church may have profited from the factions, since people had to be aggressive so as not to lose their influence. I discovered attitudes on various sides that were not exactly servant-like and I tried foster such a spirit toward all involved. But, of course, I had my own inner battles to fight against selfishness and the desire for pre-eminence. God's priests first make sacrificial offerings for their own sins, and only then for the sins of others (Hebrews 7:27). If one is going to be an interpreter of the Word of God, it must be in life as well as in word. The biblical hermeneutic is a far-reaching one: Jesus made God known as much through his life as through his teaching.

Sometimes I found myself being attacked by the professors, at other times by Crum Jenkins. In 1963 I was asked to be on a committee to prepare for our fellowship's exhibit at the 1964-65 New York World's Fair. My special assignment was to help write a Bible correspondence course. Another person on the publications committee was Roy Bowen Ward. Once, in the course of these meetings or as we planned the launch of *Mission*, Carl Stem wanted to help Roy with travel expenses. Carl had a Ph.D. in finance from Harvard. He had gone to church in Lexington and I had met him there. He was now working for the Federal Reserve Board in Washington, D. C. Perhaps as the result of our friendship, I was asked to speak at a Memorial Day lectureship at Rockville, Maryland, and several times invited to speak at the Sixteenth and Decatur church in Washington, D.C. when Ray Chester, the minister, was out of town. We stayed with the Stems a few times. They also came to visit us in State College. Crum had met Carl, and since Carl was outgoing and spent time talking with Crum and shared with him the inner workings at the Federal Reserve, Crum liked him. Carl told me he wanted to give the money to Roy through a church so he could deduct it from his income tax. He said it was too complicated to do so where he attended and asked if we could do it through the church in State College. Since Crum was either treasurer or chairman of the finance committee at church, I asked him, and he made the arrangements.

I was unprepared for the resulting furor. I had reservations, but the action certainly wasn't illegal and I wanted to help two friends. Though such practices are common in some congregations, I soon found out that it was a major bone of contention at State College. What was unusual was that the professors who jumped all over both Crum and me probably were much more sympathetic to the projects involved than Crum. They entered into a barrage of attacks because previously, in their view, Crum had, in a freewheeling manner, funnelled money to whomever he pleased, sometimes so as to gain friends for himself in the power struggles. They had closed down the practice and now I had opened it up again. I could see the problem. Both Crum and I were soundly censured in a business meeting. I felt I had it coming, so I made no defense. A proposal was put before the meeting that we accept no money from outside sources without approval of the business meeting. I spoke up and said, "It seems to me your concern is not so much who gives, but who gets. In a strict interpretation of this proposal we would have to meet to decide whether to accept a large contribution from a visitor. The rule we should make is that no funds will be spent from church monies without approval of the business meeting." This proposal was agreed upon, and soon the ill will subsided.

Later, we were looking for a preacher. One of the prospects was John T. Smithson III, who was then preaching in West Lafayette, Indiana. He was a friend of Roy Creech, a professor of horticulture who was one of Crum's opponents. Crum thought Smithson might be all right, but he feared that employing him would give Roy an upper hand in the power struggles. Business meetings on the matter were tense, with angry words flowing back and forth. I brought my Bible to one of the meetings. Someone asked why. I replied that as a people we professed to follow the Bible in all things, but in our business meetings we seemed to forget its directives about how to treat one another. I said I had in mind reading certain texts if business proceeded as it lately had. That meeting went better and I did not interrupt with a Scripture reading. Another time, however, Crum was very upset over an action (which I supported) of certain professors. In this meeting a friend of his denounced me at some length. I said nothing. The charges were not without substance, even if somewhat distorted. After some time, when it became obvious that I wasn't going to say anything, Crum became embarrassed and interrupted his friend by introducing a new topic.

Despite all these problems we felt good about the church in State College. We managed to make considerable headway despite all the controversy. The differing proposals resulted in more activities being approved, rather than less. A core of us supported any good cause, regardless of the source. Since none of these aggressive persons were squashed, as happens when only one side has the upper hand, we got much done.

This church, though atypical in educational level, was similar to a number of congregations in the 1960s in that region and throughout the United States. Few members were interested in letting teachers explore their doctrinal "hobbies." Few wished to hear the standard church-blueprint sermons. The main agenda, since we had so many children (we were in the midst of the Baby Boom), was to bring up our offspring in the faith. We put our energy into church classes, youth meetings with other congregations, and summer youth camps. We were also interested in Christian education, and, to some extent, Northeastern Christian, though Crum was far more interested than the rest because he was on the board. He was chagrined, I think appropriately so, that interest by the congregation in Northeastern Christian was not far greater. We also wanted to grow. We kept adding numbers, but mainly because of people moving in, either to teach at or attend the university. We were baptizing a few in the community and at the university, but mostly our own children. We tried several methods of reaching outsiders, but none proved imminently successful.

Our church classes, from kindergarten up, focused on the Scriptures. We were mostly interested in what the Bible said about spiritual growth, and how to live and think as Christians in our university community. We interpreted Scriptures with far different questions in mind than those of the meeting preachers of the 1930s. Already, a new hermeneutic was at the embryo stage. Whoever wished might dust off the old hermeneutic and dangle it before the church, but if it was not helpful to the perceived tasks that confronted the believers, it was not likely to receive a groundswell of support. My sense is that some convince believers that their hermeneutical priorities are "the rules by which we have always interpreted the Scriptures," and that these rules are useful in opposing certain new directions. Even then, however, the rules, much like *Gray's Anatomy*, are left on the shelf; worthy of respect, but rarely consulted.

I often taught classes, especially on Wednesday nights, since I preached once or twice a month at Carlisle, a hundred miles away. I also preached in State College, on occasion. I first proposed to teach the Old Testament prophets on Wednesday nights. This was agreed upon with some reluctance. We only had one adult class, but many of the adults were involved in teaching classes for children, nursery-age through teens. Not many of our members had studied the prophets except the few who had attended Christian colleges. I supplied some background, but focused on their message, especially the need for single-minded devotion to God, rather than simply keeping the law. I also stressed concern for the poor and needy which is so central to many of the prophets. Most of the people in the class seemed to appreciate what was going on. I always left time for discussion and questions. While one or two were insistent that we spend time on prophetic fulfillment, I did not permit that focus to become the driving force of the class. Admittedly, if someone only attended periodically, it was difficult to follow the content. A member of the church, a major potato farmer named Guy Stutzman—from the town of Indiana, Pennsylvania, to the west of us—traveled back and forth because he also had farming interests toward Scranton, to the east. He visited a few times, made a few comments in class, but after awhile seemed pretty impatient with what was going on. He was on the board of Northeastern Christian, a friend of Crum's, and usually stayed all night with him. Crum told me that Guy said the study was a waste of time, since it did not contribute to salvation.

Such reactions sometimes reveal the quirks of our hermeneutic rules. The salvation hermeneutic rule is an old one in Christendom. It was emphasized by David Lipscomb. It was not, however, intended as a criterion by which to eliminate sections of the Scriptures as worthy of study, but as a means of giving focus to whatever is studied. I think the rule has validity if applied for the latter reason. That's what we were doing in the class. I was trying to show, by looking at the message of the prophets, that God requires for our salvation a singleness of heart.

> How can I pardon you? Your children have forsaken me, and have sworn by those who are no gods. When I fed them to the full, they committed adultery and trooped to the houses of prostitutes. They were well-fed lusty stallions, each neighing for his neighbor's wife. Shall I not punish them for these things? says the Lord; and shall I not bring retribution on a nation such as this" (Jeremiah 31:33)?

God also requires a concern for others. "He has told you O mortal what is good; and what does the Lord require of you but to do justice and to love kindness, and to walk humbly with your God" (Micah 6:8)? Paul certainly thought the Old Testament was crucial for the salvation of Christians. In writing to Timothy, he said, "from childhood you have known the sacred writings that are able to instruct you for salvation through faith in Christ Jesus" (II Timothy 3:15). The New Testament did not exist in Timothy's youth, nor was it by any means complete when Paul wrote Timothy. It was the Old Testament which, according to Paul, was "able to instruct you for salvation."

One time I preached a Sunday night sermon series titled "Six Sermons on Romans Six." In these sermons I explored the manner in which Paul envisioned the Christian life from the perspective of the cross and the resurrection. Toward the end of the series I showed that Paul considered entry into Christ through baptism the ground of sanctification and eternal life. I pointed out that Paul believed in "once saved, always saved." The Christian is not precariously situated above a precipice, always in danger of falling into the abyss, I taught. One is "sanctified." Furthermore, Paul says that not anything "will be able to separate us from the love of God in Christ Jesus our Lord" (Romans 8:39). God will not capriciously deny our salvation. No exterior force will snatch it away from us. Nothing will force us to fall from grace. We can, however, turn our backs on God. If we fall from grace, though, it is our decision. After the sermon, Crum came around to talk with me. He said, "I understand the point you are making. I will have to think about it. But if this is true, how will we refute the Baptists?" I replied that

I worried more about what the Scripture teaches than about an interpretation which would refute someone, Baptist or otherwise. At one time we declared that we were willing to learn from anyone who would help us interpret the Scriptures aright. Did we really mean it?

The heirs of the Restoration in the region were of all stripes: including liberal Disciples, conservative Christian Churches, and non-instrumental churches, some of which were unaligned. We had a monthly meeting attended by preachers and others from all these groups. We carried on discussions in which we disagreed, but still treated each other as brothers. The non-instrumental churches had Sunday afternoon singings to which persons from across the spectrum came. We also visited each other's gospel meetings. An anomaly among the non-instrumental congregations was a small church in Nittany, about twenty miles east of State College. We designated them "the pinchers," because of the manner in which they partook of the Lord's supper. Their hermeneutic rule was that they were not worthy to do precisely what the Lord did when he broke the bread. Since they themselves were unworthy to break the bread, they pinched it off. I'm not sure how they applied this across the board. Does this mean that since Jesus prayed while looking into the heavens that they, in turn, prayed while looking at the ground?

Pennsylvania State University

At Penn State only two courses were required of all undergraduate students: Speech 200, and Logic. English composition, math and other requirements existed, but it was possible to CLEP out of these. The global requirement in speech was fairly recent. This meant that we taught speech to five thousand sophomores each year. This required sixty sections per term, four terms per year. Speech 200 was our bread-and-butter course. We worked hard to make it a quality experience. We had constant meetings to make sure that our syllabi, requirements and standards were essentially the same. The first year, I taught two Speech 200 courses per term for four terms. It was also presumed that I would do research for publication, though the amount was not specified.

In the fall of 1962, Pennsylvania State University was one of the few places in the country where an attempt was made to bring together those interested in philosophy and rhetoric. The initiator of these exchanges was Dr. Robert T. Oliver, then chairman of the department. Oliver was perennially obsessed with the manner in which rhetoric had been influenced throughout history by other disciplines, and what such disciplines could learn from each other. His own researches outside of speech had been in psychology and international studies. Oliver was an inveterate promoter of collegiality and of the speech discipline. He approached Henry W. Johnstone, Jr., serving in 1961 as acting chairman of the philosophy department, about appointing visiting professors in philosophy and rhetoric. Henry had engaged in exchanges with Chaim Perelman of Belgium regarding argumentation, and with Maurice Natanson, later of Yale, on other matters. Arrangements were made for Perelman to offer a graduate course as a visiting professor, in the fall of 1962. The course was promoted among graduate students in both philosophy and speech.

I, along with various colleagues in speech, attended Perelman's lectures and other functions. It was at those lectures that I got to know a few of the philosophy professors, especially Henry Johnstone, Robert Price, Joseph Flay, and Stanley Rosen. These were the beginnings of a series of cross-disciplinary exchanges which contributed to the founding of a new journal, *Philosophy and Rhetoric*. Twenty to thirty people regularly attended Perelman's lectures. The rhetoric students were interested in Perelman's focus on audience-centered rhetoric. The philosophy students were probably more interested in his reflections on logic and argumentation.

In 1958 Chaim Perelman, along with his colleague, Olbrechts-Tyteca, published a landmark volume, *La Nouvelle Rhétorique: Traité de l'Argumentation*.[1] The English translation was completed in 1969. In the introduction Perelman expressed appreciation to Richard McKeon at Chicago, and to Oliver, Johnstone, and Olbricht at Penn State.[2] Perelman became interested in rhetoric as the result of his legal training and work in international law. As he studied argumentation he found greater helpfulness in classical rhetoric than in post-Cartesian developments in logic.[3] Though he was aware of the emotional and personal dimensions of persuasion he, like Aristotle, devoted much of his attention to the logical aspects of argumentation.

Some of us wondered how to promote these interchanges and I volunteered to send out an occasional newsletter to interested persons in American universities. The newsletter was titled *Antistrophos*, a Greek word used by Aristotle in the opening sentence of *The Rhetoric*. Aristotle wrote, "Rhetoric is the counterpart—*antistrophos*—of Dialectic." The title seemed very apt for a periodical promoting interchanges between rhetoricians and philosophers. The two newsletters produced, dated November 1965, and November 1966, are available in the archives of *Philosophy and Rhetoric*.[4] It was hoped, early on, that this newsletter might be parlayed into a journal, but those with control of the budgets were of the view that these interests needed to snowball before seriously embarking upon the founding of a journal.

In 1965 Robert T. Oliver announced his retirement as chairman of the speech department, effective October 1. A search for a new chairman was launched which resulted in the appointment of Stanley Paulson, who came to Penn State from the presidency of California State University at San Francisco in the summer of 1966.

In March of 1966 I was offered a contract to teach at Abilene Christian College (now University), commencing with the fall of 1967. I was seriously interested, but did not care to make a commitment that far in advance. One of my early talks with Paulson involved my dilemma as to whether I should continue at Penn State or accept the Abilene position. I felt constantly affirmed by Paulson, who strongly recommended that I stay at Penn State. He had interest in philosophy and especially in promoting the image of the speech department. He offered constant encouragement about developing *Antistrophos* into a journal. He did not immediately develop Oliver's ties with the philosophers, but he recognized this as an area in which Penn State might enter the national limelight. Henry Johnstone also encouraged me to stay, and even offered to nominate me for his position as Assistant Vice President for Research, which he planned to abandon. It was out of these circumstances, at least as I understood them, that Paulson and perhaps others decided to commit budgetary dollars for launching the long-awaited journal. This happened either late in 1965 or early in 1966.

It was with a degree of sadness and regret that I nevertheless eventually decided to leave Penn State. Among the causes of my chagrin was the excitement over the birthing of *Philosophy and Rhetoric*. I felt something like a parent abandoning a newborn on the proverbial doorstep: an apropos metaphor, given that I have since made almost no contribution to the rearing of the child, which has now attained a mature age of thirty years.

Pedagogies, Publications and Perspectives

It was part of my agreement with Oliver that after I became experienced in Speech 200 I could develop classes which reflected my special interests. I was hopeful of teaching classical rhetoric because of my work in the classics. At one point I anticipated publishing either a commentary or book on the *Rhetoric* of Aristotle. One solution was that I teach a course that was already on the books, Continental Oratory. None of the current students had taken the course so it had no clientèle. I was somewhat reluctant to take up the course since few American speech students had an interest in European studies. Despite these reservations, I offered the course. I was pleased that the first time I offered it, nine students enrolled. The second time there were fourteen. These numbers by no means put it in the category of a popular course, but they were respectable. The course provided the opportunity to utilize my studies in classics, church history, and theology. By beginning with the Greeks and moving through medieval times to the Reformation, I covered territory with which I was familiar, and which mostly focused upon Christian discourse. We also continued into Europe during the modern period.

The course gave me a chance to pursue a major interest: the manner in which both the method and content of rhetoric is affected by cultural perspectives and ideas. I was especially interested in those aspects of rhetorical theory which view the audience as the determining factor in communication. In much rhetorical theory, especially British and American, the aims of the speaker have been heralded as the driving force of the rhetorical enterprise. This is obvious in many subtle ways. For example, in delineating types of speeches, the categories are persuading, convicting, informing, and entertaining. Insights on each type in the British-American tradition focused on divining the intent of the speaker. He was the one who determined which type of speech was presented. I argued that the speaker may have this option in a classroom setting, but that with actual audiences it is the audience which determines the viable type of speech, if the communication is to be effective. One can, in contrast, therefore, take the above categories and define them in terms of audience expectations.

As I now look back on the point of view I was developing, I am surprised to find that I was already exhibiting some of the characteristics of Post-Modernism, and that before many people in the speech discipline were similarly affected. But I need to define how my perspective differs from Post-Modernism. In effect, I rejected a major thesis of the Enlightenment, which held that in the world of nature as well as the world of men, principles and conclusions are universally applicable. As an occasional historian, it had become obvious to me that while we might wish for universally applicable insights, cultural diversity has ruled out such a prospect. One can, of course, claim that universal rhetorical principles exist, but to begin with that presumption is not helpful if one takes seriously the characteristics of effective rhetoric down through history.

I, however, did not, contrary to various Post-Modernists, reject the Enlightenment affirmation that reality is weighed, sifted and understood with the help of empirical data and reason. It is, in fact, through these means that cultural relativity is disclosed. And, while I agree with Post-Modernism that methodology is culturally relative, I am a relativist only in regard to methodology, not in respect to ultimate truth. I always have been and continue to be a monotheist. I do not see how a real monotheist can be a relativist in regard to final or ontological truth. I believe that ultimately, truth is one because God is one. But even the truth of God appears in many contexts, times, and cultures. The creations of God are multiple, not singular. The rich diversity of God's creation are clearly affirmed and praised in the Scriptures, as in Psalm 147. Hermeneutics is a methodology, not a content. Hermeneutics must therefore take into account the richness of the diverse ways in which God has revealed himself to different persons in different times. "Long ago God spoke to our ancestors in many and various ways by the prophets, but in these last days he has spoken to us by a Son" (Hebrews 1:1).

We first noted cultural differences in Continental Rhetoric by contrasting biblical speeches with early Greek speeches. The Greeks, I noted, believed with Plato that ultimate truth resides in essences; therefore, that truth is located in transcendental universals. Aristotle, likewise, posited the essences, but he concluded that essences only exist in particulars. They do not have a life apart, as Plato argued. The Hebrews, on the other hand, believed that truth resided in God alone. Truth, then, ultimately is discovered through observing the actions of the one God. Rhetorically, the Greeks sought to locate these universal truths by utilizing universal *topoi*—topics—such as cause, time, and space. They carefully utilized either inductive generalizations or deductive arguments to arrive at these truths. The Hebrews, rather, sought to trace the mighty acts of God in history as the clue to reality. Paul put it this way: "For Jews demand signs and Greeks desire wisdom" (I Corinthians 1:22). Rhetoric which is influenced by the Hebrew turn of mind is less concerned with essences than with actions. I made this point by contrasting Paul's sermons in the synagogue in Antioch of Pisidia (Acts 13:16-41), with his address to the Athenians (Acts 17:22-31). In the synagogue sermon, Paul spoke of the past specific historical relationships of God with Israel. In the speech on the Areopagus, Paul first noted the universal propensity of the Athenians to worship the gods, and the conclusion of Greek poets that "god" is immanent in all reality. It was only after he had appealed to the Greek interest in universals that he turned to the God who acted in history, specifically in the resurrection of Jesus Christ. Greeks believed that the human soul is an essence and is eternal. But they had a difficult time fathoming the resurrection of a specific human. "When they heard of the resurrection of the dead, some scoffed..." (Acts 17:32).

Because audiences are diverse, I therefore concluded that the most helpful rhetorical observations focus on the culture of the auditors. In Speech 200 we had various assignments: to present an informative speech, then a persuasive speech, for example. I became interested in the culture of the informative speech as compared with that of the persuasive. How do the audiences for the two differ? My struggles with this question took place in a philosophical and theological context. The result of these interests was the development of a class on informative speaking and the writing of a book, *Informative Speaking*.[5] The book was one in a series of paperbacks edited by Ted Clevenger, who was teaching at the University of Pittsburgh when I first went to Pennsylvania. At the time the series made its appearance, Ted was chairman of the speech department at the University of Texas, and later at Florida State.

Informative speaking was usually defined in speech texts either from the standpoint of the speaker or the content. A speaker set out to inform when she wanted to share information on some subject which, in her view, was unknown and non-controversial. From the content standpoint, informative material consists of facts or conclusions beyond dispute. The speech may include the opinions of authorities, not to agree or disagree with these opinions, but merely to report on the type of persons who hold them.

Some schools of philosophy have argued that the most valid form of communication is informative. Information consists of data and conclusions beyond dispute, which are established or verified empirically. This was the position of

Alfred Korzypski, the father of the discipline of general semantics, and before him, of the logical positivism of the famed Vienna Circle, represented by Rudolf Carnap and A. J. Ayer. These philosophers were well aware that experts argued, but they believed that when the dust cleared and unanimity was achieved, the resulting communication should be labeled as information. Argumentation and persuasion were judged as inferior activities. In contrast, other philosophers—Hegelians and the phenomenologists, for example—demoted mere factual content, and presumed that the most important communication has to do with matters that are arguable. Henry Johnstone at Penn State was of the view that the most important philosophical problems are those which philosophers argue about.

I found myself agreeing with Johnstone. I tended to think that little data is beyond dispute, especially if it is significant data. One can even argue over who hit the most major league homers in a year. Roger Maris hit the largest total number, but a reasonable argument is that the total games played had so increased by Maris's time that the former record of Babe Ruth should stand. I concluded that should we shift the definition of informative speaking to the audience, and away from the speaker or the content, we would arrive at a more helpful definition. I was struck, about this time, in reading a statement of Augustine in the *Catechizandis Rudibus* in which he declared that catechizing can take place only when the person involved has already come to believe in the truth of what the church teaches and is willing to hear out the Christian teachings. It seemed that a communication context is "informative" only when the audience accepts a speaker's insights as beyond dispute.

It is one thing for a speaker to claim that his information is beyond dispute, but if his auditors do not see it that way, he must turn to persuading them that such is the case. Informative discourse, therefore, occurs when an audience is willing to grant in advance that a speaker's content is beyond dispute. In our time, most of the information which achieves this privileged status is likely to be scientific. For example, college freshmen will likely hear out a chemistry professor's presentation of the atomic chart without dispute. They are in the same position as apprentices or catechumen. A group of the professor's colleagues, however, might wish to argue with certain points made in the same presentation.

I was additionally interested in informative communication because of its contribution to a scientific and technical culture. In the 1960s a technological world, with new communication avenues involving computers, loomed large on the horizon. Even though we eagerly anticipated the coming communication revolution, some of us perceived dangers lurking in the shadows. Depersonalization could well result. If machine data is assigned top priority, then people are incidental; little more than Social Security numbers. But some of us believed that humans have top priority. It is humans who collect the data and interpret it. They design and execute the building of the machines. We rejected a privileged role for informative communication. Some denied even the prospect of delineating an informative genre of communication, arguing that all communication is persuasive. I held, though, that informative communication has an honorific role in apprenticeship. In conjunction with the interests of Henry Johnstone in defining personhood, I came up with a perspective which I concluded was Christian, and which was philosophically interesting: Informative communication paves the way for personhood.

I came to believe that personhood provided a beginning point from which to distinguish acceptable and unacceptable modes and methods of communication. I published an article, "The Self as the Ground of Persuasion" in the *Pennsylvania Speech Annual*.[6] All forms of communication, I argued, are to be judged on the criterion of the self. The critical question is, how is the selfhood of both the speaker and the auditor to be preserved in the communication act? I concluded that in persuasion, the self is preserved when the speaker respects the commitments of the auditor and helps him arrive at a position which is consonant with such commitments. Coercion or manipulation, therefore, is the effort to force a person to accept a point of view or undertake an action which counteracts his commitments. Religious conversion, for example, is a major realignment of commitments, but should come about through honest assessment, not through subterfuge.

> For our appeal does not spring from deceit of impure motives or trickery, but just as we have been approved by God to be entrusted with the message of the Gospel, even so we speak, not to please mortals, but to please God who tests our hearts (I Thessalonians 2:3, 4).

A person, I concluded, is a being with affirmations, commitments, and a style of life consonant with them. This was biblical, I argued to myself—not in this article—because humans are made in the image of God. God is a being who declares his commitments and acts accordingly. A person is, therefore, similarly defined. And so, none of us is born a "person." We arrive at personhood when we make decisions—when we have commitments. On various matters, we may not yet have achieved personhood, even late in life. I have yet to scan pictures or text into a computer program, for example. I have few insights or commitments in this regard. I am an apprentice and I am, accordingly, willing to subject myself to someone who is knowledgeable on these matters. I have not yet achieved personhood in this regard, but once I am informed or have completed my apprenticeship, then I will be a person. Informing me on such matters will no longer be viable; only argumentation or persuasion, because I will be speaking as a peer with peers. The aim of honorific informative communication must be to work itself out of a job. The communication proceeds in such a manner as to bring the apprenticeship to completion. This means that not only are data and conclusions presented, but the history of, and reasons for these conclusions. In that way, later on, I will be able to argue the value of the presuppositions. Invalid or unethical informative communication is that which attempts to hide the controversial presuppositions involved so as to keep the informant in the state of apprenticeship: in other words, to impede the auditor's emergence as a person.

The same presuppositions are valid in hermeneutics. A biblical hermeneutic enables the one to whom the Word is being interpreted to understand not simply the interpretation, but the grounds for the interpretation. At one time we argued strenuously that believers should examine "the Scriptures every day to see whether these things were so" (Acts 17:11). I haven't heard that Scripture emphasized in a long time. Can it be that we have become afraid of people working through the Scripture on their own, for fear they will come out differently than the way we see it? Are we apprehensive lest people complete their apprenticeship and become interpreters of the Word in their own right?

Missions and Apologetics

My sister and brothers were engaged in mission activities in these years. In 1954 Nedra, who is older than I, married James R. McGill. They spent two years in Germany, first in Nürnberg, then in Munich. My brother Glenn and his family went to Germany in 1959 and stayed until 1968. He preached for both the native German and the U. S. military congregations in Nürnberg. In 1964 Owen, who was preaching in Lamar, Missouri, decided that he wanted to hold three-week summer campaigns in four towns in Pennsylvania, accompanied by Harding students. The first summer he recruited seven male students. I secured churches for him in Johnstown, Huntingdon, Sunbury, and Warrington. They knocked doors for two weeks and had one week of preaching. They baptized several that first year and were well accepted in the churches. The next year we decided to start a congregation in Altoona. The church in Cherry Tree had bought a lot there some years earlier in hopes of starting a congregation, but the effort never took off. Several members of the church in central Pennsylvania met to discuss a campaign to launch the effort, which Owen would direct. In the meantime we heard that a congregation in Freeport, Texas wanted to support a work in the northeast. We informed them about Altoona. They made a visit and decided to put their resources into a congregation there. We located a preacher, Dwight Hesson, and the congregation started with a bang. Soon an edifice was erected and above fifty persons assembled regularly. Persons from several congregations in central Pennsylvania attended the campaign meetings and encouraged the church in various ways.

Early in 1967, Glenn arranged for me to spent the summer in Europe, speaking in places from Rome to Stockholm. I first taught a class in a military retreat in Burchtesgarten, along with Stanley Lockhart. Burchtesgarten was famous during World War II as the hideaway where Hitler took Eva Braun. A military base was below and the Eagle's Nest above. The beautiful area consisted of small German villages and evergreen-covered mountains with snow-peaked summits, some of which were nine thousand feet in elevation. Then I held week-long meetings for the military congregations in Nürnberg and Munich. After that I, along with Fausto Salvoni, taught two weeks each in the Scandinavian Preacher's School in Copenhagen and the Italian Preacher's School in Florence. I ended by speaking at the annual Frankfurt Lectures. In the Preacher's School I taught biblical archaeology and Christian apologetics.

Apologetics had become one of my specialities in the eyes of some, though I did not particularly seek out that role. J. W. Roberts and the board of *Restoration Quarterly* decided to put out a special issue on Christian apologetics. I was asked to write an article on the method and content of apologetics.[7] My views on apologetics were influenced by my perspectives on argumentation and persuasion, though the content was deeply influenced by work in theology and biblical theology at Harvard. I believed that since apologetics is an effort to lead persons into the Christian faith, it had to commence from the perceptions of the person involved. This meant first that there is no universal Christian apologetic. Apologetic, if successful, must relate the faith to the views of specific persons. And again, if the person is to become a Christian, the commitments must become her own, rather than being forced upon her through manipulation or coercion. Furthermore, the God to whom she is led must be the God of the Scripture, not some philosopher's or scientist's God. Apologetic in the history of Christianity was always directed toward people. In other words, it was *ad hominem*. The problem however, was that evangelical Christians tended to employ apologetics which were created for a different place and time. These apologetics, therefore, did not relate to the new setting. In the words of LeMoine Lewis, it was similar to firing volleys into trenches that hadn't been occupied for fifty years. What is needed is an apologetic which speaks to the concerns of our day, not a different day.

I therefore needed to work out an apologetic which related to the current scene. My first major challenge came through preparing a Bible correspondence course for the 1964-65 New York World's Fair. The publications committee started meeting in 1963. The committee was of the conviction that none of the existing Bible correspondence courses were suitable as an entry-level course. The existing courses presupposed a certain disposition toward the Scriptures. If persons wanted additional instructions, then the course of greater length by Monroe Hawley would be employed. Our course was to have but six lessons.

The question was how to begin. What was the need on the contemporary scene that might lead a person to consider the biblical faith? I decided to take a clue from Paul and begin with guilt and its resolution. Paul observed to the Athenians that they sought to cover all the bases with respect to the gods. So great was their fear that they might miss a god, they even had a statue to an unknown god. I began by discussing the contemporary feeling of guilt. I pointed out that the feeling of guilt, though not its specific manifestations, is characteristic of humans. All of us feel guilty about something: inadequate work skills, neglecting family and parents, or perhaps being insensitive to associates. I then proceeded to announce the good news, as did Paul, that God in his Son addressed both guilt and its resolution.

As I had in Copenhagen and in Rome, I commenced by considering the need to know the presuppositions of the persons to whom we hoped to offer this apology for the Christian faith. Then I proceeded through the topics of standard Christian apologetics, indicating what I perceived as the helpful approaches for Europe in 1967. If the persons to whom one is communicating accept the Bible as inspired from God, then one can begin with the Bible. If the Bible is not so revered then one must start from a different place. Perhaps, it was suggested, the point of departure was to build a case for the authenticity and inspiration of the Scriptures. That was typical in our circles in the 1960s. I pointed out, however, that was not the approach of the early Christians as they faced a world that knew nothing of the Bible. If one looks in Acts at Paul's sermons to the gentiles, he discovers that Paul first identified a common ground with his auditors, then set out the Christ story or some facet of it. For example, in Lystra he declared, "...we bring you good news, that you should turn from these worthless things to the living God, who made the heaven and the earth and the sea and all that is in them" (Acts 13:15). In I Thessalonians 1:9, 10, Paul outlined his preaching to the Gentile audiences and started with the same observation. Efforts to create a loyalty to Scripture as the Word of God came later for Paul.

As to the classical arguments for the existence of God, I pointed out that while I was impressed with some, they did not necessarily lead the seeker to the God of the Scriptures. For example, Thomas Aquinas's first proof, borrowed from Aristotle, was from motion. Our experience is that nothing moves unless it is moved. It defies rationality, however, to posit motion ad infinitum—motion preceded by motion preceded by motion forever. First motion must exist, or, in the language of Aristotle, there must exist an unmoved mover. We observe motion in the world about us. What accounts for it? In Christian tradition, as Aquinas pointed out, the unmoved mover is God. I think the argument for an unmoved mover is the only rational explanation for motion. The question is whether the unmoved mover is the God of Scripture. A remote unmoved mover, such as conceived by Aristotle, one who is unconcerned for the welfare and plight of humanity, qualified quite well for the deity proved in this argument. The God of Scripture, in contrast, is a God of love who is involved with the people made in his image and faithful to his covenant community. The argument of the unmoved mover does not prove the existence of a God with the characteristics of the biblical God.

If rules of hermeneutics, as I think they must be, are designed to interpret Scripture for a particular time and place, then similar audience characteristics must be taken into account when formulating an appropriate hermeneutic by which to explain Scripture to that audience.

The Move to Abilene

After considerable anguish we decided to move to Abilene so that I could begin teaching there in the fall of 1967. All of us felt very much at home in Pennsylvania, but I had not forgotten my longtime commitment to train preachers, and Abilene offered me the chance. I was not to teach homiletics, but, for starters, philosophy and Old Testament. I could become more specialized as new teachers were appointed. I welcomed these courses, since my interests at Penn State had moved in these directions and I continued to be enamored with biblical theology, having kept up with new works as they were published.

Our decision to move was not universally applauded. People from church discouraged us. My department and friends at Penn State did everything they could to keep me around, including a promotion to associate professor and a sizable raise. My parents were not too favorable, since they considered Abilene to the left of center. Dorothy's father was appalled that the salary was one-half my projected next year's pay at Penn State. Her parents were not pleased about our going to Abilene, even though they liked the town and the people. James D. Willeford lived there and they had spent time with him and his family on more than one occasion.

Not only did Dorothy have to orchestrate the move to Abilene by herself, I also left her with seven kids and thirteen Siamese cats. At that time we were raising Siamese cats to sell. We had two females and eleven kittens. The seven kids can be accounted for in this manner: four, of course, were our own. The previous fall a woman started attending church, having been invited by Maretta Rice. She was divorced from her husband and had recurring mental problems. She was now out of the hospital and doing well. Maretta befriended her. Since her children were about the same age as ours we had them out to eat with us and baby-sat the kids on various occasions. Late in the winter she started having mental problems again. I observed that she was going in and out of the twilight zone, so I recommended that she voluntarily enter the state hospital at Holladaysburg. She resisted the idea. Then, about two weeks later, she asked if she could bring the children over for a couple of hours. We said yes. We began to worry about four hours later, when she hadn't returned. Then we received a call from the hospital, saying that she had entered as a patient. We decided that we would keep the children that night and see what could be done with them the next day.

We called the woman's parents, thinking that they would keep the children. They said they couldn't handle them and they wanted nothing to do with them, since the daughter had taken advantage of them more than once. We then called welfare and they said they would see about making arrangements, but the kids would probably have to split up. We decided that since, hopefully, the mother would be out of the hospital after a few months, and since we had the room, we would keep them. We thought that at least the parents might want to help financially, but they declined that as well. Still, it worked out pretty well, but at times all of us were tested. The kids were nice, but the youngest daughter, particularly, missed her mother.

So, Dorothy had her hands full, to say the least. As it happened, the mother would get out of the hospital about the time Dorothy went to Wisconsin before the move to Abilene, so it all worked out. This circumstance raises the question: how does one interpret the Word? It seems to me that we have do it with our lives as well as our declarations. We did not go around advertising our care of these children, but the news got out in my department since we couldn't keep it from our close friends. More than one person commended us for what we were doing. Even as I got to know people at Penn State, some of the faculty were standoffish because of my S.T.B. degree and religious commitment. But along the way we were accepted more and more. These new developments, especially, created an opportunity to put in a word for the Gospel when we were asked why we were taking care of all those children.

---

[1] Chaim Perelman and L. Olbrechts-Tyteca, *La Nouvelle Rhétorique: Traité de l'Argumentation* (Paris: Presses Universitaires de France, 1958) 2 vols.

[2] Chaim Perelman and L. Olbrechts-Tyteca, *The New Rhetoric: A Treatise on Argumentation* (Notre Dame: The University of Notre Dame Press, 1969) v.

[3] Chaim Perelman and L. Olbrechts-Tyteca, *The New Rhetoric*, 1.

[4] The archives also contain my lengthier version of the beginnings of *Philosophy and Rhetoric*.

[5] Thomas H. Olbricht, *Informative Speaking* (Glen Ellyn: Scott, Foresman, 1968).

[6] Thomas H. Olbricht, "The Self as a Ground of Persuasion," *The Pennsylvania Speech Annual*, 1965.

[7] Thomas H. Olbricht, "Apologetics in the Restoration Movement," *Restoration Quarterly*, 6 (1962) 167-188.

9
The Heart of the Scriptures: Abilene Christian University, 1967-1976

In early August 1967 we left Wisconsin for Leadwood, Missouri, where my parents lived. My mother had a year to go before she retired, at age 70, from teaching first grade. We then, along with my parents, went on south to Thayer, where my grandparents lived. From there we took my dad to Nebraska to look into business involving his ranch. We decided to combine the Nebraska trip with our move to Texas, though it was much out of the way. Once in Texas we would put Dad on a bus and send him back to Thayer. Mother stayed with her parents since Grandmother, because of a stroke, was confined to a wheel chair.

We bid my grandparents and Mother goodbye. We had a nine-seat, 1964 Chevrolet station wagon. So there we went: three adults, four children aged nine to fourteen, two cats, several house plants and our luggage. It was a full car. We made it to Nebraska without trouble, albeit with plenty of children's complaints.

That first year we rented the house of Abe and Phyllis Malherbe. Abe had taken a leave from teaching at ACC and had returned to Massachusetts to get some writing done. Our furniture had arrived and was in the Malherbe's garage. Abe's books were stored here and there, along with back issues of the *Restoration Quarterly*. Dorothy had agreed to keep the *Quarterly*'s books and handle circulation. Church was convenient, since the Hillcrest church building was only four blocks away.

I had my job cut out for me that first year. The agreement was that I would teach three classes so I could get some writing done. The standard load then at Abilene Christian was five three-hour courses. If one taught graduate courses the number was reduced to four. I taught Religious Teachings of the Old Testament, Beginning Philosophy, and Great Bible Doctrines. The second semester I taught Old Testament Introduction, Beginning Philosophy and the continuation of Great Bible Doctrines. This meant that I prepared to teach five courses that year which I had never taught before.

In addition, another responsibility was unexpectedly dropped in my lap. Walter Burch, an Abilenian for some years, suddenly decided to move to Long Island to be part of the West Islip congregation, the flagship "Exodus" church spearheaded by Dwain Evans. He twisted my arm to take over the new journal *Mission*, the first issue of which was dated August 1967. I had been involved with plans for the journal from the beginning, but by no means anticipated the mantle that descended upon me. I would have rejected the privilege hands-down, but Walter assured me that no one on the Abilene scene had the interest, skill, or appropriate insight to follow through. Abe Malherbe was a more appropriate person, but he had had the foresight to leave town for a year.

Walter Burch was the principal organizer for *Mission* even though Dwain Evans was likely the driving force who kept the dream alive. In 1963 Walter coordinated the planning sessions leading to the exhibit at the New York World's Fair. We decided, in the publications committee, that we would distribute *Twentieth Century Christian, Power for Today, The North Atlantic Christian, The Christian Chronicle,* and other journals, but we dreamed of a revamped or new journal of high quality. Some discussion centered upon upgrading the *North Atlantic Christian,* but nothing was done, probably both because of costs and the time involved. The skills of the quality writers, so it was thought, were tied up in the other World's Fair publications.

After the fair was over the discussion of a new journal continued. The camaraderie of the Fair inspired corporate endeavors by which to address the problems of the sixties. A channel of communication was needed. Several persons agreed, for different reasons. Some dreamed of a better quality of journalism, some of a higher level of scholarly insight, some of a more open environment for the discussion of ideas, and some of addressing of the problems of the sixties. Most of those involved believed that the church needed to climb out of old trenches and storm new no-man's lands.

Several meetings ensued, but the one that determined the final course of the journal was held in Memphis. In that meeting Otis Gatewood proposed that we incorporate, sell stock and establish a bookstore. He conceived the enterprise much like *Twentieth Century Christian,* in which a profit would accrue. The majority, however, were not interested in a business enterprise, but in establishing a new journalistic voice among our people. As Walter put it, "Our objectives were to: (1) to create a new editorial voice within Churches of Christ; and (2) to provide a forum in which writers with different perspectives could express themselves freely, even if their views were unpopular."[1]

The anti-*Mission* furor that soon broke out did not focus on biblical interpretation. Rather, the flap was a power struggle, only ostensibly issue-driven. It was a decade before persons writing for the popular journals became aware that the "old hermeneutic" was not particularly helpful in delineating a biblical position on these new concerns. A few articles then appeared criticizing the "old hermeneutic." I believe, however, that the new canon of questions put to the Scriptures beginning in the early 1960s had already eroded the perceived usefulness of our traditional hermeneutic methods. When questions change, then theology changes. And when theology changes so does hermeneutics. In the 1991 *Image* articles I referred to these developments as a paradigm shift.[2]

The August 1967 founding issue of *Mission* appeared without an editor, to spread the liability. The board of *Mission,* however, at some future date, anticipated appointing an editor. The first year, the journal was to be generated by a seven-person board of editors: Walter Burch, Ray Chester, Hubert Locke,

Thomas H. Olbricht, Frank Pack, J. W. Roberts, and Roy Bowen Ward. Walter solicited articles for the first issue. It is not accidental, I think, that these were popularized articles by those of a scholarly bent: Malherbe, Ward, Olbricht, Don McGaughey, Wesley Reagan, and Juan Monroy. Members of the Board of Trustees for *Mission* included all the editorial board, along with Bill Banowsky, Dwain Evans, Everett Ferguson, Abe Malherbe, Don McGaughey, Don Sime, Carl Spain, David Stewart, and Ike Summerlin.

The moment we arrived in Abilene, *Mission* was dumped in my lap, and soon Dorothy's. I coordinated the editing, took the manuscripts to the printer, and read proof—as did Delno Roberts—pasted a mock-up, and Dorothy and I, with the help of the kids, sorted the journals into zip code order, whereupon I took them to the post office for mailing. Other activities included raising money, increasing subscriptions, and worrying about paying the bills. Walter was great for initiating a project, but not strong on insuring a feasible balance of income and outgo, and carrying the burden in the heat of the day. Dorothy took over the subscriptions and bookkeeping. The next action was to find another printer. *Mission* was being printed by the company for which Walter worked, but their prices were high, even for Abilene. I called or wrote for bids from various presses. I'm not sure how I heard about Futura in Austin, perhaps through Ray Chester. With the printing cut in half, we soon had the expenses at least at a manageable level.

As the first board meeting drew near, the persons who wanted to fan the flames pushed for an editor who would initiate a distinctive platform. As a result, Roy Ward was appointed editor, and Ray Chester managing editor. Before long the influence of the educated voices was overshadowed in order to push platforms and programs. It's not that my colleagues and I disagreed with what was being pushed, we would just have gone about it differently. We were always much more interested in action than agitation. In Nashville in 1966, I remember asking a group of about ten persons who were waxing eloquent over the plight of "negroes" if they had ever entertained any in their homes. None reported they had: they said they hadn't thought of that. Persons such as Abe Malherbe resigned from the board for these reasons.

Mission continued in much the same vein until 1973. In January 1973, Vic Hunter was announced as editor. By now *Mission* had become quite controversial: my own family criticized me for my involvement. I heard of places in which I was declared *persona non grata*. Four of us at ACU were on the board, Ferguson, Roberts, Spain, and myself. John Stevens, president of ACU, began drawing considerable flak from certain ACU board members over our involvement. Carl resigned in August of 1970. In late 1972 *Mission* quit identifying the board members in the journal so schools such as ACU would not be effected by the fallout. John kept talking with us, but said he thought we were going to have to resign from the board. I decided to resign because though I had already resigned as business manager, Dorothy was still doing the books and I was being pressed into considerable work and advice. I needed to get on with my own publications and I decided the only way I could get out from under the burden was to resign from the board altogether and tell Dorothy she had to talk with Carl Stem, then dean of the College of Business at Texas Tech University in Lubbock, and business manager for *Mission*. Carl took this well and called her frequently. The person most adamant against resignation was J. W. Roberts, who told John Stevens he would not resign. It would have been interesting to have seen how this conflict played itself out. Unfortunately, J. W. died of a heart attack in April 1973.

Looking back now, thirty years later, it appears that the sentiments published in *Mission* are commonplace among the influential preachers and larger churches across the brotherhood. Those threatened in the nineties by new changes find themselves without a publication to rally around which is respected by the leading preachers. That is the difference between 1967 and 1997. In 1967 leading preachers paid deference to views expressed in the *Firm Foundation* and the *Gospel Advocate*. Now they read first *Wineskins*, then *Image*. All four journals have their clientele, but none has a privileged position across the brotherhood as the former two did, the *Gospel Advocate* for the first half of the century and the *Firm Foundation* in the sixties and seventies.

Developed Perspectives on Hermeneutics

In this book I have detailed many aspects of my years which may, at first glance, seem irrelevant to interpreting the Scriptures—to hermeneutics. But I have done so to make it clear that my perspectives were not developed solely in the classroom. They emerged in the crucible of specific churches and the struggles of Churches of Christ across the United States and other regions of the world. They were not ivory tower events, nor intended for academic consumption only. No theology which has demanded historical respect has ever been isolated from the real-life struggle to be God's people. The same is true for hermeneutics. But it was in the classroom that I gave formulation and systemization to my understanding of hermeneutics.

By the time I reached Abilene Christian, I was of the conviction that a hermeneutic method which professed to be biblical had to encompass these features: (1) It had to be dedicated to locating the central message of the Scripture. (2) God, Christ and the Holy Spirit would be the focal point for its message. (3) It must recognize that the intramural "hermeneutics" within Scripture proceed through showing that God expects of humans only what he himself has already done. (4) It must allow that much Scripture is narrative and that commands, examples, and inferences are embedded in story material. It appreciates the danger in trying to isolate the three, for polemical purposes, from the narratives. (5) It assumes narrative as essential for reports about the biblical God, for he is chiefly known through his mighty acts in history and their interpretation. (6) It must be sensitive to cultural diversity, both within the Scripture, in historical Christendom, and with respect to our own history in the Churches of Christ. (7) It does not permit the accidents of history or contemporary concerns to determine the crucial topics of Scripture. (8) Its resulting interpretation has implications for the life of the interpreter as well as his intellectual processes. (9) It recognizes that the question of what is authorized by Scripture is related to all of the above.

It was through teaching courses in the religious teachings of the Old Testament during my first year at Abilene Christian and religious teachings of the New Testament my second year that I began to see more clearly the manner in which a hermeneutic which is faithful to the biblical message may be formulated. This was so because the major question raised, when teaching either Old Testament or New Testament theology, is, what are the theological centers of the testaments, if any? If one can determine the theological centers, then one has located a framework from which the rest is to be interpreted. A method for doing biblical theology is therefore the beginning point for a hermeneutic that is faithful to Scripture.

The Teaching of Biblical Theology

Once I agreed to teach Religious Teachings of the Old Testament, the next step was to think through the goals I hoped to attain and how to proceed. I was greatly influenced by Stendahl's article on biblical theology in *Interpreter's Dictionary of the Bible* (1962), in which he argued that we need to be very careful to ask what the Bible meant in its own setting before we go on to decide what it means for us in our time. As I perceived it, this delineation was unmistakably restorationist. We have argued that we are eager to replicate early Christian faith and life as discovered in Scripture. We are therefore committed to original meanings—what it meant then—rather than the later explanations of interpreters living in other eras. In other words, if we claim to live under the word of God, to be judged by it rather than to be judges of it, we are committed to a rigorous pursuit of the theology presented in

the Scripture. My goal for the course, then, was an exacting investigation of Scripture in order to determine its theology from some central core located in the Scripture itself.

The first time I taught Old Testament theology I employed the framework set out by G. Ernest Wright in the chapter "The Faith of Israel," from volume I of *The Interpreter's Bible*. The topics in this chapter were "God and the People of Israel," and "The Worship and Service of God." I certainly could not fault positioning God as the focal point of the Old Testament. The book of Genesis starts out, "In the beginning God..." and Malachi ends by heralding the impending advent of the day of the Lord. It appeared to me, however, that Wright's headings were superimposed on the Old Testament, rather than clearly flowing from the text. One might as well, as have various authors of Old and New Testament theologies, superimpose the traditional catalogue of theological topics: faith, revelation, inspiration, Scripture, God, Christ, the Holy Spirit, creation, man, the church, the sacraments, ethics, ecumenics, and eschatology, or end things. The question I kept asking myself was whether or not it was possible to discover some sort of framework within the Old Testament, rather than importing it from without. A structure of some sort which was embedded in the text would obviously be more biblical than one imported from the exterior. If such a superstructure could be found, it would have great ramifications for hermeneutics—at least, so I concluded. This core would provide the crucial skeleton from which to view individual concepts within the text.

I searched for the core message of the Old Testament because that would provide a clue as how the details are fleshed out. If such a core does indeed exist, then the Old Testament is held together by a story line and specific problems are explained in the light of it. My task was locating such a core. By this time I had definitely arrived at the conclusion that a flat view of Scripture was not biblically defensible. James P. Sanders, the Rockford preacher, had poured the foundation for this insight, but it took a few years to finish building it inside my thick skull. Jesus spoke of the weightier matters of the law (Matthew 23:23). Paul wrote of "that which was of first importance, that Christ died for our sins in accordance with the Scriptures, that he was buried, and that he was raised on the third day in accordance with the Scriptures" (I Corinthians 15:1-9). As I explained to students who defended the equal weight of all things in Scripture—and they have been numerous—that it would seem strange indeed if Jesus' mixing spittle with mud and placing it on the eyes of a blind man somehow was of equal importance with his own resurrection. Not only, therefore, did I reject the flat view, I perceived that in some way the most important concepts in Scripture provided the foundations from which the interpretations of specific commands to action arose.

About this time I came upon an illustration in John Bright's *The Authority of the Old Testament* which helped allay the fears of those who insisted that distinguishing the important from the unimportant is dangerous, because it is a human enterprise. People of this mindset are afraid that if you turn someone loose to determine what is important, they will surely declare unimportant whatever they do not like or that which opposes their traditions. It is therefore much safer to assume that everything in Scripture is of equal importance to free interpretation from the stratagems of those with an ax to grind. In our heritage we have avoided all efforts to ascertain what is of most importance because we are aware that the rest of the evangelical world assigns baptism to the realm of items that may be meaningful under some circumstances, but are basically unimportant. We also know that certain persons—Thomas Jefferson, for example—were embarrassed by the miracles of Jesus and deleted them, preparing truncated versions of the Scriptures.

Bright, however, said that concepts in Scripture are like different-size bills. All currency has value; it's just that some bills are worth much more than others. Counterfeit money is worthless for commerce, but all legal tender has worth. Similarly, even though some concepts in Scripture are more important than others, each has a value. If this can be understood and accepted—and this is a view which comes from both Jesus and Paul, in such passages as "These you ought to have done, without neglecting the others" (Matthew 23:23)—then how can we determine what is most important in Scripture in a manner unaffected by human preference and prejudice? Are we subject to the whims of every Tom, Dick, and Harry who sets himself up as the final arbitrator? Perhaps. But what if the Old Testament itself provides clues?

I struggled over this conundrum, seeking a solution for over a year, but without success. In 1968, Abe Malherbe returned to Abilene Christian from his year's leave. I was now asked to teach New Testament theology. Once again I faced the tough task of determining how I would structure the course. I was convinced that superimposing the traditional theological topics was forcing a set of categories upon the Scriptures, and being derelict in the duty to seek out the center which emerged from within Scripture. When I raised this matter with Abe, he said, "I would take clues from C. H. Dodd's little book on apostolic preaching." Dodd proposed that the theology of the New Testament is fleshed out from the *kerygma*—the preaching of Christ found in the sermons in Acts and the various confessions of faith elsewhere in the New Testament. The topics for New Testament theology should therefore be the basic items preached in regard to Jesus. I thought about this and it seemed like an important and biblically-grounded perspective. Before working all this out in regard to the New Testament, however, I backtracked to the Old.

Old Testamant Theology

I was convinced by G. Ernest Wright, through his lectures and writings, that the central story line of the Old Testament was the mighty loving acts of God and their interpretation. Wright often spoke of certain catalogues of these acts. As I thought about it I wondered why he had not employed these acts as the basic structure of Old Testament theology. After all, they were derived from the Old Testament itself. Gehard von Rad, perhaps the premier Old Testament theologian of the twentieth century, had perceived that the theological underpinning of the hexateuch revolved about certain basic themes. For him the most important were the promise to the fathers, the exodus, the deliverance at the sea, the revelation of Yahweh at Sinai, and the bestowal of the land of Canaan.[3] With this beginning I developed, after an examination of several Old Testament credos, a nine-point catalogue of the items from the Old Testament. Later, I was impressed that before his death, G. Ernest Wright, in the outline of his Old Testament theology course, was moving in the same direction.

The Old Testament credos, such as Deuteronomy 26:1-10, Psalms 105, 106, 136, and Nehemiah 9, as an aggregate, identify nine important actions of God as foundational for all Old Testament thought. Many of the nine are contained in all the credos. These credos agree that the beginning point for the faith of Israel lies with Yahweh, the God who acts lovingly on behalf of his people. A few years later I wrote a book in a popular mode on the theology of the Old Testament, *He Loves Forever*. In that book the first nine chapters revolve about the ways in which God acts mightily and lovingly. He is the God (1) who creates and sustains, (2) who made promises to the fathers, (3) who acted in Egypt and at the sea, (4) who trains his son in the wilderness, (5) who puts it in writing with his people, (6) who shows his care by giving law, (7) who commands the heavenly armies, (8) who gives his son an inheritance, and (9) who makes a promise to David.

These topics are the fundamental skeleton upon which the whole of the Old Testament is fleshed out, according to the credos of the Old Testament, not according to my preferences as to what that skeleton might be. It provides not only a clue to the most important actions and ideas, it also serves as a starting point for addressing concrete situations. If this is the case, then the proper interpretation of the Bible commences with this skeleton and pays particular attention to the manner in which Israel's laws and ways of life are encased in the narrative description of these events. Only by noting these contexts can a hermeneutic which identifies commands and examples be truly biblical. Specifics are to be understood or interpreted in the light of these mighty acts. For example, the loving actions of God in the Exodus serve as the basis for the way Israel is to treat aliens in its land. "The alien who resides with you shall be to you as the citizen among you; you shall love the alien as yourself, for you were aliens in the land of Egypt...I am the Lord your God who brought you out of Egypt" (Leviticus 19:34, 36).

Psalm 136 shows clearly the same manner of proceeding. The Psalm commences with a praise of the Lord whose love endures forever. He alone works great marvels (v. 4). His actions are two; first, in creation, and then in history. But how do God's past mighty acts impinge on the present? Does this catalogue in any manner help interpret what is happening in one's life, even now? That is what a hermeneutic is supposed to do. It should provide a means of establishing the rules, blessings, and insights for life in the present. At the close, the psalmist goes on to establish just such insight: the God who acted powerfully in the past is the same God who remembers us when our fortunes are low, who rescues us from our enemies, and who gives food to all flesh. We are therefore to interpret what is happening to us right now from the perspective of this catalogue of past mighty acts.

If we choose one of these themes—the promise to the fathers—we can briefly show how it is the skeleton upon which Genesis is fleshed out. The theme proceeds throughout the Old Testament and into the New. The promise to Abraham is found in Genesis 12:1-3 and repeated to Isaac, Genesis 26:4, and Jacob, Genesis 28:13, 14.

> I will make you a great nation, and I will bless you, and make your name great, so that you will be a blessing. I will bless those who bless you, and the one who curses you I will curse; and in you all the families of the earth shall be blessed.

I would like to dwell particularly on the last point: that all the families of the earth will be blessed through the descendants of Abraham.

Genesis 1 provides an account of God's creation of the world as a dwelling place for man. The world as God created it is good. But because Eve and Adam violated the rule about the tree of the knowledge of good and evil, human life went from bad to worse and dragged the rest of creation with it. God was so distraught he determined to destroy the whole of creation, but because of Noah, eight were saved. Again, though, man reveled in sin, even challenging God by building a tower. What was God to do? He determined to continue his good gifts to humankind through a family and their descendants—Abraham's. These gifts started immediately. God's blessings on Abraham flowed over onto Lot, his nephew. Isaac, in a time of drought, went to live among the Philistines, and as the result brought a blessing upon that nation. After Jacob lived and worked for Laban a number of years Laban grew more and more affluent. He was puzzled as to the cause of all his good fortune and finally became so curious he resorted to divination. He reported to Jacob what he learned: "If you will allow me to say so, I have learned by divination that the Lord has blessed me because of you…" (Genesis 30:27). It was Joseph, however, who brought the blessing to all nations. As a major drought afflicted the entire ancient world, people learned that grain was available in Egypt. "Moreover, all the world came to Joseph in Egypt to buy grain, because the famine became severe throughout the world" (Genesis 41:57).

The promise of God to Abraham runs like a thread, a story line through the book of Genesis. To fail to see this is to incorrectly interpret the book and its specifics. In Exodus through Deuteronomy, even the details of the law are related to this promise. The laws are given to Israel for her good and the good of her neighbors (Deuteronomy 6:1-15). The promise is remembered later in the Old Testament, as in Isaiah 49:6: "I will give you [Israel] as a light to the nations, that my salvation may reach to the end of the earth." Paul picks up on the same theme in Galatians and elsewhere. The promise was realized by Israel and her neighbors many times in the past. Now it is realized in a new and special way through the crucified and raised Messiah. "And the Scripture, foreseeing that God would justify the Gentiles by faith, declared the gospel beforehand to Abraham, saying, 'All the Gentiles shall be blessed in you'" (Galatians 3:8).

As I began to grasp the manner in which the Old Testament is held together by a story line which in turn informs the specifics, the old dichotomy of my youth finally began to fade away. Mother's introduction to the Scripture through story turned out to be very biblical, though in certain ways different from what she imagined. But likewise the views of my grandfather and father could not be discounted. The Bible consists of facts, but not just a series of independent, isolated items that chiefly require the inductive and generalizing skills of an empiricist to render them palatable. The data in

Scripture is ensconced in a major framework which runs throughout the whole. There is, after all, as our forefathers supposed, a "scheme of redemption," even though at times the trail gets faint and one is compelled to backtrack to pick it up again.

A major problem with the approach of those who wish to envision Scripture as chiefly a book of discrete data is that they miss the story line. In fact, they are not even likely to be looking for one. In the most extreme devotees there may even be a denial that a story line exists, or if it does, it is basically unimportant. In fact, if the skill required in interpreting Scripture lies in tracking down the story line—however faint—these authorities are unemployed, because this is a different hermeneutical job description. Their expertise lies rather in amassing, concordance-style, volumes of data related to a topic in which they are interested, and, with uncommon cunning, locating a thread running through it which supports the doctrinal positions they push. This they do while all the time claiming—no doubt, sincerely—that their conclusions are uncontaminated by the doctrines of men, since they range over such a wide territory of biblical facts. They categorize their conclusions with the famous term—famous with us, anyway—"necessary inference." But what can these inferences be but doctrines of men, since they are the creations of adroit workmen, of those persons who conceived the generalizations to synthesize and bring to a conclusion the large body of data they compiled? Thomas Campbell recognized how inadvertent human inference may be in the *Declaration and Address* and therefore, while he does not deny its usefulness, does repudiate such conclusions as being the very word of God or as beneficial in distinguishing Christians from those who are not.

My proposal is not that inference should be rejected as a feature of biblical interpretation, but that the role for inference as we have commonly perceived it runs counter to what is appropriate when the nature of biblical materials is taken into account. Rather than inferring how data of Scripture are held together at a higher level of abstraction through our own inductive skills, we should be locating the skeletal core, the redemptive scheme evident in Scripture itself. The person we have been describing employs his own glue to hold together the facts in the Scriptures. I contend that he should leave his glue at home. It is not needed, since Scripture itself supplies the glue. The finely-tuned skills of inference should be employed instead for ascertaining how the story line in Scripture casts a long shadow over all the individual facts. The story line from the Scripture itself is the glue which holds together the discrete entities. The story line found in Scripture is not a doctrine of men. The "necessary" inference of the skilled polemicist may, in fact, be an unneccessary doctrine of men.

New Testament Theology

In the spring of 1969 I embarked upon a course titled, "The Religious Teachings of the New Testament." As mentioned above, I found Malherbe's proposal suggestive. I was now convinced that the New Testament, just like the Old, had a story line. In the New, the focus is on what God has done through Jesus of Nazareth. Jesus is the apex, the culmination of God's mighty acts. Central to God's action is the death, burial and resurrection of the Son. The proclamation of this incredible accomplishment, according to Paul, is the good news, and initiated the Corinthians into the New Israel—the church.

The sermons in Acts, as noted by Dodd, contain the earliest statements of faith. They clearly focus on Jesus and set forth the salient features of God's work in him, and of his words and works. Peter's sermon to the household of Cornelius in Acts 10:34-48 is the most complete statement of the preaching: (1) that Jesus is the Son of God, Messiah, (2) that he was conceived and anointed by the Holy Spirit, (3) that he was announced by John the Baptist, (4) that he went about teaching, and (5) doing good, (6) that he was crucified, and (7) raised, (8) that he was seen by many witnesses, (9) that God is no respecter of persons, (10) that through baptism, all are (11) added to the church and (12) receive the Holy Spirit, and (13) that he is coming again as judge of the living and dead. This basic *kerygma* is also expressed in embryonic form in I Corinthians 15:1-9, I Thessalonians 1:9, 10, and I Timothy 3:16.

In the Old Testament, the mighty acts are the skeleton upon which the various books are fleshed out, and in the New, the core preaching concerning what God has done through his Son informs the specific guidelines for believers. The New Testament code of conduct grows out of a replication of the actions of Christ. "Be imitators of me, as I am of Christ" (I Corinthians 11:1), "Christ also suffered for you, leaving you an example, that you should follow in his steps" (I Peter 2:21). To collect and generalize from specific commands of Christ while ignoring the basic proclamation is a human enterprise, resulting in a doctrine generated by humans. We only interpret aright the commands of Christ when we are aware of the manner in which they replicate Christ's own actions. Just as in the Old Testament the commands are grounded in the prior actions of God, —the treatment of aliens, for example—so in the New, the commands are empowered through the antecedent actions of Christ.

A demonstration of this point is obvious in Jesus' command to the disciples to wash one another's feet. Jesus came from God and he was returning to God (John 13:3). It was he, uniquely identified with God, who washed the disciple's feet. He ministered to the disciples, who wore sandals and walked dusty Palestinian trails, at the point of their dirtiest bodily aspect—the feet. After so doing, Jesus said to the disciples, "So if I, your Lord and Teacher, have washed your feet, you also ought to wash one another's feet" (John 13:14). The command had no significant life of its own apart from Jesus' unprecedented action. The command did not precede, but followed the actual washing. God never requires anything of humans which he himself has not modeled beforehand. "We love," wrote John, "because he first loved us" (I John 4:19). We ought to wash one another's feet, not because of a universal imperative, but because our master washed feet. Because he addressed life where it is the seamiest—the feet—we are propelled to servanthood, to wash one another's feet. Furthermore, by his action he frees and empowers us to serve, regardless of how repugnant and smelly our fellows.

Baptism and the Lord's supper are not, as our logic-oriented friends envision, mere statutory entities. They are rather the channels through which we replicate and remember the astonishing love of God as disclosed in the death and resurrection of Jesus Christ. "While we were still sinners Christ died for us" (Romans 5:8). It is a grand paradox: that there

are commands, as well as examples, in regard to baptism and the Lord's supper, is indeed the case. But these identify the nuts-and-bolts aspects. At center-stage, however, is the model of the divine-human relationship. The disciple acts as he does because of the manner in which his Lord acted. Because Christ took up the way of the cross in his ministry and ended his life on the cross, the disciple takes up his cross and follows the master. In baptism she emulates Christ's death and resurrection by going down into the water and coming up out of it. In the same manner, in the breaking of the bread, we replicate the body of Christ broken on the cross. By drinking the fruit of the vine, one reproduces the blood of the Lord which flowed from the cross. By simply seeing these through the spectacles of the logicians, we disregard God's overpowering, unprecedented love and His eliciting of our grateful response. We best interpret the Scripture aright when we instead constantly perceive our acts as replications of the actions of God through Christ which are first conveyed to us in narrative form.

Paul clearly offered guidelines for the relations between husband and wife, parent and child, and master and slave in Ephesians 5 and 6, which flesh out the ramifications of the cross. In 5:1, 2, believers are charged to imitate the love of God which he exhibited through Jesus Christ. "Therefore be imitators of God, as beloved children, and live in love, as Christ loved us and gave himself up for us, a fragrant offering and sacrifice to God." What a God! What an unparalleled action! God, who is master of the universe, the maker of heaven and earth, through the Son gave himself up for you and me. He subjected himself to us! Unbelievable! What we have in Ephesians is not a call to bare-boned

obedience, but a challenge that we submit ourselves to others, just as Christ submitted himself to us.

In regard to every human relationship, Paul spelled it out: "Be subject to one another out of reverence for Christ" (5:21). The first charge is specifically to the wife. How does her subjection to her husband reverence Christ? It reverences him because that is precisely what Christ did. He subjected himself; gave himself up for us. The wife is subjected when she gives herself up to her husband. The charge to the husband is to love his wife. Several have tried to delineate a difference between being subject and loving. But if one takes seriously all of Ephesians 5 that distinction is purely academic. It has no basis whatsoever in the text. Look again at 5:1, 1: love has to do with giving up. Being subject has to do with giving up. The charge to the wife and husband therefore is exactly the same; they are each to give themselves up for each other. They are both to love the other. They are both to submit to each other.

In chapter 6, speaking of parents and children, Paul exclaims, "Children, obey your parents in the Lord, for this is right." What does "in the Lord" mean? It may mean, "obey your parents who live under the demands of Christ, since their requirements will be his." But it may also imply that just as Christ obeyed his father, so children who are in him will obey their parents, precisely because they are in the Lord. Fathers, in turn, are to submit to their children. They are "not to provoke them to anger." This does not mean that parents are to supply every whim and wish. But they submit to their children so that their welfare will be addressed. They are to encourage rather than alienate.

Slaves are to obey their masters "as slaves of Christ, doing the will of God from the heart" (6:6). Because Christ submitted to the will of his father for the salvation of sinners, even unto death, so slaves are to submit to their masters. Masters, in turn, are to subject themselves to their slaves: to look after their welfare, rather than autocratically issuing continuous threats. They are to do so because God is their master. God had concern for all of humankind, causing the rain to fall on the just and unjust. Since he is a caring master, earthly masters likewise should be caring.

It takes time to work through all the ways in which the *kerygma*—the gospel proclamation—colors commands, examples, and implications. When our hermeneutic is biblical, our inferences focus precisely upon the ways in which the actions of Christ inform our actions. I have taught New Testament theology with the kerygmatic outline more than thirty times, yet I continue to discover new ways in which this proclamation informs specific injunctions. God still has light to shed on his word, as John Robinson, a seventeenth-century Puritan, once remarked.

About fifteen years ago I gave a name to this "new" hermeneutic. I labeled it the "Christ" or "Christological" hermeneutic. I did so because if one is mostly working from the New Testament, the guidelines for the church and the individual are fleshed out from the preaching concerning Christ: that he died, arose, and is coming again. Later it occurred to me that the rule of Scripture is larger than the Christ rule. It is the "God, Christ, and Holy Spirit" rule. The mighty acts of God in the Old Testament reach fruition in Jesus Christ and in the work of the Holy Spirit. We need to see the Godhead shining through the specific commands of the total Scriptures, both Old and New Testaments. Inference is, in fact, necessary, but it must debark from the story line of Scripture, not from generalizations drawn by those who ignore or are not even aware of the story line.

At the end of these courses in biblical theology I began reflecting on the implications of what we had gone through in the class for interpreting the Scriptures. I proposed that the requirements for a hermeneutic are: (1) that it be biblical. The trifold hermeneutic—command, example, and necessary inference—is never explicitly found in Scripture, nor, as a formula, implicitly. It may be discovered at the earliest, perhaps, in writings of leaders of the reform wing of the Reformation—Calvin and Zwingli. (2) A hermeneutic must recognize first of all him who is the focus of Scripture—God, revealed as Father, Son, and Holy Spirit. (3) A hermeneutic must take seriously the basic story line which runs from the Old Testament into the New, highlighting the mighty works of God on behalf of Israel, and for all men through Jesus and the Holy Spirit. (4) A hermeneutic must give attention to how this basic story line incorporates specific examples and ordinances. And (5) it must encourage the believer to action which emulates the Lord's prior action.

Admittedly, with this hermeneutic, which I believe to be profoundly biblical, I have still never been able to settle beyond dispute all the concerns of either my students, my critics, or myself. What is troublesome to those who want to nail all matters to the wall is that this hermeneutic may, in the final analysis, result in a degree of open-endedness. This does not set well with those who demand black-and-white decisions on all questions. But I hope I am more swayed by what is biblical than by the scruples of those with bipolar agendas. Interestingly, though many of these profess to admire the person who "examines the Scriptures daily to see if these things were so" (Acts 17:11), they do not submit this fundamental presupposition of theirs—that answers must be either yes or no—to the Scriptures. For example, when John asked Jesus, "Are you the one to come, or are we to wait for another?" (Matthew 11:2), Jesus answered neither "yes" nor "no." But one who is aware of the implications of Isaiah 61:1 knows what is behind Jesus's response, and surmises the answer.

In my classes, I also reflected briefly on specific matters that have historically occupied our attention. I have already shown that baptism and the Lord's supper clearly proclaim by re-enactment the good news of the crucified and resurrected Lord. Likewise, the music suitable for the assembly of Christ's people is that which best sheds light upon the Godhead. The ministry of music is a teaching ministry, according to Paul (Colossians 3:16).

> Let the word of Christ dwell in your richly; teach and admonish one another in all wisdom; and with gratitude in your hearts sing psalms, hymns, and spiritual songs to God. And whatever you do, in word and deed, do everything in the name of the Lord Jesus, giving thanks to God the Father through him.

The value of worship music which provokes mood and emotion without drawing its hearers to reflect on God's indescribable acts of love through Jesus is questionable. Traditions which highlight instrumentation, whether they be high liturgical or "low-church" charismatic, have often primarily sought to produce mood and emotion, sometimes devoid of any real theocentric context. Vocal music which tells the old, old story, which feeds and edifies and moves the believer, was the music of the early Christians.

Leadership in the church is also informed by the cross. The style is that of servanthood. Christian leaders should sidestep any style which models authoritarian governmental and military methods, in order to serve as their Lord served (Mark 10:45). Cross-centered polity avoids the hierarchical ecclesiology of much traditional Christianity.

The practices of the church or individual Christians are judged right or wrong based upon whether the forms themselves proclaim the Christ of the *kerygma*. The social-custom criterion is a dead end, since every biblical form and institution seems to have a cultural history, even baptism and the Lord's supper. Baptism and the Lord's supper are significant not as the result of being non-cultural, but because in their very forms they proclaim the action of God, Christ, and the Holy Spirit in death and resurrection: the candidate actually goes down into the water and is buried and raised; the communicant actually eats the meal which Christ ordained as his memorial feast. The holy kiss and the washing of feet, in contrast, do not by their forms alone proclaim the life and death of Christ. They certainly, however, declare his spirit of welcoming: that as Christ welcomed us through his death, so we should welcome one another (Romans 15:7), and that we should serve each other even in menial tasks, just as he served (John 13). Still, the specific form in these cases do not announce the death and

resurrection as do baptism and communion. Greeting and serving are imperative. The Lord did both. But in our time and place, a handshake or opening the door for a visitor achieves a similar end.

Church Life

We were glad that we lived near the church building. It was a new experience for us. We were also pleased that in a congregation so large that every member of the family had several choices for peers. The kids were unaccustomed to finding so many friends their age at church. The schools in Abilene were at some distance and, being without the sort of busing system we had in Pennsylvania, we had to car pool. Each of the four kids were in a car pool with members at Hillcrest. The congregation and people were friendly. It was a good congregation in so many ways, but we still had problems adjusting.

Nevertheless, we were soon immersed in the activities of the congregation. I taught adult classes of various sorts. Dorothy taught children's classes. The second year I was appointed a deacon. The minister was Jimmy Jividen, who was interested in helping small, struggling congregations in other regions; especially New Mexico, Arizona and Nevada. He felt that college students could be very helpful in inviting people to the short meetings he held in these places. He also aspired to encourage and help train budding preachers. The way to address this, he felt, was to create a program. I was not involved in the discussions of the elders and others in planning the program, but soon I was approached about directing it. I agonized over whether to do so. I had more than enough to do with my classes and *Mission* and my aspirations to be a publishing scholar. I finally decided, however, that if the focus was upon servanthood and included both male and female college students I would consent to direct it. We called it the Discipleship Program because a disciple is one who takes up his cross and follows in the footsteps of Jesus.

The object of the Discipleship Program was to give students a biblical perspective on serving others. The involvement was geared around summer efforts, though some activities were planned during the school year, such as going with Jimmy for a short meeting. We met each Wednesday night to study the Scripture and discuss practical aspects of serving in churches and other programs. Some of the males served as apprentice preachers. Eddie Sharp, in our first group and now minister of the University Church of Christ in Abilene, went to Las Vegas, Nevada as an apprentice to Gary Workman. Others, including females, worked in meetings and vacation Bible schools. Still others went out as camp counselors. We had a well-organized program overseen by a committee. We interviewed all the candidates and administered the Minnesota Multiphasic Personality Inventory exam. Some opposed giving the exam on the grounds that Paul might not have passed. I was not overly turned on to the idea and said that we should not bar persons because of the exam. But after two years it became apparent that every time a problem surfaced in an exam, a problem occurred in the field. So, at minimum, we could predict which persons would require long talks with supervisors.

The program went very well and I was able to establish close ties with the students involved. I always considered myself an outsider to my Abilene peers. I had not gone to Abilene Christian, as most had, and I was not a part of the network. But it was easy to enter into close relationships with students both at church and on campus, so that through the years I discovered that the persons with whom I identified most were students. The key players among my peers in Abilene liked gung-ho promoters, whether they had any substance or not. I reacted negatively to these types: it was not my style. I may have been respected, but I was not a part of the "old-boy network." Instead, my network consisted of students.

Restoration Quarterly

My official connection with *Restoration Quarterly* began in 1963, when I was appointed to the board. J. W. Roberts took a trip around the world in 1965-66. Even though I was teaching at Penn State, I was asked to edit the *Quarterly* while he was gone. I edited three issues and was identified as Acting Editor in issues 9:3, 4 (1966), and 10:1 (1967). Dorothy served as business and circulation manager in 1967-68 while the Malherbes were in Boston, then permanently after they left Abilene. Abe returned to Abilene from Boston and taught from 1968-69, then accepted a position at Dartmouth. He had become disenchanted with the growing carping over liberalism. He aspired to be a publishing scholar and he viewed the Abilene teaching load and the constant need to put out brush fires as prohibitive to his goals. He also felt that Abilene Christian was more interested in athletics and fine buildings than in scholarship.

When J. W. Roberts died suddenly in 1973, the board appointed me editor. Under my encouragement we appointed additional members to the board. In turn, the new board reviewed our mission. We wanted to give the scholars among us the opportunity to share their insights, but we decided that our target audience would be graduate students and preachers. Further, we decided that our focus should be on biblical studies and Restoration history, though we would not exclude other topics. Since we hoped to increase our appeal to preachers, we decided to print a sermon in each issue. With this revised mission and a clearer focus, as well as some other promotional activities, we were able to up our subscriptions to about 1,400. It was difficult to maintain that level, however, and more normally the number totaled 1,200. The *Quarterly* was sometimes positioned as left of center, but since the material was scholarly, not promotional or agitational, the brotherhood watchdogs seldom stirred when it appeared.

These were difficult years for Abilene Christian. College campuses in those days were famous for protests and riots. Our constituency expected us to take stands against "hard rock" music, long hair, beards, straggly, unkept hair on women and unisex, grungy clothing. Church members did not like what was happening to their college-age students, even at the Christian colleges. In the decade of the 60s, Abilene Christian had consistently improved the scholarly quality of its undergraduate and graduate offerings in religion, but mainly in the areas of biblical studies and church history. The foremost teachers were John Willis and Tony Ash in Old Testament, Abe Malherbe, J. W. Roberts, and Neil Lightfoot in New Testament, and LeMoine Lewis, Everett Ferguson, and Bill Humble in church history. The practical areas remained much the same. Those of in-depth scholarship and charisma typically taught in biblical studies and church history. Abilene also became more venturesome for a time in topics and speakers at its annual lectureship. Dwain Evans, who had achieved great name recognition because of Exodus Bay Shore (later West Islip), was invited to speak on the Holy Spirit in 1966. His views were far from conventional among our preachers and caused quite a stir.

As a result, Abilene Christian had became something of a question mark with church members and preachers. We still recruited many students, but the complaints were widespread. The big preacher's gatherings in the large cities of Texas frequently resonated with anti-Abilene Christian rhetoric. In the middle sixties the college addressed the situation by asking certain teachers to resign. At least two resigned under pressure from 1965 to 1968, though they were good teachers and highly respected by the students. Another outstanding person or two left because of the criticism and turmoil. We were on a powder keg. The relations with administrators and preachers for someone in my position were not affirming, but my support group was the students. Abilene Christian had many outstanding students, now evident by the numbers who have become internationally-known preachers, professors, lawyers, doctors, and business professionals. Despite the external criticism, then, as Malherbe remarked, at that time we were euphoric over what we might accomplish as scholars. Most good ACU students thought they could be admitted to the best universities and seminaries and become leading scholars in their area of expertise. It was exhilarating to be around students like that.

By 1974 I had accumulated enough credit for directing theses to take off a semester at full pay. I inventoried what contribution I might best make to biblical studies and decided that with my special interests and training I should write a history of biblical studies in America. In order to do so I needed to be in New England, because I had in mind starting with the Puritans. The best libraries were at Harvard, Boston Public, Massachusetts Historical Society, and the American Antiquarian Library at Worcester.

In the meantime, Tony Ash left ACU to become chair of the Religion Division at Pepperdine University, leaving the Minter Lane congregation without a preacher. Landon Saunders was at first invited to fill in. Soon arrangements were made for him to preach whenever in town. The rest of the time we dispersed the duties among various others including Randy Becton, Art McNeese, and myself. Landon and I began periodic talks about a program he wanted to call "Heartbeat." I was quite interested in the program because, as Landon hoped to position it, unique communication, apologetic, and hermeneutic tasks were involved. Landon was not simply interested in being a good communicator. He wanted to be a faithful conveyor of the Word. He perceived that I could add a special dimension to the ministry.

Various factors fell in place that made it possible for us to spend fifteen months in New England. 1976 was the year of Bicentennial celebrations in the United States. The Herald of Truth radio program planned a special series of fifteen-minute presentations designed to celebrate our religious heritage. Herald of Truth and Heartbeat were then both under the umbrella of the Highland congregation. I struck up a deal with Landon and Randy Becton whereby I would write foundational pieces for the heritage programs and materials for

Heartbeat, including position pieces, response letters, biblical expositions, and a few scripts for the broadcasts. We left for New England in late May 1975 and remained until late August 1976.

Landon, in five- and one-minute Heartbeat programs, set out to surface unchurched people who wouldn't be attracted to the good news through ordinary religious discourse. He was not opposed to in-house discourse in the churches or among the committed, but that was not his targeted audience. Without knowing or admitting it, traditionalists among us have been true children of the Enlightenment, supposing one universal audience and one mode of discourse in proclaiming the Gospel. It's like the universal garment: "One size fits all!" I was attracted to Heartbeat because of my view of communication and apologetics, which dictated that discourse must be geared to the language and mode of the auditor, not the speaker. Traditionalists among us had little communicative insight or imagination. They listened to Heartbeat and declared that Landon came off as a humanist. It certainly wasn't the Gospel in their view, since he referred little to Scriptural narratives or statements. Landon was under constant fire at one stage. He had become well-known, especially among college-age persons in our Christian colleges and elsewhere, and was in big demand as a speaker. Among us, a high-profile and unconventional proclamation have always been fair game for the critics. A second reason was that Heartbeat was under the auspices of the Herald of Truth, which was the national "brotherhood" program. About the Herald of Truth, Carl Ketcherside once made the wry remark that the people in the brotherhood who supported the Herald of Truth never listened to it, while those who refused to support it always did. Heartbeat was designed intentionally for people other than its critics, and those for whom it was designed loved it.

The question was, what were the needs of people out there who for some reason or another were unattracted to religion? In 1974 Heartbeat had been broadcasting for about three years; at first, only on a few stations. The stations often carried the programs as a public service and arrangements were made by people in local settings who had taken up the burden of the ministry. By that time, Heartbeat had received about 4,500 letters. I set out to read them and establish content analysis categories. It is true that messages create their own audiences, so responses may have mostly surfaced reactions to the topics discussed, but we anticipated that listeners would mention additional needs. The number-one problem of Heartbeat listeners was loneliness. Related to loneliness was desertion by spouses, children, parents, or friends. Another major condition was boredom. Many persons expressed a lack of challenge in their job. This ran all the way from assembly-line workers to highly-skilled executives. As Landon put it, the question was whether they had any reason for getting up in the morning. Meaninglessness was related to all this, but despite the existentialists, few put their fingers precisely on a despair conditioned by generic emptiness. The correspondents gave concrete reasons, having to do with other people, as the source of their anxieties.

After categorizing and describing the targeted audience I then proceeded to struggle with the question of how these persons might be addressed so that eventually they would open their lives to the good news of Jesus Christ. The approach of Landon's short broadcasts was to identify a single problem, then suggest that answers might be available from unexpected quarters. These cryptically referred to "another dimension to life." One of Landon's favorite illustrations was of a fish which struggled to live on dry land and almost died because it was out of its element. That is the reason so many were struggling, he said: they were attempting to live out of their element. Once in a while Landon quoted a saying of Jesus, usually introduced by the phrase, "A great teacher once said..." Jesus was always, "The Teacher."

My work focused on the second level of communication. The radio programs were designed to pique an interest. Responses generated a list of prospective seekers. Landon spent much of his time doing workshops at motels in cities where the program was popular. The workshops were announced on the program. Landon spoke at these gatherings so that listeners could meet him in person. He had a very melodious and winsome voice. He exuded even more charisma in person than on radio. After Landon spoke, attendees were divided into small groups, led, in each case, by local members of the church. The Heartbeat design projected layered communication, which worked wonderfully well through the first two stages: the radio program and the seminars. Large numbers attended who had never darkened the door of a Church of Christ, or, in some cases, of any religious assembly—sometimes as many as four hundred. They were normally turned-on after the sessions. The follow-up procedure called for the small groups to continue to meet periodically, as agreed upon by those involved. The attrition after a few meetings was, in some cases, considerable. The church wasn't to be brought up in the early meetings. The introduction of the church occurred after the leaders had created rapport with the people as individuals: the third stage. Not too many leaders were successful, however, in getting people to attend church. Marge and Claude "Gil" Gillis of Leominster, Massachusetts—who were likely more adaptable than some since their background was not in Churches of Christ—said that, though they loved their group and the group loved to meet, they were only able to interest one or two in attending church and then not for any sustained period. The third stage was always the big hurdle. We kept thinking there might be a better way. It might involve better training for the group leaders or improved materials for discussion. But Landon was a front man, in the best sense of the word. He was not a follow-up person. He despaired of employing a large staff. The persons who worked for Heartbeat were involved in stages one and two. A larger staff would force him to be more of a fund raiser than a front man. He wanted to be free to proclaim the Gospel and relate to people.

This was an exciting opportunity for imaging and execution for someone with my background. Not only did it put to the test my communication theory, it also kept my hermeneutics honest. Ivory tower theories faced the test of real life. We sought to apply theory to real audiences, or, as Mike Hawkins, one of Landon's associates, put it, "where the rubber meets the road." The layered communication was not fully my idea, but I gave it philosophical underpinning. The first master's thesis I directed at Penn State was by Michael Sexton on Sören Kierkegaard's theory of communication. While Landon's stages did not fully follow those of

Kierkegaard, the targeted outcome was the same: genuine conversion to the Christ of the Scriptures.

My task was to generate materials for the second stage. The workshops were designed to address the audience with more explicit biblical insights, but not as yet in "church language." What I set out to do was locate biblical materials which spoke to current needs. We attempted to translate these into fresh language so the ideas could be communicated to persons without explicit religious backgrounds. I worked on materials in Genesis and elsewhere in the Old Testament which had to do with the promise to bless the nations. I also worked on I John, Colossians, and Hebrews. What we sought was not so much a specific biblical text for what we perceived to be a question in the audience—we weren't looking for a "local" weather forecast. What we wanted, rather, was a "national" weather projection which addressed the larger picture. We had no illusions that this "national map" was true of everyone in the country, but hoped it was accurate for our targeted audience.

In late December 1975 I took twenty-five ACU students to Aspen, Colorado. We talked to people on the streets and invited them to come at night and listen to Landon Sauders speak in the Aspen Chapel. It seemed to me, because of experiences in Aspen, that Colossians provided a valuable backdrop for understanding our audience. For example, we had run into people who were governing their lives by astrological signs. I talked with one woman at some length, asking her how she thought God was related to the configuration of the stars. She said she believed in God, and that she had now become convinced that knowing a person's horoscope really provided insight into the person, but she didn't connect the two statements. The kind of people we were reaching were influenced by powers of various sorts, but God was only one among the powers. In Colossians, likewise, persons were addressed who gave deference to many diverse powers in the universe. They recognized Christ as one of the powers, but he was only one from among many. They worshiped angels (2:18) and attributed extraordinary influence to the elemental spirits of the universe (2:8).

The question now was, how did Paul set out to combat the veneration directed toward these powers by his readers? He did not immediately decry the existence of the powers, nor did he address their existence directly. Rather, he focused on the powers of Christ. He was adamant that Christ was not one power among many. "For in him the whole fullness of deity dwells bodily and you have come to fullness in him, who is the head of every ruler and authority" (2:9, 10). We attempted to employ the same strategy. We identified the felt need of our target group to access "powers from beyond." We sought to be specific as to what our auditors revered and feared. We did not seek merely to destroy the consequences of these powers, but to introduce the Teacher, before whom all powers pale in comparison. He is the very Son of God and partakes fully of God's nature. Why revere and fear these other powers? He releases us from them all, we proclaimed.

I proposed this as a "national weather map"—a far-reaching hermeneutic. The procedure was to find the mind-set of a targeted audience, then locate in Scripture materials that address persons of similar outlooks. The next stage was to communicate to the contemporary audience in the same manner, and with the same conclusions, as found in Scripture. The final goal was to bring people face-to-face with the God of Scripture and his Son, Jesus Christ. Everytime anyone in Scripture interpreted the faith to persons in a specific context, God always came to the forefront, sooner or later.

In early 1974 Landon mentioned that it was important to start our Minter Lane students talking with outsiders, one-on-one. We had a few sessions in Abilene designed for this purpose. We invited persons in the Air Force and others to meet at a neutral location. After thinking it over, I put a proposal before Landon. I told Landon that I knew a place where we could meet face-to-face with plenty of unchurched people without knocking on a single door (Landon had several reservations about door knocking). I proposed that we take a group to Aspen during ski season. He thought it sounded like a winner.

I called Jack Hicks, then preaching in Glenwood Springs, Colorado, and asked him about the proposal. Would it be possible to find a place where Landon could speak in Aspen? Would the church in Glenwood Springs be supportive? Would the members be willing to house the students? Jack seemed hopeful and said he would check it out. The answer was "yes" on all counts. He found a modern chapel in Aspen which could be rented for three nights. We started recruiting students and designated the effort, "Mission Snow". It ended up that we took twenty-two students, making twenty-five in all, counting Dorothy, Erika, and myself. The results were impressive, in certain respects. We talked with numbers of people on the streets and in restaurants. We had a total of some thirty different persons we contacted who showed up for the meetings, and some were good prospects for the kingdom. The students stayed in touch through correspondence, and one or two of our contacts visited Abilene. The result was that two persons were later baptized. The main problem was that the time was too short to achieve major permanent results.

Mission Snow fueled another outreach. Wayne Anderson received an M.Div. from Abilene Christian in 1973. He accepted a position as associate minister for outreach for the College Congregation in Fresno, California. Wayne had been involved with my brother Owen in Campaigns Northeast. He had talked with me about establishing a summer program comprised of Abilene Christian students, to be called Western States Outreach. He wanted me to sponsor and help train the students, and establish Minter Lane as the Abilene base during the school year. I told him I would, but that the best manner of recruiting was by student leaders. I proposed that he come to Aspen so that he could meet these students and perhaps recruit among them, so Wayne worked with us in Aspen. Some of the Mission Snow students were interested and they recruited others. The summer of 1975 was the first year for Western States Outreach. In the middle of the summer, while we were in Massachusetts, I received a call from a Western States Outreach student reporting that Wayne Anderson had been killed while riding a motorcycle in Yosemite National Park. Western States Outreach lived on for about ten years, and I helped them as I could.

Western States Outreach was the model for yet another outreach team. Bill Porter and David Malone, the latter of whom had been involved in Western States Outreach, decided to start a similar group called "Good News Northeast." I helped them get started. They, too, were based at Minter Lane, and we trained the two groups, in part, together. They commenced in the summer of 1977. I did the preaching for them in Storrs, Connecticut. Good News Northeast was sponsored by the congregation in Arlington, Virginia, which was Bill's home congregation. The preacher in Storrs was Cloyd Taylor, whose father was an elder at Arlington. Good News Northeast continued for about five years. Upon receiving their M.Divs., Bill and David moved to New England and helped launch churches northwest of Boston. Bill was an outstanding student and team leader. The participants raised money from relatives, friends and congregations for their summer work. Bill told them that God had treasures stashed away all over: all they needed to do was ask for it. His team was very effective in fund-raising.

These were interesting experiences in which we attempted to share God's voice in the Scriptures with people who were often unchurched and knew little about God or the Bible. We were reminded that interpretation involves the whole of life. We certainly made use of examples, but those offered were the narratives containing the words and actions of Christ: enfleshed examples, not rational models from logic textbooks.

---

[1] The Memphis statement was modified until it became officially titled, "The Task of *Mission*" and appeared in volume 1:1, 3-6. I have written a more detailed account of the beginnings of *Mission* which may be found in "New Journals For The Sixties: *Restoration Quarterly* and *Mission*" and located in Payson Library, Pepperdine University.

[2] Thomas H. Olbricht, "Hermeneutics: The Beginning Point," *Image*, Part I, September 1989, Part II, October 1989.

[3] Gerhard von Rad, *Old Testament Theology*, translated by D. M. G. Stalker (New York: Harper & Row, 1962) I, 69.

10

New Topics for Interpretation: 1977-1996

We returned to Abilene from New England in the fall of 1976, having stopped by Wisconsin and southern Missouri to visit relatives. I continued my teaching duties, spending one class session talking about hermeneutics in both Old and New Testament theology. I also spent a bit of time discussing hermeneutics in a course which I developed in the early 1970s, "Introduction of Doctrinal Studies." I first organized the course along the lines of my theological training at Harvard Divinity School. Regardless of efforts of college administrators to change pedagogy, my impression is that most faculty follow the model of what they perceived to be successful in the courses they took. I employed the text I found meaningful as a student, Gustas Aulén's *The Faith of the Christian Church.*[1] I also required additional reading: Paul Tillich on theological methodology, Karl Barth on God, and

Donald Baillie on the atonement, among others. I organized the course according to the standard theological topics (*"Regula Fidei"*) listed in Chapter Seven, and repeated here.

1. Faith
2. Revelation
3. Scripture
4. God,
5. Christ: Savior and Salvation
6. Holy Spirit
7. Man: Sin and evil
8. Creation
9. Church
10. Worship and sacraments
11. Ethics and Morality,
12. Ecumenics
13. Eschatology

I believe that theology proper has a useful function apart from biblical theology. Just as a preacher is not worth his salt who cannot explain a text in such a manner that it can be understood by a specific audience, so biblical theology is not helpful unless it can be brought to bear upon a specific context. The effort to do so is what I designate "theology." Biblical theology is an undertaking which focuses only upon the message found within in the Scriptures, the message located in the inspired text. It is once for all, and sits in judgment on all subsequent theology. Nevertheless, the church cannot do without theology, which is the effort to communicate the theology of the Scriptures to a specific age. While biblical theology is immutable, theology should change as needed to communicate with its own era and social context. The theologian, in my view, should know from the outset that his theology is doomed. He should highlight the self-amortizing nature of theology. I did not, for example, teach theology by using Charles Hodge's three volumes, since he wrote for a previous century and focused, in part, on concerns that were not shared by me or my students.

My approach was to bring to bear the outlook of Churches of Christ on the above topics, set out the perspectives of the current theologians as well as the history of theology found in their works, and critique both from the standpoint of the theology of the Scriptures. I would have loved to have had a book by someone in our heritage which addressed the same topics. I asked students to purchase Royal Humbert's *Compend of Alexander Campbell's Theology*[2], which was of some help, but much theological water has gone under the bridge since Campbell's time. We have not had, to date, doctrinal statements of any depth in book form.[3] I therefore included in my lectures the perspectives of Churches of Christ, as well as the biblical critique of those perspectives.

I also developed a second course which might be described as "Systematic Theology for the Churches of Christ." In the catalog it was designated "Restoration Doctrine." The title was certainly safe enough, but probably prosaic, from a student perspective. The course was not required for any degree except the master's in doctrine, but eight to fifteen students usually took it. I wanted the students to read their papers in class and the smaller numbers made that possible. The first third of the course was dedicated to hermeneutics. I then took up four or five of the theological topics above, and worked on them in some depth. I had students buy a paperback on each topic when I could discover an appropriate one. I followed this pattern in my lectures, presenting a historical perspective of Christendom, setting out restorationist outlooks, discussing the current climate in regard to the topic, then proposing a current theology which I perceived compatible with biblical theology. The hermeneutical methodology I proposed provided guidelines for the outcome. I required a three-part paper on one of the topics discussed in class. The first part consisted of a discussion of hermeneutics, the second, reflections on the historical perspectives on the topic, and the third, a theology of the topic for our time.

I commenced the section on hermeneutics by struggling with a definition. I pointed out that traditionally, hermeneutics is defined as the rules by which exegesis proceeds. Since World War II, however, under the influence of Bultmann, the term came to focus on the presuppositions of the interpreter. For the Bultmannians these presuppositions were the mindset of contemporary culture. Bultmann argued that in his epoch, the consensus culture was best located in the work of the Marburg philosopher, his colleague, Martin Heidegger. Heidegger can be classified as an existentialist or a phenomenologist. What the Scripture means for the latter half of the twentieth century, therefore, is what it means through the eyes of the existentialists, Bultmann held. His New Testament theology, then, was in effect a theology encased in the categories of existential philosophy. To put the matter in our traditional vocabulary: for Bultmann, what is authorized for the Christian today is whatever in the New Testament reflects an existential perspective. He located this core, or *kerygma,* almost exclusively in the writings of Paul and John. The rest of the New Testament, declared

Bultmann, must be demythologized and ignored. I pointed out that Bultmann's program was interestingly similar to ours. The difference is that for us, the New Testament must be interpreted from the perspective of empirical facts. Whatever meets this test is authorized. Whatever doesn't, while not rejected—Zechariah, for example—since we must always embrace the whole of Scriptures, is simply ignored. The Bultmannian approach was at the heart of this "new hermeneutic." I pointed out to students the view of the British scholar Alan Richardson that Rudolf Bultmann is a heretic. I agreed, because I did not, nor do I presently, think that the presuppositions of the New Testament are those of Martin Heidegger—or Francis Bacon, for that matter. I therefore rejected the basic thrust of the "new hermeneutics" of the Bultmannian school.

I pointed out that today one needs to distinguish traditional hermeneutics from the "new" hermeneutics. I then observed that our hermeneutics has had two parts, though in the current discussions of hermeneutics in Churches of Christ only one part is identified as hermeneutics. The first part has to do with what is authorized for our churches today and the hermeneutic is the tripartite formula: command, example, and necessary inference. It is here that our hermeneutic is in the same category as the Bultmannian "new hermeneutic"—drawing its criteria from a system of thought, rather than from what Scripture reveals as important. It is also interesting that Bultmann, after demythologizing the New Testament, believed that the remaining preachable message rested in the New Testament *kerygma*—the preaching about Jesus. Nevertheless, he passed this message through the filter of Heidegger's existentialism. Similarly, we have seined the New Testament with the command-example-necessary inference net and declared our catch as authoritative. The rest of the Scripture we have often left adrift in God's vast ocean of revelation.

The second part of our hermeneutic was what the Scripture meant in its own context. It was this second part that our nineteenth century forefathers called hermeneutics. This hermeneutic was the standard or classical hermeneutics which served as the presuppositions for grammatico-historical-literary biblical criticism. That was what Alexander Campbell presented in his essays on the "Principles of Interpretation."[4] We have therefore had a two-part hermeneutic, the second part of which is either dismissed or ignored by those who oppose the "new" hermeneutic among us. Whatever our new hermeneutic may be, I am not aware of anyone among us who wants to interpret Scripture by the dictates of Rudolf Bultmann's program.

In the course I prepared two annotated bibliographies, one for the Bultmannian "new hermeneutics" and another for classical hermeneutics. Both I and the students added to these bibliographies as I continued to teach the course. Insights of this sort may not be needed for most persons who are seeking what God wants them to do, but they may be imperative for those who seek to lead believers and criticize their brothers for getting it all wrong. After offering a perspective on hermeneutics, we spent some class time on the history of classical hermeneutics. Classical hermeneutics is alive and well among evangelicals at such places as Wheaton, Fuller, Trinity, and Bethel Seminary in St. Paul, Minnesota.

What has concerned me most of all in regard to the history of hermeneutics and the plethora of books on traditional hermeneutics is that certain obvious, basic insights have been ignored. Who can dispute that in the Old Testament God takes center stage, or that in the New, 'God is revealed through' his Son and his Holy Spirit? What good is a hermeneutic which fails to home in first on these matters? Only then can one properly struggle with whatever details remain uncertain in one's walk with God, since what we are to be is what Christ is. "Therefore be imitators of God, as beloved children, and live in love. . ." (Ephesians 5:1, 2). Those who limit hermeneutics to technical questions regarding exegetical rules have set their sights far too low. They are willing to relegate hermeneutics to the nuts-and-bolts aspects of philology, history, and literary genres. But the ultimate end of the interpretation of Scripture is to come face-to-face with the living God.

In Restoration Doctrine I handed out a schematic itemization of the hermeneutics which I proposed as useful for the course. The hermeneutics might best be described as global or theological, as compared with local, borrowing again from the weather forecast analogy. The itemization was as follows.

1. Locate the centers of the Scriptures: that is, God, Christ and the Holy Spirit, so as to be familiar with how the Godhead informs specific commands, examples and observations.
2. Locate the mindset of the culture being addressed.

3. Select a section of the Scriptures which seems to speak to this contemporary context.
4. Notice how the persons in this Scripture are addressed from the perspective of God, Christ and the Holy Spirit.
5. Employ a similar approach in bringing the Godhead to bear on the contemporary context.
6. Relate the specific action or understanding to the larger narrative of God's mighty works for his world through the Son and the Holy Spirit.
7. Undertake this interpretation as members together in the church of the living God.

This outline is abstract without the backgrounds provided by this book. This is the reason why I have felt inadequate to write a how-to-do-it book on hermeneutics. The same can happen as the result of reading this book, but perhaps the likelihood is less. I would argue, however, that the method outlined above is profoundly biblical, dependent at all stages upon the Scriptures themselves, not upon "common sense" or manuals of logic. My proposal is, in fact, not particularly revolutionary. Something along these lines occurs whenever most people take up the Bible in an effort to discern God's will. A journey as long as this book may be necessary, if only to undo the effects of centuries of misfocused hermeneutics.

Two Examples

I now offer two examples which set forth more concretely how I think this hermeneutics works in actual situations confronting the church. Both commence with descriptions of the Minter Lane church in Abilene and the Malibu church in California. Each example pinpoints a major trouble spot in most Churches of Christ today. The first regards the church's worship, and the second, the role of women in the life of the congregation and in the assembly.

The Church's Worship

I will first set out the context. In 1980 Minter Lane had two Sunday morning services. Our building could not accommodate everyone from late August to early May, when the students were in Abilene in full force. We thought of building a larger place of assembly, but we had reservations. We wanted to spend our money for the many mission programs we supported. The solution was going to two services. This likewise accommodated more persons of varying schedules. Our experience was that the total attendance was about one hundred more when we had two services. The first service was at 8:15 A.M., classes at 9:30 A.M., followed by a second service at 10:30 A.M. Minter Lane has since revised the service to one continuous assembly with a break in between and no classes on Sunday morning. The situation at Malibu in 1996 is much like Minter Lane fifteen years ago.

At Minter Lane, most of the older persons attended the early service, along with other families. The second service was principally made up of students and singles. The complexion is much the same at Malibu, except that families driving from the valley areas, fifteen to twenty miles away, by majority attend the second service. For many years at Minter the same song leader led identical songs in both services, under the supposition that since we could not be together on Sunday morning at least we could have the same worship experience. Several, however, did not agree with this song leader. In the 1960s college students commenced singing different songs than those in *Great Songs of the Church*. They learned songs in youth meetings and summer camps which made their way into chapel at ACU, and occasionally, if a student led singing, into church. Jack Boyd, an ACU professor of music, resisted these songs at Minter as long as possible. The same developments occurred in Malibu.

Sometime in the middle seventies a few persons in the church at Minter became interested in neo-charismatic outlooks and worship. Certain popular television shows such as the PTL Club, The 700 Club, and the programs of Oral Roberts and Jimmy Swaggart, also contributed. These persons favored a less structured worship, using some of the new songs from charismatic circles as well as short songs based on Scripture passages. Songs from contemporary Christian music were also introduced. The decision was made that the songs at the second worship would be led by a different song leader who most likely would be a student. The songs were to be selected by this song leader in expectation that he would use more of the short Scripture songs, normally sung in unison. The same developments, without the direct charismatic influences, occurred at Malibu. Students in Malibu have mixed preferences. Some like the short Scripture songs and some do not. Most of those who came to the Minter Lane second service were pleased to sing the short Scripture songs.

At Minter the second service remained basically conventional until those with charismatic propensities campaigned for greater flexibility. The second service became independent of the first in tone and content, sometimes omitting any sermon. If a sermon was preached, the preacher was not the regular Minter minister. The pattern for this assembly was mostly short talks interspersed with songs and Scripture readings. Most of those who attended liked the new format and those who didn't began attending the first service. The numbers in the second service remained about the same, since some new people in Abilene started attending and made up for those who left for the first service. Though the formatting of the service was independent, the persons involved remained coordinated with the larger body because Max Tipton, one of the elders, was a leader of this service, along with at least two of the deacons, Cotton Hance and Stan Shewmaker. A second elder, John Elkins, was also very supportive. Finally, though, the leaders in this service decided they could not do what they wanted at Minter, so about forty members left, including Tipton, Hance and Shewmaker, and founded the Abilene Community Church. From then on the Minter congregation opted for one Sunday morning service.

At the second service in Malibu the music and other aspects of the worship have become more fluid, but the preaching remains and is the same as in the first service. Some use has recently been made of worship teams for the singing, which include both men and women. Such teams are now being used in several Churches of Christ. None were employed ten years ago, to my knowledge.

Other congregations have faced similar scenarios in recent years. How are we to address these changing approaches to worship? I will respond by taking up each step of my hermeneutic proposal. For reasons which will become clear, I will start with Step 7.

Undertake this interpretation as members together in the church of the living God. Before making any decisions or pronouncements, that is precisely what we did. While various individuals struggled with these matters, we studied worship as a congregation and the elders studied together. Our actions and decisions related to our understanding of the Scriptures, which informed every subsequent response.

Step 1: Locate the centers of the Scriptures: that is, God, Christ and the Holy Spirit, so as to be familiar with how the Godhead informs specific commands, examples and observations. We agreed that regardless of any thought or action we had regarding worship, the main purpose was to glorify God, who is the father of the Lord Jesus Christ and the giver of the Holy Spirit. No specifics of worship could be isolated from the question of whether God was being glorified. Almost every Scripture commenting on the assembled believers and what they did has God in the forefront.

> Let the word of Christ dwell in you richly; teach and admonish one another in all wisdom, and with gratitude in your hearts sing to God. And whatever you do, in word or deed, do everything in the name of the Lord Jesus, giving thanks to God the Father through him (Colossians 3:16, 17).

Step 2: Locate the mindset of the culture being addressed. Above I have identified some of the major cultural changes involved in these situations. Some of these were from outside the church and some from within. Worship assembly changes have been continual in our movement. One hundred-fifty years ago, our worship followed Scottish patterns: the songs were often Psalms put to music. But then, as noted previously, popular English and American hymns began to invade our services, especially those coming from the Awakening.

By time I attended Harding in 1947 a concentrated effort was being made to upgrade the music in the churches by encouraging the purchase of either *Great Songs of the Church* or L. O. Sanderson's *Christian Hymns*. These hymnals, while including some gospel songs, emphasized the more stately classics of the British and American evangelicals. By the 1970s *Great Songs* became the most popular single hymnal, but winds of change were already at work. Those of us who worked so hard to stamp out Stamps-Baxter were appalled when several of the "big" preachers argued that growing churches needed more popular hymns and announced a preference for Alton Howard's *Songs of the Church*. At the same time we were bombarded with what some termed "camp songs," such as "Blue Skies and Rainbows" and "The Steadfast Love of the Lord Never Ceases." We also—in some cases, reluctantly—began to include in the canon songs by various evangelicals, especially the Gaithers.

Our hymnody is changing. But that same thing has happened in the past. For about twenty years we have had a canon centered in the Howard hymnal which is basically static, though even he has added a few songs, and in the latest version, several of the "camp songs," some with words only. Some seem to think we have "always" had a static song tradition. Those preachers and leaders who may be older, with short-term memories or an axe to grind, have done little to disabuse churchgoers of this fallacy. Once again we are entering into a more fluid approach to music in the church. We are adapting to new hymns which address God, Christ, and the Holy Spirit directly, which employ fresh language and are more attuned to metropolitan and cosmopolitan ears than the favorites of the past. The hymns are sung, sometimes interspersed with Scripture readings, throughout the service—even during the sermon—and may be led by a music team. Now solos, quartets, choirs, or other musical groups may be heard, containing women as well as men. Some may argue that by elevating worship teams and their leaders, we are tending toward professionalism, but I would argue we are doing so no more than the song leaders who made the meeting circuits of the 1930s—the Austin Taylors and their ilk. It is clear that we have had various traditions over a two hundred year period, and that traditions continue to evolve.

Step 3: Select a section of the Scriptures which seems to speak to this contemporary context. Rather than selecting a smattering of Scripture to fling at a question, which tends to be our practice, we can be more biblical through looking in some depth at a section which addresses a situation similar to the one confronting us. In the case of worship, the best section of Scripture seems to be I Corinthians 11-14.

Step 4: Notice how the persons in this Scripture are addressed from the perspective of

God, Christ and the Holy Spirit. Clearly, the church at Corinth was in chaos over aspects of the assembly. In chapter 11 Paul discussed the head-covering of females. We will come back to this passage when scrutinizing the role of females. Following 11:17, he focused on the manner of taking the Lord's supper. The problem arose because people ate as they arrived, rather than waiting for one another. Paul's ultimate concern was that the believers emulate the motivations and actions of the crucified Lord, who lived and died for others. When the Corinthians ate together they should therefore, out of respect for Christ, have waited for each other. Human needs were to be recognized—they should eat at home if necessary—but they were not to overthrow the manner in which the serving Jesus was to be emulated in the gathered body.

In chapter 12 Paul addressed the matter of spiritual gifts. I suggest that since in all of Paul's writings he only takes up ecstatic tongues in the Corinthian correspondence, that these activities were unique in Corinth. The Corinthian phenomenon was different from that in Jerusalem, since at Jerusalem "each heard in his own language," whereas at Corinth no one understood the utterances without an interpreter (14:5, 8). Cultural influences from the outside obviously affected worship in the Corinthian church. Paul did not oppose these developments simply because they were cultural. Instead, the question in his mind was how they impinged upon the centrality of Christ. He provided guidelines for coping with these powerful forces. The first was that whatever happened in the assembly, Christ must be recognized as Lord (12:3). If someone were to blurt out, in the excitement of ecstatic utterance, "Let Jesus be cursed," they should be clear that whatever empowered such an utterance was not from God.

What is the criterion, then, that determines whether what happens in the assembly is acceptable to God? First, and foremost, the answer is: if, by the action, the lordship of Christ is being affirmed, it is acceptable. Paul goes on to evaluate the various gifts in terms of whether they contribute to the church, the body of Christ (12:27). Gifts from God are never flashy or showy or intended simply to enhance the status of the person exhibiting them. They are given by God for the "common good" (12:7). Furthermore, the highest gifts are not to be weighed by the human standards of how extraordinary they are, but whether they exhibit faith, hope, and love, all of which are directed toward God and the fellow believers (12:31; 13:13).

In chapter 14 Paul addressed more directly what went on in the assembly. Whatever occurred there should be for "upbuilding and encouragement and consolation" (14:3). These are attributes received from God through his presence with the believers. Not only is the worshipping church lifted into the very presence of God, but an outsider, if worship is appropriately focused, senses God's presence. "After the secrets of the unbeliever's heart are disclosed, that person will bow down before God and worship him, declaring, 'God is really among you" (14:25). The ecstatic utterances, by the manner in which they disturbed the assembly, even though claimed for God, were not from him. "For God is a God not of disorder but of peace." I may be wrong, but I think both we and the charismatics have misread this section of I Corinthians. We have done so because we have focused on the exterior manifestations, rather than the ways in which God does or does not show his characteristics through these manifestations. We have often assumed that the tongues being exhibited in the Corinthian church were from God. Paul, on two counts, declared they were not. First, they did not exhibit the highest gift by enhancing the love of Christ in the church. Second, they brought confusion to the body. Whatever denigrates love and results in confusion is not from God.

Step 5: Employ a similar approach in bringing the Godhead to bear on the contemporary context. How, then, does Paul's word from God help us address the disturbances over the assembly at Minter Lane and Malibu? At Minter Lane we discussed I Corinthians 11-14 in a long elders' meeting and, from time to time, afterward. What conclusions did we draw?

First, cultural influences from the outside are to be expected. Those among us who write on such matters, who oppose new developments in the church simply because they are culturally driven, are wrong on two counts. First, those who criticize current worship-style changes tend to measure the new aspects against worship in our churches in the 1950s. But what this criticism fails to take into account is that the worship of the the 1950s had changed considerably from the worship of the 1930s. In other words, culture influenced our worship in the 1930s, the 1950s, and continues to do so in the 1990s. Even the worship of the New Testament churches—which differed in various regions—was influenced by the local culture. This is even more clear if one reads accounts of Christian worship in the second century. Culture has always influenced worship in the church, and the worship-style critics only assume otherwise because they are historically illiterate, presumably by choice. Second, and more importantly, they are wrong because Paul did not reject what was going on at Corinth on the grounds that it was "outside" or culturally motivated. He rejected it on the grounds that the Holy Spirit was impugned (12:3), the lordship of Christ denied (12:3), or the presence of God obfuscated (14:23).

Next, we decided that the first and foremost goal of the assembly was to recognize the power of the Holy Spirit, the lordship of Christ, and the peace of God. In another passage which is also worthy of study for this situation, Paul wrote, "For the kingdom of God is not food and drink but righteousness and peace and joy in the Holy Spirit" (Romans 14:17). Where these are recognized, upbuilding, encouragement, and consolation occur.

Third, we recognized that no present congregation of the Lord's people worships exactly like the early Christians did. One reason is that the New Testament churches themselves did not worship exactly alike. A second reason is that we do not fully know how they worshiped. We know, for example, that they probably chanted psalms, but we do not know what psalms, or exactly how they sounded when chanted. We know something about the times of worship, which varied according to place and date, but little about the order in the assemblies. If I Corinthians 11:23-26 is standard, they broke bread first, then they ate a common meal. After the meal they drank the fruit of the vine.

Fourth—a point already mentioned above—we knew that standard worship practices in Churches of Christ, about 1950, contained as much extra-biblical tradition—four-part harmony in singing, for example—as strict imitations of New Testament worship. I am at a loss to explain the grounds on which singing groups are opposed today. I prefer congregational singing. I love it, and I always have. Still, I cannot ignore that I Corinthians 14:26 likely includes solos. Singing groups, as far as I can see, are mostly opposed on the grounds of "unnecessary inferences." Similarly, when four-part harmony was first introduced into British churches, the furor was loud and long.[5] Many of the same arguments were made against four-part harmony that now appear against singing groups. But if challenged, how can anyone establish that four-part harmony is authorized by the Word of God? There is no doubt in my mind that it is a tradition of men. So how are worship traditions to be evaluated? We have great aversion to tradition—the traditions of others, not so much our own. We must remember that Paul was not opposed to traditions, but they had to be weighed and sifted through a recognition of the power of the Holy Spirit, the lordship of Christ, and the peace of God. Sometimes traditions fared negatively in his judgment—the Corinthian manner of taking the Lord's supper (which, by the way, we do not precisely practice, since we have eliminated the common meal), and the length of hair on males and females (11:16), for example.

Fifth, we concluded that whatever worship traditions we had, whatever traditions we wanted to break, and whatever changes we wanted to make must be evaluated on the grounds of whether God was glorified and whether the people of God were built up, encouraged, and consoled. We are not to reject changes in the assembly simply because they are new. Neither are we to insist on changes that are disturbing to the body and which violate the consciences of sincere and dedicated believers. We are in trouble, however, if we always give in to those who cultivate cantankerousness and care more about tradition than about God. God does not approve of furor and disorder in his body (I Corinthians 14:33). He does not approve of running rough-shod over believers with sincere convictions (Romans 14:20-23). But neither does he approve, I believe, those who object to changes because they are uninformed about historical perspectives, and who will fight to the bitter end to "keep things as they are."

Step 6: Relate the specific action or understanding to the larger narrative of God's mighty works for his world through the Son and the Holy Spirit. We therefore concluded, in the two churches under consideration, that our hermeneutics enabled us to proceed as best we knew how, according the to light which God gave us. It was appropriate that we approve new songs and approaches in the second worship assemblies. We were right to constantly weigh the new directions according to Paul's criteria. I might observe that arguments from inference were constantly employed, but we knew the beginning points from which valid inferences were derived: the love and peace of God, the lordship of Christ, and the empowerment of the Spirit to produce faith, hope, and love in the body. We were also correct to maintain a place for traditional approaches to worship, insofar as they fulfilled the same requirements of glorifying the Godhead. We did not permit people to be at ease with these traditions simply because that was what they knew and preferred. We let them know that unless God somehow shined through these forms, our worship was in vain.

It was also appropriate that we attempted to keep peace between the traditionalists and the neo-charismatics. We were challenged by some from both sides for being derelict in our duty because we did not support their understanding and put down those who opposed it. We did not succumb to these pressures, however, because we emulated Paul's hermeneutics: we kept our eyes on God. We believed that the "parties" were at times more wed to their preferences than to the love of God. We opposed various innovations recommended by the neo-charismatics, for example, because they seemed more designed to call attention to certain "gifts" than to the Lordship of Christ.

We ourselves were mostly at peace with God, even though not always with our brothers and sisters, because we believed that we were living under the word of God and interpreting his Scriptures in the manner of his apostles, rather than according to a schematic formula derived from men. We were also at peace because we constantly sought wisdom from God. More than once, we quoted James to remind ourselves that our decisions did not rest simply on our own shoulders. "If any of you is lacking in wisdom, ask God, who gives to all generously and ungrudgingly, and it will be given you" (James 1:5). We did what we knew to do and trusted God for his faithfulness in supplying any requested insight. Our specific actions may not be what any other congregation should do: in some situations developments are so volatile and the position of the leaders so precarious that the whole church might go out of control. But I believe that any congregation needs to follow the same criteria we followed, because these were not ours, but those set forth by the servants of the living God who walked with the resurrected Lord. At Malibu the situation has been different than at Minter Lane, but we have still attempted to keep God at the center of our weighing and sifting of developments.

The Role of Women

When we arrived at Minter Lane, women were actively involved in the life of the congregation as church school teachers and coordinators of programs. It was not uncommon in some of the classes for women to take a turn teaching mixed adults when multiple teachers were used. Women have also taught mixed classes at Malibu under the same arrangements. The Minter classes were delineated by age levels and it was in the age groups from twenty to fifty that this was most likely to happen. All the time we went to Minter we lacked a full-time preacher: even if someone preached regularly, he was also a professor at the university. On occasion, we rotated preaching duties among several men for several months at a time. The only full-time employee of the congregation was a church secretary. She was, therefore the congregational coordinator, kept books for the congregation and the mission efforts, and was authorized to co-sign checks with one of the elders. The situation was much the same at the Malibu congregation when we arrived, except that the church secretary did not function as the main coordinator to the same extent. The Minter building was several miles from where most of the elders lived, and those who lived close worked several miles away. At Malibu, in contrast, we have had a full-time minister who offices on campus and most of the elders live close to the church office, permitting males—elders and others—to be more active in the coordination of activities.

At Minter Lane, women prayed aloud in the "sharing groups"—later changed to "shepherding groups"—when several short prayers were requested, but in most groups they were not singled out to lead a prayer alone. They did not often pray in classes at church with the probable exception of one class. The practices at Malibu are much the same, except more recently women—mostly students—have prayed in Sunday night services when multiple "chain" prayers are requested, and are sometimes asked to lead prayers in sharing groups. Women at Minter headed such ministries as the library, children's worship, children's classes, women's Bible study, and book review sessions. Minter was famous over the years for short devotionals on Sunday morning and night, prepared and presented by members of the church. These included short remarks, Scripture readings and appropriate songs. Sometimes these were prepared by a husband and wife, but the husband made the presentations. Sometimes they were prepared by a woman, and a man—not necessarily her husband—made the presentation. One or two women who liked to prepare devotionals refused to continue, on the grounds that if they couldn't present them, they wouldn't prepare them.

Later, Minter introduced a ministry system where each deacon headed a ministry, but since there were not enough deacons to cover all the bases, others, including women, also headed ministry teams. After a couple of years the decision was made that unless a person headed a ministry team they were not really deacons, so all the deacons resigned and those who chaired the ministry teams became the official servants (in the Greek, *diakonos*) for the church. In this manner, women became official servants, except that we had dropped the title "deacon," and certainly did not introduce the word "deaconess." The same scenario occurred at Malibu about five years later. An elder at Malibu, John Wilson, pointed out that "deaconess" is not actually a biblical term. In Scriptures there are servants—deacons, and the same term applies both to male and female servants. The question therefore is whether there is a biblical use of "servant"—*diakonos*—which distinguishes between general servants and those who hold a special office.

In both congregations various people were uncomfortable with women praying and teaching in the different meetings. The other roles for women did not receive much comment. The persons most vocal tended not to be males in the congregation, but older women. The older women considered the younger women who aspired to participate "out of line." They may not have put it this way, but they looked with disdain at these "pushy" younger women. If both husband and wife were upset, the family usually departed for another congregation.

In leader retreats at Minter we sometimes selected women to address the participants. Women also served as small group discussion leaders. The women who were willing to take these roles were not necessarily the ones in the congregation who were best educated. We had on occasion a few women with Ph.D.'s who taught at the university. All of the women willing to take over these tasks were college graduates and some had master's degrees. Their main qualification was communication ability and spiritual discernment. Some of them worked in public schools as teachers or librarians. None were the wives of elders. The situation is much the same in Malibu, except that more of the women have Ph.D.'s and are professors or attorneys.

Over the years in both congregations, women's voices have been heard in assemblies. At Minter in Wednesday night devotionals, women sometimes read Scriptures into a microphone while seated in a pew. In one period at Minter we had an occasional solo singer, and while these were mostly men, on an occasion or two a woman sang. Women made comments when children's classes gave special presentations on Sunday or Wednesday nights. When mission teams were sent out or MARK ("Missions Apprentice Recruitment Korps") persons departed or returned, women made reports in the same manner as men: this has been also the case at Malibu. A few women in both congregations, as well as men on the behalf of women, agitated for more participation. Members in both of the churches have strong views, pro and con, on the matter, and any changes have been preceded by much discussion. In both congregations, the Scriptures have been studied carefully and repeatedly for insight on proper women's roles.

What do we conclude about the role of women if we apply the above hermeneutical principles? First, of course, it is a church matter (Rule #7). It is the church which must stand face-to-face with the Scriptures and decide what to do and think. Second, we must approach the matter from the center of the Scripture (Rule # 1). Surely, the Scripture begins and ends with God.

Rule #2: Locate the mindset of the culture being addressed. We live in an age in which women are perceived to be free to enter any profession whatever. This is not altogether an accurate version of history or the current situation, but it is true that

American women are now accepted in more professions than at any time in American history. Because this is true, many argue that it should apply across the board, in matters of ministry as well as in law or medicine. Dorothy and I recently sat at a dinner with a man, about twenty-five years of age, and his father. The son said that women should be permitted to become ministers because they are being widely accepted today as leaders in all areas of life. Since they are now accepted it would be improper to object to them as ministers. Whatever society favors is adequate justification for him. The father was embarrassed, and countered by saying that women are accepted in most societal roles, but religious decisions are based on the Scriptures, not on what people approve in any given time. Neither father nor son made headway in convincing the other.

The role of women in society has changed, especially since the 1950s. When Americans think of the benchmark from which women's positions have deteriorated—or risen, depending on the view involved—the point of departure is usually the 1950s. In the 1950s the ideal American family lived in the suburbs. The husband left home each day for the inner city because that was where the jobs were. Few women worked, because a single salary was considered adequate, and they too would have needed to travel to a worksite—considered a difficulty at that time. Household appliances were in developmental stages but in most households the necessary tasks of the day were adequate to keep women occupied. In the 1960s and 1970s, schools relocated to the suburbs. With the increase in automatic household technologies, women now had time to do things other than domestic chores. Jobs also moved to the suburbs. Soon, more women were working than not. In the 80s, women sought both management positions and entry into the professions. The roles for both men and women became filled with peril as jobs shifted from the manufacturing sector to communication and service-related businesses. Many men suddenly found their skills obsolete.

Regardless of whether the 1950s image of the family was ideal, it was not that way from the beginning, even as late as the 1920s. The majority of Americans in the 1920s lived on farms or in small towns, including most members of the Churches of Christ. In the majority of the families I knew in the early 1930s, the men did not "go off" to work. Most of my cousins and uncles were farmers who worked at home on the farm. My grandfather ran a gas-station and grocery, but his house was a hundred feet away: Grandma sometimes took over when he had to leave. My best friend's parents ran a Benjamin Franklin five-and-ten-cent store. They worked equal hours there and lived within a few blocks. When I went home with Sammy after school, we first went by the store. They gave us candy and then we played at his house—he scarcely fit the current profile of a "latchkey" child. Another friend's parents ran a small grocery and grill near the elementary school: the husband took care of the store and the wife ran the grill. Most husbands and wives were partners in the full sense: they made business decisions together. If the woman happened to be the most ambitious or the most businesslike, it was not normally a reproach to the man, since they were a team. My uncle's wife, who was my mother's double cousin, had enough ambition for both my uncle and herself. She was the dreamer and the brains of the family. My uncle was a hard worker, though, and carried his share of the load. The Sausers were admired widely. They were a team. No one put him down because he was the brawn and she was the brains and spokesperson.

At church it was a bit different, in that the women played no active public role except for teaching children. Decisions, however, according to the normal societal way, were made by both husbands and wives. Often, actions taken at church owed more to the women than the men. In my family, anyway, women never took a back seat when it came to the work of the church. They put in their opinions, whether it was to their husbands, or their brothers or male cousins. My impression was that my cousin, Bynam Dunsmore—an elder—never had any original ideas for the church. His suggestions mostly came from the women in the family. I know he got plenty of advice from that quarter. Still, it was no reproach to him that he depended on female advice, since that was the culture in which we lived. Our churches changed when men began working away from home, became executives, and spent long hours in elder's meetings without the women near at hand. Actually, the influence of women in the decisions of the church declined from the 1920s onward. Our changing culture definitely influenced this decline.

According to the 1950s benchmark for the role of women, the culture of the 1920s was a failure. Few care to remember those days, for the feminists have their rhetoric and the anti-feminists have theirs, and both can best make their cases if the benchmark is pegged at 1950. The role of women in the early times certainly did not measure up to the 1950 benchmark. Women, as well as men, were entrepreneurs, according to Proverbs 31. They moved about in order to conduct business, as did Lydia (Acts 16:14). Aquila and Pricilla were an entrepreneurial team (Acts 18:1-3), and she was possibly the brains of the family since, when they undertook to explain to Apollos ". . .the way of God. . .more accurately," Pricilla was named first (Acts 18:26). In Palestinian Jewish circles, the roles of women were more limited. A woman could not help make up the synagogue quorum. There is no known example of a woman reading Scripture in the synagogue. There is no known account of a woman going out by herself on a religious mission or traveling with a rabbi.[6]

Women had a more visible role in early Christianity. Unlike the practice of the rabbis, women were included among Jesus's traveling companions (Luke 8:1-3, 10:38-42). Women were among the special witnesses to the resurrection of Christ (Luke 23:48. Acts 13:31) and, in fact, were the first to discover that the tomb was empty and have their eyes opened by the appearance of the resurrected Christ. Paul also accepted among his traveling companions women who "struggled along beside [him] in the work of the gospel" (Philippians 4:3).[7] In the early church, women were clearly called servants (Romans 16:1, I Timothy 3:8-10)—*diakonoi*. That may not have designated an office, but again, from all we can learn from the text, it may have been as much an office as that of the male servants, since the same Greek word is used for both.

Culture has always affected the role of women, in the church and out. Rather than going off into pseudo-history, psychology and Bible studies in order to prove whatever it is we already want to prove about the role of women, we ought to ask how Paul or someone else in Scripture approached the whole matter. Those who want to play to a jury of their own choosing can always find readers with itching ears (II Timothy 4:3).

Rule 3: Select a section of the Scriptures which seems to speak to this contemporary context. While various Scriptures are possible, I will again take up I Corinthians 11-14, since we have already established the background.

Rule 4: Notice how the persons in this Scripture are addressed from the perspective of God, Christ and the Holy Spirit. Paul addressed the hair- and head-covering of women in I Corinthians 11. As usual, the perspective had to do with God and his relation to the world and humans. Paul's hierarchical order is: God, Christ, husband, wife. Here, however, the hierarchy is one of source, not of authority, as is clear by his reference to Genesis 2:22: "Indeed man was not made from woman, but woman from man" (11:8). For Paul, God is the source of Christ. Does this mean that God has authority over Christ? In 8:6 it would seem that the authority is mutual in that the same statement, "from whom are all things and for whom we exist" applies equally to both. Men and women also seem to share this same mutuality. "Nevertheless, in the Lord woman is not independent of man or man independent of woman" (11:11). Paul argued that since man is made in the image of God, that glory is announced to all by his uncovered head. But since woman is made of man, her glory should be reserved for her husband. In the assembly, therefore, she is to be veiled and her hair kept long. When she prays to God she needs to be veiled. The reason for the veiling is to show proper respect to her head—meaning, apparently, her husband (11:5). The principle at work depends upon whatever it is that shows respect to

God. The particular form by which the respect occurs is not the main criterion. Just as, in greeting, what is important is that others be welcomed just as God has welcomed us (Romans 15:7), whether by kiss or handshake, so here the crucial point is that the woman's attire shows clearly her commitment to her husband, whether by veil or, in our time, by a modest dress. Paul seems to admit as much by saying that in the final analysis, the veil and the long hair is the way to demonstrate such commitment for the place and time he addressed (11:13-16).

The prayer of the woman to God (earlier, prayer and prophecy in 11:5) is interesting. Where does it take place? The discussion of veiling pertains to the public appearance of women. They are not veiled in the private presence of their husbands. Furthermore, prophecy presupposes an audience (14:1, 29). The prayer and prophecy therefore took place in public, in the presence of others when the believers assembled. If so, women both prayed and prophesied in the assembly. (Women prophets may certainly be found in the first century church, since Philip had four daughters who prophesied, as in Acts 21:9). Paul's main concern is that God be glorified, which will not occur if conflict persists over the hair and veiling requirement (11:16).

The second statement about women in the assembly is found in the context in which Paul addressed the confusion rampant in the assembly in Corinth. Paul declared, "Women should be silent in the churches" (14:34). Paul cannot mean by his phrase, "should be silent," that women are not to open their mouths at all. The charge to sing and make melody applies to both men and women. Furthermore, I Timothy 3:16 was likely a confessional statement pronounced in unison, and if so, by both men and women. Some Psalms were repeated antiphonally, such as Psalm 136. The repeating of confessions—the so-called "Apostles Creed," for example—and antiphonal reading, obviously practiced in the second century, never excluded women. Women did not proclaim (*kerygma*) in the assembly, but they prophesied. Prophecy (*propheteia*) seems to be differentiated from announcing the basic Christ story (*kerygma*) and teaching (*didache*), instead being assigned a role of personal admonition (14:24, 25) and future disclosure (Acts 21:10-12). So why does Paul say that women must keep silent? Does he speak out of both sides of his mouth?

Some believe that 14:33b-36 is an editorial addition, but this has no real basis. I have read an argument to the effect that the prayer and prophecy referred to here is that which is Spirit inspired (12:8, 14:15). When, therefore, these gifts ceased, it is supposed that women ceased to pray or prophesy in the assembly. This seems a strange conclusion, since men with the same gifts did not cease to prophesy and pray. Another observation builds on the fact that the women are to "ask their husbands at home," therefore limiting the silence to the married women only. What this indicates is that married women had lots of questions, perhaps in regard to what the prophecies meant. The single women, probably few in number, nevertheless would have belonged to a household, and could have asked the male head. A modern proposal, built on single women slipping under the wire and having the privilege of raising questions, seems risky.

Others suggest that the silence edict applies specifically to the church in Corinth. They suggest that women were the main contributors to the confusion, so that extreme measures were necessary.

Some weight may be assigned to this observation, since the passage commences with the charge, "As in all the churches of the saints, women should be silent in the churches" (14:33b). The verbal output of the women in Corinth was therefore much more in evidence than in the other churches. At the same time, in whatever regard the women are to keep quiet in Corinth, the same silence (14:33b) is already stated as characteristic of the rest of the churches. We would like to know much more about the implication of Paul's edict, but this much is clear: women's voices were permitted in the church in singing, praying and prophesying. They were not permitted, however, to interrupt with questions, thereby taking over the assembly. The confusion at Corinth was, apparently, mostly engendered by the exclamations of women. But for both men and women, the assembly was to glorify God, not satisfy the inquisitiveness of the participants (14:25).

One other statement of Paul's should be considered: Galatians 3:28 states, "There is no longer Jew or Greek, there is no longer slave or free, there is no longer male and female, for all of you are one in Christ Jesus." Paul was obviously not making empirical observations on prevailing conditions: the gulf between Jew and Gentile was still in evidence, slavery was rampant, and the roles of men and women remained much the same. Rather, he believed that in the resurrection of Christ, the seeds had been sown for a new humanity. The breaking down of walls was already in evidence, Paul believed, in the Christ-redeemed community. What was already in evidence would blossom. "We must grow up in every way into him who is the head, into Christ" (Ephesians 4:15). What he wrote, both in I Corinthians 11 and in Ephesians 5, indicated that men and women were to submit to each other because of Christ. For Paul, the advent of the Messiah heralded the first signs of an emerging new universe (Romans 8:22), a new ethnicity, a new humanity, and a new gender (Galatians 3:28). Paul believed the universe was in the early stages of being set free from the bondage of decay. He also believed that the wall of separation between Jew and Gentile had been torn down and the passage back and forth had commenced. He also believed that the wall between slave and free had dissolved in the community of faith and would expand in the future. The total abolishment of slavery took eighteen centuries, but was finally achieved. Is it just possible, as Stendahl asks, whether on analogy with slavery, which had ups and downs, and reached its heights about the time it was abolished, the walls of distinction between males and females will finally be overcome, both in the world and in the church?[8] If so, then the grounds for increased roles for women is not simply a matter of what culture dictates, but rests upon the foundations of what has already been announced in the advent of the Lord of Scripture.

Step 5: Employ a similar approach in bringing the Godhead to bear on the contemporary context. At the forefront of any discussion of gender roles in corporate worship must be the requirement that God is to be glorified in the assembly of his saints. Everything we set out to do in the contemporary church must be to the glory of God. No gain is made in the church of the living God if the reassessment of gender roles proves to be for the glorification of gender rather than the God who created gender. God is glorified when all his people, regardless of race, social status, or gender, can exhibit their faith in the assembly of the saints. The question, then, comes down to whether the manner in which that faith is exhibited should differ according to gender.

Paul clearly affirmed differing gifts and roles among those in the body. Not all Christians make the same contribution to the body. ". . .there are varieties of activities, but it is the same God who activates all of them in everyone. To each is given the manifestation of the Spirit for the common good" (I Cor. 12:5-7). Not all persons have the same role in the church.

> Now you are the body of Christ and individually members of it. And God has appointed in the church first apostles, second prophets, third teachers; then deeds of power, then gifts of healing, forms of assistance, forms of leadership, various kinds of tongues (I Cor. 12:27,28).

As noted above, Paul seemed to distinguish contributions to the assemblies of his time by gender. Women prayed and prophesied in the assembly, but they did not serve as the main proclaimers. Women did not proclaim in the synagogue, nor do we have evidence that they preached in the second century church except in the "heretical" sects, such as Montanism. Whatever Paul may have envisioned for the future, for that present time he insisted that the churches follow the common roles for women (14:33:a).

We should therefore be guided, I think, by the Pauline principle that even if an action is "authorized" in a given time and place, traditions may necessitate the foregoing of that action. Paul, for example, was "authorized" to be supported by the Corinthian Christians, but because of the situation he did not exercise that option (9:3-14). Our rule, in contrast, is that whatever is "authorized" must be enacted. Elders are authorized for the church, and we make churches feel somehow unlike real churches unless they have elders. Of course, Paul sometimes took a stand against traditions in the church, but only if a major principle was at stake. The tradition and conviction of Jewish Christians was that males should be circumcised. Paul did not oppose circumcision of Jewish Christians—that was their tradition. But he adamantly opposed the forced circumcision of gentile Christians (Galatians 2:3). To require gentiles to submit to circumcision was to elevate circumcision to a requirement for salvation. Some Jerusalem Christians held that to be the case (Acts 15:1), but Paul vehemently controverted such a conclusion.

Certain traditions prevail in Churches of Christ (as well as in denominations) which are based on age-old Christian practices. In many denominations a principle is involved—ordination, for example. We in Churches of Christ argue that the New Testament did not require ordination in the modern manner. In denominations, the question of ordaining women is crucial if women's roles are to change, since many roles are open only to ordained persons—preaching, baptizing, and administering the Lord's supper, and even "starting songs" if in the pulpit, for example. We hold that one does not need ordination to undertake any of the four, and in fact, women may proceed with any of them as long as no man is present. As I mentioned earlier, when I was a student at Harding I preached once or twice for a congregation east of Newport, Arkansas. I was warned that I might have to do everything in the service because I would probably be the only man there, and such was the case. I asked if they met if no man showed up. They answered "yes," in which case the women took care of the "five acts" of worship. Such could not have happened—at least, in that day and age—in a standard Methodist, Baptist, or Presbyterian church, not because only women were present, but because no one was ordained.

In our churches we have followed certain denominational customs, even though we have rejected the denominational principles. I will mention two. In the past in denominations, women have not been involved at all in the Lord's supper, since ordination was required. We have followed the same tradition. In our assemblies women can pass the trays for the bread or the cup as long as they simply hand it to the next person. They may even rise and carry the trays, in case a gap in the audience makes the nearest person too far away simply to hand it to them. But they cannot "officially" pass out the trays. Why? In the denominations the reason is that they are not ordained. We can say it is not biblical for women to so do, but on what grounds? Passing the trays is certainly not exercising any authority over males. It seems best to locate the reason in tradition. It was the case in the Roman Catholic tradition that women could not move the elements of the Lord's supper from one place to another, since they were not ordained. But we have never had a problem with women preparing the Lord's supper and placing it on the communion table. We would probably frown if they placed it on the table after the service commenced, but mostly if they did it with an inflated spirit. If they exercised a humble, "you-don't-really-see-me" attitude, it would be all right, at least once.

A second matter has to do with leading songs. Our hangups with songleading have more to do with tradition than with Scripture, at least as far as the language of Scripture goes. There is no reference in scripture that indicates anyone "led" prayer or "led" singing, whether male or female. We object to a woman praying alone and out loud (as opposed to a unison prayer, such as the Lord's prayer) or starting a song, on the ground that they are usurping the authority of men. True, Paul worried about women taking over the service. But if the male who organized the service asked a woman to start songs, no authority would be usurped. No one has any problems with a woman "leading" singing in a women's Bible class. It is also the case that early in our movement women sometimes "led" singing, though not while standing in the pulpit.

In interpreting the Scriptures in regard to women's roles, as in most matters, we are usually concerned with what is Scriptural, but also in a major way with what is traditional. I do not wish to downplay the significance of tradition. It is biblically appropriate to have traditions. Nor do I wish to discount the deep emotional aspects of tradition. If for example, a woman has always cooked on Thanksgiving as long as she can remember, we do not fault her for being despondent if, on one occasion, as happened to Dorothy, she was not able to cook because she was returning home from a trip. We would also not put down a person who, having always had matzos as the bread in the Lord's supper, became disoriented upon biting into rye crisp, as I did once in Stockholm. I told myself that rye crisp was no problem biblically, nevertheless it just did not seem to me the proper bread of the Lord's supper. If we decided that women may stand at the back of the building and pass the Lord's Supper from row to row, and we all agreed that it was Scriptural, we still must cope with the fact that some may respond with emotional trauma. Interpreting the Scripture for and in the context of the life of the church, we must therefore consider the traditions of our specific congregation as well as that of the brotherhood at large. We continually remind ourselves that whatever we decide must glorify God the father, Christ the Son, and the Holy Spirit. Traditions may help in the praising of God, but they may also counteract the praising of God.

Step 6: Relate the specific action or understanding to the larger narrative of God's mighty works for his world through the Son and the Holy Spirit. At Minter Lane and in Malibu, several of us believed that according to our reading of I Corinthians, women prayed and prophesied in the assembly of the church. We were aware, however, that since our tradition had from the beginning stood against women's participation in the worship service, that in the present climate it would be traumatic to designate women to pray or perform other functions. We therefore permitted women to teach in adult classes and pray in home gatherings. We also permitted women to make statements of various sorts, but not from the pulpit. At Malibu we have had women make presentations on Sunday night, but not in the place of worship. We have not had women participate in the distribution of the Lord's supper. What we have done in both cases pleased some very much, and caused consternation on the part of a few. Paul called for a similar approach in a context of strong differences of opinion in regard to what practices made a difference and which ones did not. "Those who eat must not despise those who abstain, and those who abstain must not pass judgment on those who eat; for God has welcomed both" (Romans 14:4). The avenue of escape from the morass of our emotional responses is to see, in the sister or brother, one for whom Christ died (Romans 14:15). God desires that all persons be given the opportunity act upon their faith, even though their manners of doing so may differ.

Because of God's prior action, Paul called upon believers to "Welcome one another, therefore, just as Christ has welcomed you, for the glory of God" (Romans 15:7). Because Christ submitted himself to us, we are to submit ourselves to each other. The strong are charged with a "giving up" kind of disposition: "We who are strong ought to put up with the failings of the weak" (Romans 15:1). This is a charge to the strong, but the weak person who is also trying to be a servant has no right to quote it to insist upon his own way. "Love is patient; love is kind; love is not envious or boastful or arrogant or rude. It does not insist on its own way" (I Corinthians 13:4-6). It is not wrong to insist upon God's way, but one is not required to, except when major beliefs are involved, if too many people are hurt in the process. It is not wrong to prefer tradition, nor is it wrong to agitate for change, as long as our top priorities are the love of God and an attitude of service toward the saints. If these two criteria are not furthered by maintaining tradition or pushing ahead to the new, then whatever the subsequent action, the church will not grow spiritually, neither will God be praised.

A servant heart may push for God, but never for himself. When I came to Malibu a woman was recruiting the worship assembly participants. Often church secretaries do this, but this woman was not a church secretary. She asked me to lead prayer at night services, with good reason. She told me that she could always find someone to participate in the morning service, but night was not as simple and she knew I would be there if in town. My presence and willingness helped her in situations where she might have had to make many calls to locate a participant. I was willing to serve in this way. I would have admit, however, that I sometimes chafed because I was never asked to wait on the Lord's table. Because of my status and experience in the church I might rightfully expect to wait on the Lord's table. Had I chosen to insist on my preferences, I could have said that since I was never asked to wait on the Lord's table I would not lead a prayer on Sunday night. As related previously, I once asked a women to prepare a devotional and inform her husband as to how to present it. She refused, saying that she would not prepare it if she could not present it. I appreciated her reason, but feared she did not have a servant heart. At Malibu, we have discussed the prospect of having women pass the communion trays, but never seriously, because the women desiring a more active role have made it clear to us that they would refuse if that was all they could do in the service. I understand the thinking, but again I believe the motivation is wrong. If our interest, whether female or male, is centered in serving God, the significance of the role matters little. At Minter I often passed the trays, even though I was an elder. We have discussed having elders do so at Malibu, but it is thought that many can serve in this manner and the elders shouldn't, by their participation, deprive others of the privilege.

These matters under discussion are not easy to resolve in a real, live body of believers. We are charged, however, to run rough-shod over no one. At the same time we are not to permit others to set the course of action by their personal scruples. Instead, we are called upon to serve God together so that those who come into our midst from the outside can declare, "God is really among you" (14:25).

What does it Mean, and How Does it Apply?

In the New Testament the church, in conjunction with its leadership, is assigned the task of interpreting the Scripture. We have sometimes failed to recognize the church's role in interpretation because we have been so adamant about denying the claims to official interpretation by the Roman Catholic church. In times of consensus breakdowns, however, we have insisted that the elders not only must ascertain the right interpretation of Scriptures, but must apply the interpretation by quelling or dispelling the dissidents. The favorite text for this conclusion has been Acts 20:28, 29.

> Keep watch over yourselves and over all the flock, of which the Holy Spirit has made you overseers, to shepherd the church of God that he obtained with the blood of his own Son. I know that after I have gone, savage wolves will come in among you, not sparing the flock. Some even from your own group will come distorting the truth in order to entice the disciples to follow them.

This text declares that the church consists of more than a conglomerate of individuals, each marching to her own drummer and interpreting the Scriptures as she sees fit. Rather, the church—especially the elders—are charged with correctly discerning the Word. The citing of Acts 20 has not been without controversy. Does Paul assign the elders such an authoritarian role, that they are to see after every aspect of the member's lives and keep them in line? Probably not. But it is clear that the elders, if decisions are to be made in light of the Scriptures, must lead the church in interpreting the Scriptures and applying them. The church must therefore corporately be involved in interpreting the Scriptures.

I was appointed an elder at Minter Lane in 1974. We elders continually invited the members to spend time with us in applying the Scripture to the life of the congregation. The church year commenced with a retreat of all the congregational leaders, both husbands and wives: elders, deacons, ministry leaders, and anyone else who wished to attend. From a church of three hundred resident members, we had about eighty at the retreat. The retreat lasted from Friday night into Saturday night. The agenda was created by asking members of the congregation to nominate items we should address for that year. A committee of deacons was then assigned the task of determining which items were to be discussed, usually limited to four topics. The retreat included Bible studies related to each of the items, break-out discussion groups where women served as leaders as well as men, then discussions by the whole group. Items might include the preaching ministry, the construction of an activities building, the differences in characteristics of two morning services, the youth ministry, the college ministry, the character of our worship times, the role of women, or various small group ministries. After the retreat the elders decided how to implement any conclusions that were reached. Some tasks were assigned to the deacons, others to a particular ministry, and still others were retained by the elders.

I was always impressed that, as elders at Minter Lane, we often studied the Scriptures together before proceeding in new directions. Before significant actions were taken, elders or preachers often examined appropriate sections of the Scriptures in the services. We tried to be a congregation involved in interpreting the Scriptures and applying the outcome for our lives together in the church. I came to see that it is, in fact, the church, the community of faith, which must corporately accept the responsibility for interpreting the Scriptures. A complete hermeneutic must take into account this corporate dimension.

At first I thought the amount of time we spent in elder's meetings was a waste. Every Wednesday night we started meeting about 8:30, except when there was a deacon's or congregational meeting. We seldom ended before 11:00 P.M. and occasionally left after midnight. A different elder chaired the sessions each month, so our meetings were not ad hoc. He planned the agenda and determined who else from the congregation might meet with us, which was often necessary. After the agenda was completed we proceeded, elder by elder, identifying special concerns that hadn't been expressed yet. This round-robin alone could sometimes take an hour. With some frequency, the items had been discussed previously. My first two or three years I thought the meetings could be much more efficient. After a time, however, it dawned on me that the elders were a microcosm of the congregation. All the concerns of the congregation seemed to be placed on the table, sooner or later. In fact, we could, in effect, poll the congregation right in the elder's meeting. Each member was known well enough by at least one of the elders so that the elder could report that member's views on a number of specific topics. This also included the views of vocal student members. But we never took our discernment for granted. We conducted congregational polls and held congregational meetings.

Another reason we knew the views and aspirations of almost every member was because of our shepherding groups. When we first attended Minter Lane there was a sharing program, in which persons got together for a time of Bible study and fellowship. We were always active in such groups. They sometimes met in our home and when they didn't, I still sometimes served as the discussion leader. Then we changed the sharing groups to shepherding groups, which was feasible when the number of elders doubled. The object of the new groups was for the elders to get to know more about our members than we knew already, especially in regard to their spiritual needs and insights. We had eight groups: two of the eight met each Sunday night from 6:00 to 9:00 P.M. Each group had a deacon and wife who served as facilitators. We encouraged all the family members to be present. We also welcomed the students who wished to be involved, but we didn't recruit them since the numbers would have become unwieldy. We ate first, then studied some section of the Scriptures. We normally identified a biblical book as the basis of our study over an extended time. We discussed matters facing the congregation when appropriate, using the groups as one method of polling the congregation. In these ways we were able to be a body living under the Word of God, and interpreting it together, both in conception and application.

Each congregation of the Lord's people lives under the authority of the word of God. It is the congregation, along with its leaders, that must pass muster for its interpretation of the Scriptures. Congregations must not be derilect in duty by ceding the interpretation of Scriptures to brotherhood leaders who are eager to pre-empt the local mandate, nor to preachers or even the elders of the congregation. Certainly, the preachers and elders are key players, but all people of God are charged with interpreting the word correctly. Elders, are, of course, to take the lead in calling the congregation to assess the Scriptures and make decisions based upon them. We have always charged the congregation to read the Bible's directives for elders so that they may nominate qualified persons. Why shouldn't the same charge apply to other matters facing the congregation?

---

[1] Gustas Aulén, *The Faith of the Christian Church*, tr. Eric H. Wahlstrom and Everett Arden (Philadelphia: The Muhlenberg Press, 1948).

[2] Royal Humbert, *Compend of Alexander Campbell's Theology* (St. Louis: The Bethany Press, 1961).

[3] Recently, Rex A. Turner, Sr. has published *Systematic Theology: Another Book on the Fundamentals of the Faith* (Montgomery: Alabama Christian School of Religion, 1989). The topics are essentially typical of the classical theological topics.

[4] Alexander Campbell, *Christianity Restored* (Rosemead: Old Paths Book Club, 1959 Reprint) 15-19.

[5] J. R. H. Moorman, *A History of the Church in England* (London: A. C. Black, 1980) 314-337.

[6] See Ben Witherington III, *Women in the Ministry of Jesus*, (Cambridge: University of Cambridge Press, 1984), and *Women in the Earliest Churches*, (Cambridge: University of Cambridge Press, paperback, 1992)

[7] Florence M. Gillman, *Women Who Knew Paul* (Collegeville: The Liturgical Press, 1992).

[8] Krister Stendahl, *The Bible and the Role of Women*, (Philadelphia: Fortress Press, 1966).

11
The Church in the World: Controversies and Conclusions

Dorothy and I grew up in regions of the United States which were, at least at that time, mission areas, in the sense that the Churches of Christ were just beginning to gain a toehold. After we were married the congregations where we were involved were in similar regions, and were young and small. We felt more at home with people in such settings. I was not always perceived as a suitable proclaimer in our regions of strength, but I was regularly invited to be with and address mission groups.

The first group outside of the United States where we were invited to spend time was a mission team which worked among the Quichè Indians in Guatemala. Two members of the team, Ralph

McCluggage and Roger McCowan, had worked with Owen's Campaigns Northeast when we lived in Pennsylvania. The couple we knew best in the group, however, was Richard and Karen Rheinbolt. I first met the Rheinbolts when I taught domestic missions for a week in George Gurganus's Mission Workshop at Harding College in 1966. Richard had just completed his first year in medical school at the University of Arkansas. He was from the region around Mansfield, Ohio. Karen was from Ft. Smith, Arkansas. Richard mentioned to me that they would like to do some work with a congregation that summer for about a month and also be able visit his relatives in the area. I said, "Why don't you come to State College, and go around town or the campus, talking with people?" I said I thought the congregation could help them a bit financially and they could stay with us or some of the other members, so they came. In 1968 George Gurganus came to Abilene Christian as professor of missions and after that did his summer workshops there. Ralph then came to work on a master's degree at Abilene. Another member of the team, Pat Hile, did graduate work, eventually leading to an M.Div. Richard and Karen came to Abilene for Mission Workshops and for courses at Abilene Christian, taking a course in Old Testament from me.

The mission team made their way to Guatemala in the early 1970s. In 1973 they invited Dorothy and me to come down during spring break at Abilene Christian. The team was then living in Sacapulus, about a hundred miles northwest of Guatemala City. Richard had started a medical clinic and they had converted a few Guatemalans. They were especially interested in studying Scriptures which related to their mission efforts. I met with the guys twice a day; the women met separately. Then we sometimes ate together at night. We went to bed early, since electricity was uncertain. Sacapulus was in the valley of a region which was mountainous, but not high mountains. The Quichè were poor. Their houses were adobe, the blocks usually formed from soil on the building site. Sacupulus was selected as the team's base because it had been recommended as a good place to learn Quichè. After the team had been there for awhile, however, they discovered that the village language was a variant of Quichè found nowhere except in this small region.

We studied two parts of the Scripture: first, Genesis, and then sections of the New Testament which focused on those sent to various regions of the world. The reason for selecting Genesis was that the team had concluded that the part of the Scripture which might speak best and first to the Quichè was the Old Testament, especially Genesis. I thought the hermeneutical ploy involved was admirable: God, not the ancient order, was the focus of Genesis. Of course, the principles of interpretation involved in starting with Genesis violated the supposition of many that one hermeneutic will fit all. The views of the Quichè were basically animistic. They believed that spirits inhabited all objects: trees, rocks, and lakes. They believed that major deities lived in certain specified regional mountains. The lightning and thunder around the mountains were expressions of the gods' power.

The book of Genesis addresses the same sort of worldview. The ancient peoples believed that within natural phenomena, especially in the oceans, were great powers. The deities had to battle against the oceans in order to form dry land. The opposing forces were so mighty that the gods barely eked out a victory by sheer exertion. Yahweh, however, was not a god within nature. He, in fact, created nature. He did not have to struggle mightily with the primeval waters: he created them. The fearful sea monster was only a plaything to Yahweh. "…and Leviathan that you formed to sport in it" (Psalms 104:26). The hermeneutical strategy of the team was, therefore, not to train the Quichè to re-imagine the natural world or to become scientific in the manner of the Enlightenment; to learn to view nature as impersonal and inanimate. The point was not to destroy their perception that power resides in the lightning, thunder, and rain, or that mountains exhibit forces unseen by humans. The approach, rather, was to move them from the belief in many powers to faith in one powerful deity, the God of Abraham, Isaac and Jacob. It was in this same manner that the writers of the Old Testament countered the gods of the Canaanites. They did not begin by denying the existence of such. They contended, rather, that these gods were pointless because Yahweh-God was the maker of heaven and earth and everything in it.

This, too, was Paul's approach at Athens.

> The God who made the world and everything in it, he who is Lord of heaven and earth, does not live in shrines made by human hands, nor is he served by human hands, as though he needed anything, since he himself gives to all mortals life and breath and all things (Acts 17:24, 25).

The writers of the Scriptures were involved in demythologizing, but their efforts were directed toward the myths of the ancient peoples. As Frank Cross once remarked, Bultmann's project was abortive, since Genesis was already the result of demythologizing. On the mountain, Elijah set out to establish that Yahweh alone had power (I Kings 18). He didn't need to deny the existence of the baals. Instead, Elijah reasoned, why would anyone pay attention to them if they failed to come through in the area of their speciality—hurling the thunderbolt? Who wants to worship an impotent deity?

Pat Hile made special efforts to understand the Quichè perspective on the gods and nature. He and the rest of us agreed that, in fact, the Old Testament remains authoritative for believers in such a world as Guatemala, and that it is the place to begin. To commence with the need for people to leave sectarianism for the New Testament church had no immediate relevance for these people. Inferences may be at work in bringing these Indians to believe that God is the Creator and the Father of the Lord Jesus Christ, but commands and examples—at least, as we have ordinarily conceived them—made little contribution until they were more firmly grounded in the faith.

We also began from the Old Testament as we considered going forth into the world in the name of God. Abraham was told to go from his own country to a place God would show him. He would in turn be blessed and "in you all the families of the earth shall be blessed" (Genesis 12:3). Just as Abraham, Isaac, Jacob, and Joseph were a blessing to their neighbors and eventually to the whole world, so also were those who came to Guatemala. The one who goes forth in the name of God is involved in his ministry of reconciliation.

> All this is from God, who reconciled us to himself through Christ, and has given us the

> ministry of reconciliation; that is, in Christ God was reconciling the world to himself, not counting their trespasses against them, and entrusting the message of reconciliation to us. So we are ambassadors for Christ (II Corinthians 5:18-20).

We enjoyed our time together very much. Both God and the Scripture became more alive through this ministry and in this special setting.

In the summer of 1978 we bought "Herbie II" (a Chevrolet Suburban) and headed for New England. In the arrangements under a new dean and chairman of the Bible department, I taught four courses per semester, but could take summers off. We continued contacts with Landon Saunders. Stanley Shipp, who also was in Landon's orbit, launched an internship program in St. Louis. The goal was to train teams for planting new congregations in a mission region of the United States. On the first team were Ken and Jeanette Danley. They were previously involved in Goodnews Northeast. They also grew up in the Arlington, Virginia, congregation. Partly because of their having worked around Lowell, Massachusetts, the decision was made to start a congregation there.

When Landon heard we planned to spend the summer in New England he twisted our arms to attend the congregation in Lowell, to help and encourage them. We found a campground called Emerson's in Hampstead, New Hampshire, about twenty-five miles away, which had summer programs for children of Erika's age. By then our oldest daughter, Suzanne, and her husband had completed M.D.'s and were living in Boston, completing residencies at Boston City Hospital.

When I needed to go to the library we went in and stayed with them.

It was an interesting summer. Four or five men from the Lowell team came to the campground once a week and we studied Scripture and discussed approaches to their work. They had the right idea that they needed to create new forms of worship and structure to adapt to the setting. They were especially trained by Stanley in one-on-one evangelism and they were highly motivated. They had already won area residents to the Lord; mostly singles their own age. The team worked well together and wanted to demonstrate results, since they were the flagship group. They were apprehensive of layered organization, however, and went out of their way to avoid traditions, even their own. They attempted to approach everything by consensus, without any stated leaders. This might have worked, had someone in the group been able to provide leadership without "being in charge," but no one had such skills or ability. Every worship was different in both form and content. This pleased them very much and satisfied their needs, but it was very difficult for outsiders since, for example, the newcomers did not hear songs repeated often enough to learn them. The Shipp group spent much time trying to think up creative ways to reach people. They established a service center and through it made numerous contacts. They kept busy teaching people. But they could never seem to capitalize upon and solidify their accomplishments. After staying about the same in numbers for several years, they finally closed down. They had the right idea—that the Bible must be interpreted for people in a specific context without all the freight imported from another region—but they could never lay permanent foundations. In fact, their strategy probably mitigated against permanence.

In some ways Dorothy and I identified more with my former students, scattered throughout the world as missionaries, than with members of the church in the southwest. Through the next decade, 1976-1986, we traveled to many parts of the world. In 1979 we were invited to teach in Sao Paulo, Brazil and Buenos Aires, Argentina. I taught a graduate course in biblical theology to the missionaries and Dorothy spent a few hours a day teaching the wives. In 1981 we returned to Guatemala, where we spoke at a retreat for central American missionaries at Lake Atitlán. In 1983 we traveled Europe for six weeks, looking in on the Stephen Bilaks in Lausanne, who then were engaged in a radio ministry, "Slavic World for Christ," sponsored by the Minter Lane congregation. We also made contact with participants in the Minter Lane MARK program, in Mannheim and Cologne. In each case we sooner or later discussed the interpretion of the Gospel in these different contexts. In 1984 we traveled to China and Russia, in a Peoples to Peoples program where, with communication professors from China and Russia, we attempted to share (interpret) each others' cultures. All of these different contexts brought to mind once again the difficulties of moving from one culture to another. It is the same when we attempt to move from biblical times to our times.

The Rising Controversy over the New Hermeneutics

In the fall of 1985 I was approached by Monroe Hawley of Milwaukee, Wisconsin, to be the featured speaker at the annual preacher's retreat, held at the Wisconsin Christian Youth Camp in Black River Falls. He wanted me to speak on hermeneutics, but I told Monroe that I had much rather interpret Scripture than speak on its interpretation. It had been my experience that people were more interested in digging into the Word than listening to somewhat abstract discussions of hermeneutics. In the past I had been able to convince those inviting me. Monroe, however, was of a different opinion. He said the preachers explicitly wanted to discuss hermeneutics. It was "a new world out there." When the term "hermeneutics" first hit the brotherhood publications in a major way, people used to joke, "Herman who?" But by the middle 1980s, no one was joking.

Before the Black River Falls retreat, however, our family made a major move. In late May, out of the blue, I received a call from Jerry Rushford, asking if I would consider taking the religion chair at Pepperdine. I had some signs that I might be asked earlier but I kept nominating other prospects. Someone in Abilene told me, when they heard we were moving, that they were very surprised: they thought we were a permanent fixture in Abilene. I responded, "You are no more surprised than I. I thought we'd be buried in Abilene." I responded to Jerry, "A. Craig Baird used to say, 'Don't turn down a job until it is offered to you.' I have always thought this good advice. I can't encourage you to think I am interested, but I am willing to hear what Pepperdine has in mind for the religion division."

Dorothy told me she was not interested. Furthermore, it would be a very bad move for Erika, who would that fall be a junior at Abilene Christian High School. She said, however, that if I really wanted to go talk with them, it was fine with her. So, I called Jerry and told him I would come out to talk with them. The conversations went well: I was particularly pleased with the opportunity to appoint almost an entirely new faculty, since several persons were retiring and it seemed that one or two others would leave because of the changeover. For some years now I had given thought to the persons I would appoint to create a premier graduate program for training ministers. Now, an opportunity opened up to do just that. The decision whether to move to Pepperdine proved difficult. When I returned home, Dorothy was not too turned on by my excitement. We informed Erika and she was apoplectic. There was no way she was going to leave her school and friends! I told Dorothy if we were serious at all I thought we had to make up our minds fast. I didn't want to be a lame duck at ACU, and we would have to move in about two months. We therefore arranged for the three of us to visit Malibu about three weeks later. Subsequently, despite Dorothy's misgivings—mostly due to Erika's reaction—we made the move.

Perhaps as great as any other reason for my desire to move to Pepperdine was my perception that I was really an "apostle to the gentiles." The premier work of my life had not been in the "Holy Land"—the southern and southwestern "Bible Belt"—but in the mission regions. Pepperdine seemed a strategic location. I was impressed by the observation of Hans Küng that civilization had moved from the Indian Ocean to the Mediterranean, then to the Atlantic and now was in the process of moving to the Pacific. The futurists were of the opinion that Los Angeles would be the cultural capital of the Pacific Rim countries. Los Angeles had a larger variety of sizable ethnic groups than any city in the world. By leaving ACU, however, I would not train as many preachers, that was clear. It was also clear that we could not build the sort of program I envisioned in the ten years I would devote to Pepperdine, but if a solid foundation were laid, the prospects for the future might be unlimited. I have always seen myself as a planter, a visionary, a missionary. I was not of the "have-it-now" generation. I was of the generation who grew up in the Depression, who were willing to work many years so as to lay a foundation for a bright future.

In the 1980s certain preachers among us began criticizing the manner in which church leaders had employed the command-example-inference hermeneutics, and proposed other means of interpreting the Scriptures. The result was that those loyal to the consensus hermeneutics attached the appellation "new hermeneutics" to the views of those who called for changes. One of the seed beds for the "new hermeneutics," according to the critics, was the Christian Scholars' Conference. The charge circulated that the Christian Scholars' Conference was well-organized and highly funded, and specifically designed to overthrow traditional brotherhood views, especially in regard to hermeneutics. Terry M. Hightower, who edited a book intended as a rebuttal of the "new hermeneutic," inserted the following statement in an article by Roy C. Deaver.

> It should be obvious to all that the road to liberalism has been and is being "paved" by numerous brethren for many years now. It is a highly organized, well-financed, very sophisticated scheme involving: *The Restoration Quarterly, Abilene Christian*

> *University, Pepperdine University* (esp. the so-called Christian Scholars Conference papers and Thomas Olbricht), *Image Magazine, The Sweet Commentaries*, Unity Meetings with the ICC, and Michael W. Casey's 1986 Ph.D. dissertation at the University of Pittsburgh entitled "The Development of Necessary Inference in the Hermeneutics Of The Disciples of Christ/ Churches of Christ."[1]

A copy of the book was sent to me, compliments of the elders of the Shenandoah Church of Christ in San Antonio. I wrote the elders, expressing my appreciation, and noted to Terry Hightower, the minister, that I wished the Scholars' Conference was as well-financed as their own efforts: they, after all, had the resources to print books. We had to rely on electronically-reproduced copies. From the early days of the conference, hermeneutics has been a constant topic. Since 1988 Gary Collier has organized at least one session focusing on hermeneutics.

The Christian Scholars' Conference commenced in 1981. That summer at ACU, special celebrations were being planned in order to commemorate the 75th year of the school. J. D. Thomas was chairman of the celebration and I was charged with bringing together Bible faculty from our Christian colleges. The first conference focused on religious topics and the presenters were mostly religion professors. But soon we tried to involve more and more teachers from all the disciplines. Some academic areas have had many participants and others not so many. It has depended, in part, on whom we could get to organize programs. The first seven conferences, 1981-1986, were held at Abilene

Christian. The next three were held at Pepperdine, from 1987 to 1989. The conferences then moved about: Abilene in 1990, David Lipscomb in 1991, Oklahoma Christian in 1992, Harding University in 1993, Pepperdine University in 1994, Lubbock Christian University in 1995, and David Lipscomb University in 1996. I have spoken on hermeneutics at least twice in these conferences. The focus of my presentations has been the history of hermeneutics in our movement and why we are in a hermeneutical crisis at present.

It is not clear how much headway has been made in the conference in regard to hermeneutics. In the early years we thought it was best to make hermeneutical observations through addressing specific topics—congregational polity, worship, or the role of women, for example. While we recruited some of the presenters, many were persons who responded to the call for papers. We made no effort to turn down presenters on the grounds of their points of view. We accepted all papers as long as we had slots on the program. Admittedly, few speakers at the Christian Scholars' Conference have supported what would be considered, by the right wing of our movement, "our historic hermeneutics." On the other hand, none of the speakers have employed the "love letter" analogy for the Bible or proposed an "anything goes" hermeneutics, as charged by detractors. Most of the conferences have focused on some topic on which Christian teachers could bring their insights to bear, regardless of academic discipline. For example, we have had conferences on ethics, leadership, and pedagogy. In 1994 our theme was, "Through the Eyes of Faith," in which persons from different disciplines reflected on how faith influenced their perspectives and actions in the classroom and on campus.

The interest in hermeneutics resulted in invitations to speak at the 1989 Oklahoma Christian lectures and, that fall, at the Preacher's Forum at Freed-Hardeman. Leonard Allen of Abilene Christian and I were characterized as embracing the new hermeneutics, and we were opposed by Howard Norton and Earl Edwards. Then I presented some of the material from this book at the Lake Geneva, Wisconsin Encampment, the Annual Bible Lectureship at Abilene Christian in 1993, a retreat near Regina, Saskatchewan, and a preacher's day at Camp Ganderbrook in Maine. I also spoke to a group of persons from restorationist backgrounds at Princeton Theological Seminary, to a group of preachers from both Churches of Christ and Southern Baptist churches in Nashville, and at annual preacher's week in Beamsville, Ontario. In all these settings I explored the viewpoints on hermeneutics expressed in this work.

In the winter semester of 1991, upon returning from teaching in London, I taught a course in theology at Seattle in our off-campus program (I normally teach biblical theology in our off-campus programs, but I had already taught it at Seattle). Pepperdine did the first two-year stint at Seattle from 1988-90, and immediately started a second two years, back-to-back. We decided to teach different courses this time, so that a student at Seattle could get more courses toward completing an M.Div. I decided that I must start with the theological topics central to Churches of Christ, since we are starting to lose them. In our lectureships and sermons, and especially since the accelerating demise of the "gospel meeting," these topics are no longer being highlighted. This means that persons under thirty have rarely heard a systematic presentation of our standard doctrines of the 1930s and 40s. Also, younger preachers are no longer much committed to these topics as critical. I reproduced a series of readings from journals and lectureships to provide primary source materials and also had the students purchase Donald Bloesch's *Evangelical Theology* to provide historical and current reflection upon "our" theological topics. The students seemed to appreciate the course. They said their eyes were really opened to the thought of leaders in Churches of Christ.

In comparison to the standard theological categories of historical Christendom as presented in Chapters Seven and Ten, what are the topics of our restorationist theology? We have had opinions on these traditional topics, but in a rhetorically-prioritized, rather than philosophically-oriented framework. I proposed the following set of topics, in order of priority, within our history not only from the last century, but also as evidenced in the books and periodicals of the major opinion makers in Churches of Christ from 1920 to 1960.

1. The unity of the church
2. Scripture
3. Hermeneutics
4. The Church: The Ancient Order
5. Digression: Innovation and Disfellowship
6. Salvation: The Ancient Gospel
7. Jesus Christ
8. Man: Sinner and Struggler
9. God: Creator and Provider
10. The Holy Spirit: Inspirer of the Scripture
11. Worship: Preaching and Complying
12. The Judgment: Accounting and Separating

The priority of unity in our discussions has eroded immeasurably in the last thirty years. For more than a century we perceived this to be our means of getting a foot in the door of a world weary of sectarianism. But sectarianism—at least of the kind we opposed—is essentially dead. No American denomination is wed to its creed any longer. Now, worship has perhaps replaced unity as the number-one interest in the Churches of Christ.

The question is: how shall we evaluate "our" theological topics? We need to evaluate them as we claim to weigh all matters—according to the Scriptures. The classical theological topics reflect the mindset of western philosophers. Answering the question, how do we know what we know? precedes any decision about whatever it is we know. According to classical theology we know through faith, revelation, and Scripture. What we know commences with God as foundational and proceeds through the chief realities related to God in something of a hierarchical order. Theology in western history has therefore achieved its archetypal form because of its perspectives on first matters, inter-relationships, and perceived hierarchy. If this particular structure is imperative for fielding a viable theology, then obviously restorationist theology has never ventured past the turnstiles.

The order of our topics, ranked in significance as shown above, have been primarily based on putting what we perceive to be our best foot forward: we have highlighted those topics which we thought would secure us the best hearing from our audiences. I do not fault such a rhetorically-based strategy, but these topics have also tended to shape our thinking about the the New Testament and its implications for the Restoration Movement. Instead, we should see what topics are most important in Scripture, as I have tried to show in Chapter Nine, for both the Old Testament and the New Testament. I have also provided the list of the classical theological topics which, I argue, are ordered according to a philosophical hierarchy and therefore not as appropriate as a biblically-ordered perspective.

A Critique from the Scriptures

I argue that the theology of the Scriptures is neither chiefly concerned with philosophical methodology or ecclesiological and rhetorical strategy, though the latter are not absent. The focal point in Scripture is the mighty loving action of God in his created universe and on behalf of man, who is made in his image. These actions culminate in the Son, tying together the testaments. I am well aware that in over three hundred years of the academic discipline of biblical theology, many other proposals have been set out which seek to define the centers and structure of biblical theology: covenant, *heilsgeschichte*, Christology, credo, *kerygma*, theology, soteriology and anthropology, among others.[2]

The biblical topics have a different focus than those of either classical or Restoration theology. They focus upon God—his action rather than his essence—or even the results of his actions in the church. Our restorationist topics, because they are ecclesiologically and rhetorically derived, tend to get us off on the wrong foot. It is no problem that we address these topics, but we need to assess their relative importance in the light of Scripture. Our topics, while misordered, nevertheless provide certain emphases very important in Scripture.

With this larger critique in mind we can now turn to comments on each of our theological topics. Unity is not the foundation of the biblical faith, but rather a God who loves. The love of God, however, leads directly to unity. We live under the Scriptures, hence all theologies must be evaluated by it, even our own. The Scriptures, nevertheless, are not an end in themselves. They are, as Luther declared, the swaddling clothes in which the Christ child is wrapped. They lead us to God, not to themselves. They demand our loyalty in that they lead us to God. The beginning point for hermeneutics, therefore is God, Christ, and the Holy Spirit, not commands, examples, and necessary inferences, regardless of how helpful these may be in regard to specific matters of church order.

We have been correct that the foundation of the church is Jesus Christ. But we have often ignored the Founder and chiefly discussed that which he founded. That is why I have placed the church prior to Christ in our topics. In the affirmation of Paul, the church is the body brought forth by Christ's body on the cross. The risen Lord continues his earthly ministry through the church. In regard to our view of the history of Christianity, we have been correct that the church is always falling away. For that reason, two thousand years of Christian history may be more important than we have supposed. We have much to learn from the mistakes of others—and from our own. The developments of history are always to be judged by the Scriptures, but we can profit from situations and responses. The fact is that we embrace more of the results of two thousand years of Christian reflection in our own theology than we are aware.

We have viewed Christ chiefly as the foundation upon which the church is built, and his blood as the ground of our salvation. We have not probed in depth any biblical doctrine of atonement or of Christ's word and work as formative for our life style. We have focused, rather, on a plan of salvation which culminates in baptism. Indeed, our most thoroughly nuanced theological topic has been baptism. We have made many of the right biblical observations, but we have sometimes stressed more the mechanics of obedience than the new life to which baptism points. While we suppose God to be very important as creator and sustainer and the father of our Lord Jesus Christ, we have reflected little upon his steadfast involvement with humankind. This, in part, has resulted because we have cut ourselves adrift from the Old Testament. We have been so intent on how God authorizes and authenticates our church, our theology, our style of life, our good fortune, that we have sidestepped his love and continuing struggle with his world. We have truncated the Trinity by limiting the work of the Spirit to the inspiration of the Scripture, rather than giving him his place in the ongoing empowerment of the church. We have viewed man as sinner and in need of salvation, but chiefly as a violator of rules rather than one who fails to love God with all of his heart, soul, mind, and strength.

We have been strong in affirming the desirability of right worship, but not always so interested in its result—glorifying God and edifying one another by focusing upon Christ. We have argued well the focus and frequency of the Lord's supper, but we have sometimes missed the deeper implications of banqueting with our Lord in anticipation of his return; his invitation to the heavenly banquet. We have preached long and hard on the judgment, but perhaps more to plunge people beneath the waters of baptism than to incite them to offer themselves as living sacrifices to God, and to long for his Son's appearance and kingdom.

We do indeed have a theology with a method and center. We have focused upon most of the topics of classical theology, but with a different priority and content. The question, to my way of thinking, is not whether our theology is viable from the perspective of classical theology, but whether it is viable biblically. From a biblical perspective certain positive claims, I think, can be made. (1) Our basic orientation is biblical rather than philosophical. (2) We have a highly developed doctrine of the significance of the church which, in turn, elicits a strong sense of community. Outsiders often remark how surprised they are that we know members in many other regions of the world. (3) We have a highly developed Christology—Jesus is the head of the church—even though we have not developed the spiritual significance of that headship and its ramifications as we might. (4) We have assigned an elevated significance to baptism and the Lord's Supper. (5) We have encouraged a strong sense of personal responsibility for the church and its tasks—Luther's emphasis on the priesthood of all believers. (6) We have maintained a strong sense of sin and the need for faith in God's saving actions. (7) While we have sometimes abandoned our commitment to unity, the need repeatedly resurfaces in our reflection upon God's will for us. (8) While we have made many accommodations to the culture which surrounds us, we have done so with an uneasy conscience and have been responsive to those who call into question our commitments and assimilations.

By Way of Conclusion

The journey has been long. Along the way, as with all people, I have been blessed by the love and grace which comes from God, who is the Father of our Lord Jesus Christ. I have not settled all the hermeneutical questions: possibly, I have settled none, in the opinion of some. But I have subjected many aspects of interpreting the Scriptures to the rigorous scrutiny of the Scripture itself. I have not offered a simple, how-to-do-it hermeneutical formula, since I do not believe such possible. But I have indicated the lines along which Scripture must be interpreted. I believe that any hermeneutic must highlight the obvious focal point of Scripture: God, who reveals himself as Father, Son and Holy Spirit. I further believe that the interpreter, in word and deed, is inextricably a facet of interpretation, and that interpretation takes place in a body of believers, and is made real in the life and action of that body.

The Unfolding of My Reflections on the Nature of Scripture

I began this journey by reflecting on whether Scripture is best characterized as fact or story. I concluded that it is both, in that the facts are endemically imbedded in story. An interpreter who ignores the narrative in order to rush ahead to the facts inevitably misconstrues the Scriptures. A misinterpretation likewise occurs when an interpreter treasures the narrative, but denigrates the significance of the facts.

A second station along the way was the imaging of Scripture. Is the Scripture mostly a source book for resolving the puzzlement of constant searchers? Is it a blueprint or pattern book for those who would replicate the New Testament church? Is it a manual to resolve the issues created by the leaders of the church? Is it a handbook for the proper ethical and moral life? Is it a chart for identifying the plan of salvation, as well as the fundamentals of the faith? Is it a how-to-do-it book for planting an aggressive, growing church? Is it a reference on the standard theological agenda—the *regula fidei*? The answer is that in a limited sense, it is all of the above, but none highlight its main purpose. The main purpose of Scripture is to set forth the mighty actions of God as Father, Son, and Holy Spirit, and to explain what these actions mean to a humanity which often focuses on its own agenda rather than God's. Many of the classical hermeneutics books get sidetracked with technical grammatico-historical matters, and fail to address the central focus of Scripture. We in the Churches of Christ have tended to limit hermeneutics to a method whereby we can rule on the implications of a specific Scripture for a specific practice.

A third way station had to do with the biblical relationship of God with his world and with a humanity made in his image. The Enlightenment and scientific visions of reality have posited a world which functions as it does because of impersonal, natural laws. The biblical vision differs. The regularity perceived in the universe is not because of natural laws which exist apart from God, but precisely because of the ongoing faithfulness of God to his creation. As Son, he "sustains all things by his powerful word" (Hebrews 1:3). The extraordinary

mighty acts may have ceased, but God's relationship to humans and to the universe remains the same. A hermeneutic which repostures God and the world according to an Enlightenment scientific vision is not biblical. The Scripture is always misinterpreted when forced into the straitjacket of human models for reality. Scripture is not susceptible to a Platonic, Aristotelian, Ramian, Baconian, Lockeian, common-sense, Hegelian, scientific, Heideggarian, New Age, postmodern, or any other brand of re-imaging.

A fourth stop had to do with whose list of topics or questions best help us interpret the Scriptures. Our set of special questions for the Scriptures have focused on the features of the church and the plan of salvation. We have argued that when we obtain biblical answers to these questions we can unify Christendom and restore the church of the New Testament. We inherited these questions through the Zwinglian and British reformers, and reformulated them in such a manner as to address nineteenth century America. These questions, while implied in the Bible, are not the main questions of Scripture. Other confessional groups have focused on the standard theological topics to provide a checklist of the important questions to put to the Scriptures, a practice which began with the *regula fidei* of Origen in the third century. Again, however, though there are biblical answers to each of these questions, they do not place the focus exactly where Scripture does. The biblical questions may be found in the Old Testament, in the professions of the faith of Israel—the credos. In the New Testament they are found in the sermons preaching Christ (the *kerygma*) and other short statements of faith. These focus on the mighty works of God and what they mean, culminating in God's ultimate work through the Son. Culture, even our own, influences hermeneutics far more than we realize. We discover cultural influence through examining Christian history as well as that of our own movement. Books on the history of hermeneutics, unfortunately, tend to focus on the technical aspects of interpretation and unfortunately do not situate the larger matters in the context of the culture.

A fifth way station had to do with the aspects of the Scripture under which Christians live. While, in a sense, Christians live under the New Testament, not the Old, yet New Testament writers—Paul among them—commend the Old Testament as authoritative for Christians. A statement more compatible with the New Testament is that Christ replaced the institutions of the Old Testament, but the actions of God and their interpretation in the Old Testament remain an authoritative word for Christians. The similar view that the Gospels may be pushed aside to highlight Acts through Revelation has no New Testament support. This bias is only possible on the grounds that God's chief concern is the restoration of the New Testament church. The Gospels say little about overt structures of the church, but they provide an irreplaceable narrative in which the characteristics of those who comprise the kingdom of God are set forth. The New Testament church exists, not so much as a perfect pattern, but as an assembly of redeemed people. The Gospels make clear how those people act. Christians live under the whole council of God, not an emasculated canon. A hermeneutic which denigrates the authority of the Old Testament and the Gospels is not supported by the New Testament.

A sixth stop focused upon the translation of Scripture into life: the ultimate aim of hermeneutics.

When God set out to interpret himself to humanity he sent his Son, not a handbook of hermeneutical rules. "No one has ever seen God. It is God the only Son, who is close to the Father's heart, who has made him known." The Greek word from which the last phrase is translated is the root for our English word, "exegesis". Those who ultimately interpret the Word of God do so in action as well as in word. Despite our polemics to the contrary, the principal setting for interpreting the word of God in the New Testament is the church. Hermeneutics should therefore be church hermeneutics. By that, I mean hermeneutics should focus on how the leaders of the church arrange for the interpretation of the Scripture in the teaching and life of the congregation. The guidelines thus advanced have to do with activation as much as conception. The same focus holds true for individual understanding and application. Hermeneutics is much more far reaching than observing the Lord's supper with correct regularity. It has to do with the total life of the congregation and individuals vibrantly eating the Son's meal as God's people. Perhaps these parameters for hermeneutics are too expansive. But if in some way hermeneutics does not recognize the full dimensions of life, the subsequent reductionism encourages varying degrees of lifeless Christianity.

Seventh, within the theological and hermeneutical method of the Scripture itself, the explicit statements and examples of what humans should become are always drawn from what God has already done, as set forth in His interpretative word. Three statements from Scripture come to mind.

> He has told you, O mortal, what is good; and what does the Lord require of you but to do justice, and to love kindness, and to walk humbly with your God (Micah 6:8)?

All the traits mentioned in Micah's statement are repeately professed in the Old Testament, especially in the Psalms, to be the very characteristics of Yahweh. In fact, the phrase "love kindness" is a repetition of the same Hebrew word, *chesed*, which almost always is employed for God's steadfast love, and very seldom used to depict human love for God.

> If any want to become my followers, let them deny themselves and take up their cross and follow me (Mark 8:34).

It is clear that the taking up the cross, even for Jesus, was a style of life as well as a manner of death. "For the Son of Man came not to be served, but to serve, and give his life a ransom for many" (Mark 10:45). The rules for the life of the disciple are derived from the servant-styled life of the Savior. They are more than mere commands, examples, and inferences from the logician's handbook. They are the emulations of the life of the very Son of God.

> So if I, your Lord and Teacher, have washed your feet, you also ought to wash one another's feet. For I have set you an example, that you also should do as I have done to you (John 13:14, 15).

Finally, there are admittedly various levels of hermeneutics. The analogy with different genres of weather forecasts may help. We have claimed universality for command, example, and necessary inference, both in terms of Scripture's content and in respect to time and place. In other words, we situate our hermeneutics in the category of a global forecast. But if I am correct in the observations throughout this book, the manner in which we have employed commands, examples, and necessary inferences is more parallel to a regional forecast. Don't get me wrong: we need the various forecast levels! We need, in addition, national and local forecasts. It is imperative that our hermeneutics be nuanced in such a way as to give recognition to these different levels.

With these preliminaries always in mind, an enumerated hermeneutics may be advanced. The employment of it, however, requires a greater or lesser degree of sophistication, depending on the use to which it is put. I do not expect that these steps will be appreciated apart from some of the insights provided in the text of this book. An instantaneous objection might be that if a hermeneutic, for example, the one I propose, is not immediately perceptible, then, on that ground alone it is non-biblical. I must reply, however, that the contention that the biblical message is simple is itself not biblical. II Peter says, of the writings of Paul,

> So also our beloved brother Paul wrote to you according to the wisdom given him, speaking of this as he does in all his letters. There are some things in them hard to understand, which the ignorant and unstable twist to their own destruction, as they do the other Scriptures (II Peter 3:15, 16).

We usually explain that Jesus spoke in parables in order to capture people's attention and put complex ideas in simple, everyday words and concepts. But, according to Matthew,

> Then the disciples came and asked him, "Why do you speak to them in parables?" He answered, "To you it has been given to know the secrets of the kingdom of heaven, but to them it has not been given...The reason I speak to them in parables is that 'seeing they do not perceive, and hearing they do not listen, nor do they understand'" (Matthew 13:10-13).

Because we have grown up with our hermeneutic we think it's simple. I have observed that persons who come to us from other backgrounds do not find it simple, and even the most perceptive require a year or two to in order to employ it in such a manner as to end up with the proper conclusions.

And so, I end as I began.

In a real sense hermeneutics is the interpreting of God to those who wish to be his. Even God did not propose to do that by a few simple rules. He did not offer rules, but a Son. "No one has ever seen God. It is God the only Son, who is close to the father's heart, who has made him known [exegeomai]" (John 1:18). Jesus Christ is therefore the ultimate hermeneutic. If God can best explain himself in person, we can best explain him too in his body, that is, his living church.

Our charge is clear. The right interpretation of Scripture places God, in his Son, at the center.

> You know what time it is, how it is now the moment for you to wake from sleep. For salvation is nearer to us now than when we became believers; the night is far gone, the day is near. Let us then lay aside the works of darkness and put on the armor of light...put on the Lord Jesus Christ (Romans 13:11-14).

"The grace of the Lord Jesus be with you. My love be with all of you in Christ Jesus" (Romans 16: 23, 24). "The grace of the Lord Jesus Christ, the love of God, and the communion of the Holy Spirit be with all of you" (II Corinthians 13:13).

---

[1] Terry M. Hightower, Ed., *Rightly Dividing the Word,* (Pensacola: Firm Foundation Publishing House, 1990) 505.

[2] See Gerhard Hasel, *Old Testament Theology: Basic Issues in the Current Debate* (Grand Rapids: William B. Eerdmans, 1991). *New Testament Theology: Basic Issues in the Current Debate* (Grand Rapids: William B. Eerdmans, 1976).